MYSTERY
IN MADRIPOOR

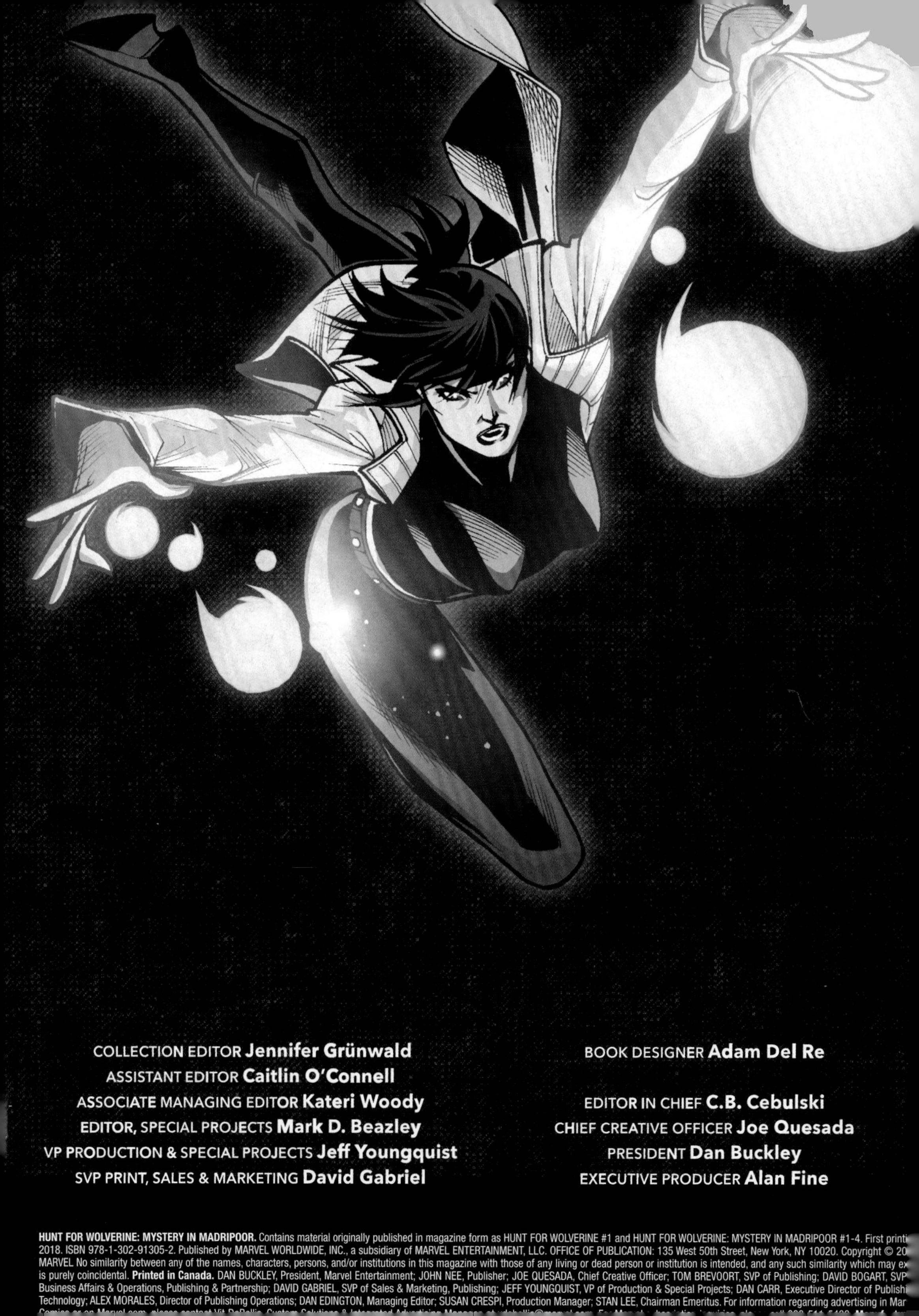

COLLECTION EDITOR **Jennifer Grünwald**
ASSISTANT EDITOR **Caitlin O'Connell**
ASSOCIATE MANAGING EDITOR **Kateri Woody**
EDITOR, SPECIAL PROJECTS **Mark D. Beazley**
VP PRODUCTION & SPECIAL PROJECTS **Jeff Youngquist**
SVP PRINT, SALES & MARKETING **David Gabriel**

BOOK DESIGNER **Adam Del Re**

EDITOR IN CHIEF **C.B. Cebulski**
CHIEF CREATIVE OFFICER **Joe Quesada**
PRESIDENT **Dan Buckley**
EXECUTIVE PRODUCER **Alan Fine**

HUNT FOR WOLVERINE: MYSTERY IN MADRIPOOR. Contains material originally published in magazine form as HUNT FOR WOLVERINE #1 and HUNT FOR WOLVERINE: MYSTERY IN MADRIPOOR #1-4. First printi 2018. ISBN 978-1-302-91305-2. Published by MARVEL WORLDWIDE, INC., a subsidiary of MARVEL ENTERTAINMENT, LLC. OFFICE OF PUBLICATION: 135 West 50th Street, New York, NY 10020. Copyright © 20 MARVEL No similarity between any of the names, characters, persons, and/or institutions in this magazine with those of any living or dead person or institution is intended, and any such similarity which may ex is purely coincidental. **Printed in Canada.** DAN BUCKLEY, President, Marvel Entertainment; JOHN NEE, Publisher; JOE QUESADA, Chief Creative Officer; TOM BREVOORT, SVP of Publishing; DAVID BOGART, SVP Business Affairs & Operations, Publishing & Partnership; DAVID GABRIEL, SVP of Sales & Marketing, Publishing; JEFF YOUNGQUIST, VP of Production & Special Projects; DAN CARR, Executive Director of Publishi Technology; ALEX MORALES, Director of Publishing Operations; DAN EDINGTON, Managing Editor; SUSAN CRESPI, Production Manager; STAN LEE, Chairman Emeritus. For information regarding advertising in Mar

MYSTERY IN MADRIPOOR

HUNT FOR WOLVERINE #1

WRITER **Charles Soule**

"SECRETS AND LIES"

ARTIST **David Marquez**

COLOR ARTIST **Rachelle Rosenberg**

"HUNTER'S PRYDE"

PENCILER **Paulo Siqueira**

INKER **Walden Wong**

COLOR ARTIST **Ruth Redmond**

COVER ART **Steve McNiven, Jay Leisten** & **Laura Martin**

MYSTERY IN MADRIPOOR #1-4

WRITER **Jim Zub**

ARTISTS **Thony Silas** WITH **Leonard Kirk** (#4)

COLOR ARTISTS **Felipe Sobreiro** WITH **Andrew Crossley** (#4)

COVER ART **Greg Land** & **Jason Keith** (#1);
Greg Land, Jay Leisten & **Jason Keith** (#2);
Giuseppe Camuncoli, Roberto Poggi &
Dean White (#3); **Giuseppe Camuncoli,
Roberto Poggi** & **Morry Hollowell** (#4)

LETTERER **VC's Joe Sabino**

ASSISTANT EDITORS **Christina Harrington, Chris Robinson** & **Annalise Bissa**
EDITORS **Mark Paniccia** & **Jordan D. White**

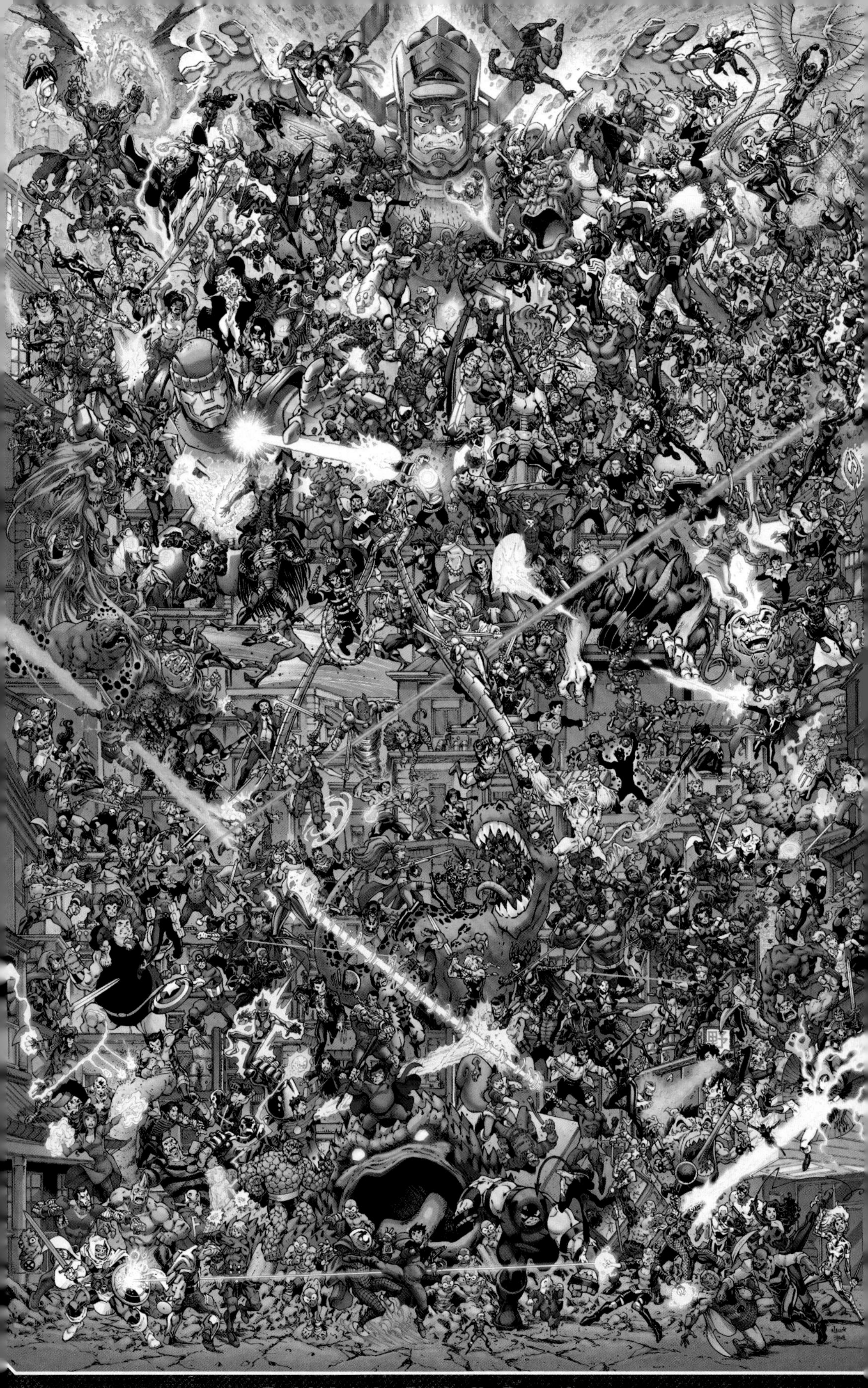

Todd Nauck & Rachelle Rosenberg

WEAPON LOST #1, ADAMANTIUM AGENDA #1, CLAWS OF A KILLER #1 & MYSTERY IN MADRIPOOR #1 CONNECTING VARIANTS

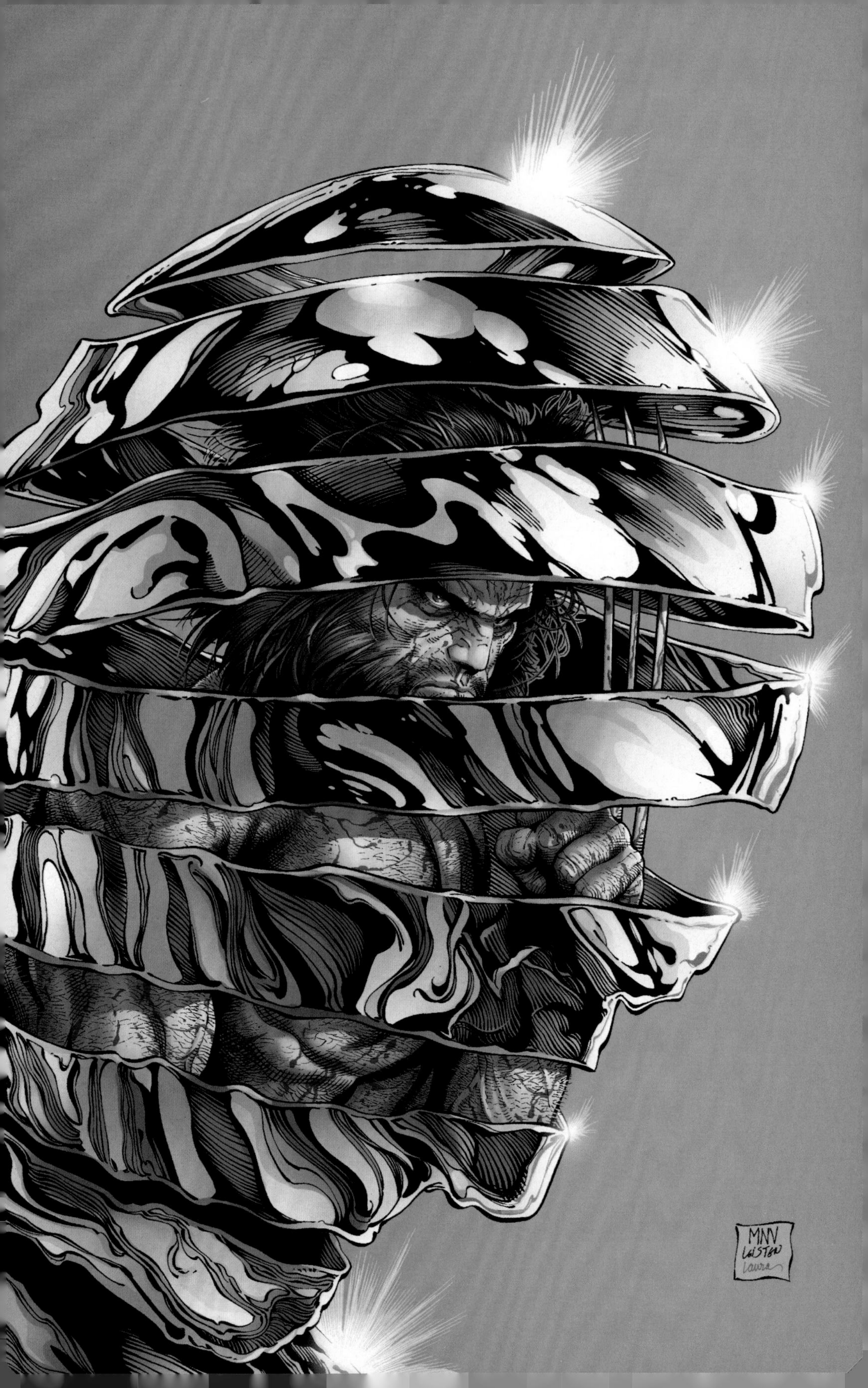

WOLVERINE DIED,
ENTOMBED IN
MOLTEN ADAMANTIUM.

THE X-MEN TOOK HIS
METAL-ENCASED BODY
AND HID IT AWAY,
KEEPING ITS LOCATION SECRET.

BUT NOTHING STAYS BURIED.

IT WAS ONLY A MATTER OF TIME.

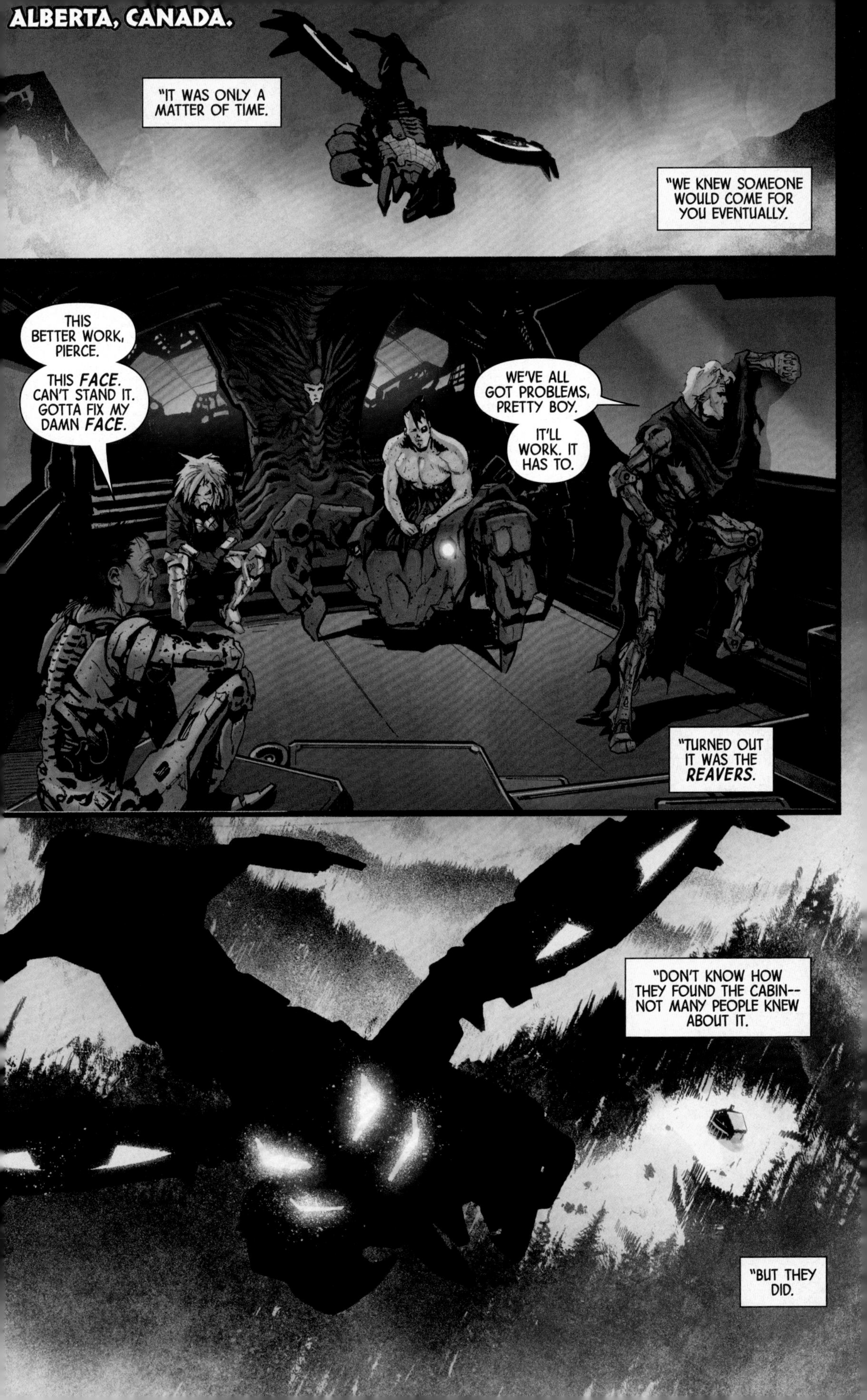
ALBERTA, CANADA.
"IT WAS ONLY A MATTER OF TIME.
"WE KNEW SOMEONE WOULD COME FOR YOU EVENTUALLY.
THIS BETTER WORK, PIERCE.
THIS FACE. CAN'T STAND IT. GOTTA FIX MY DAMN FACE.
WE'VE ALL GOT PROBLEMS, PRETTY BOY.
IT'LL WORK. IT HAS TO.
"TURNED OUT IT WAS THE REAVERS.
"DON'T KNOW HOW THEY FOUND THE CABIN-- NOT MANY PEOPLE KNEW ABOUT IT.
"BUT THEY DID.

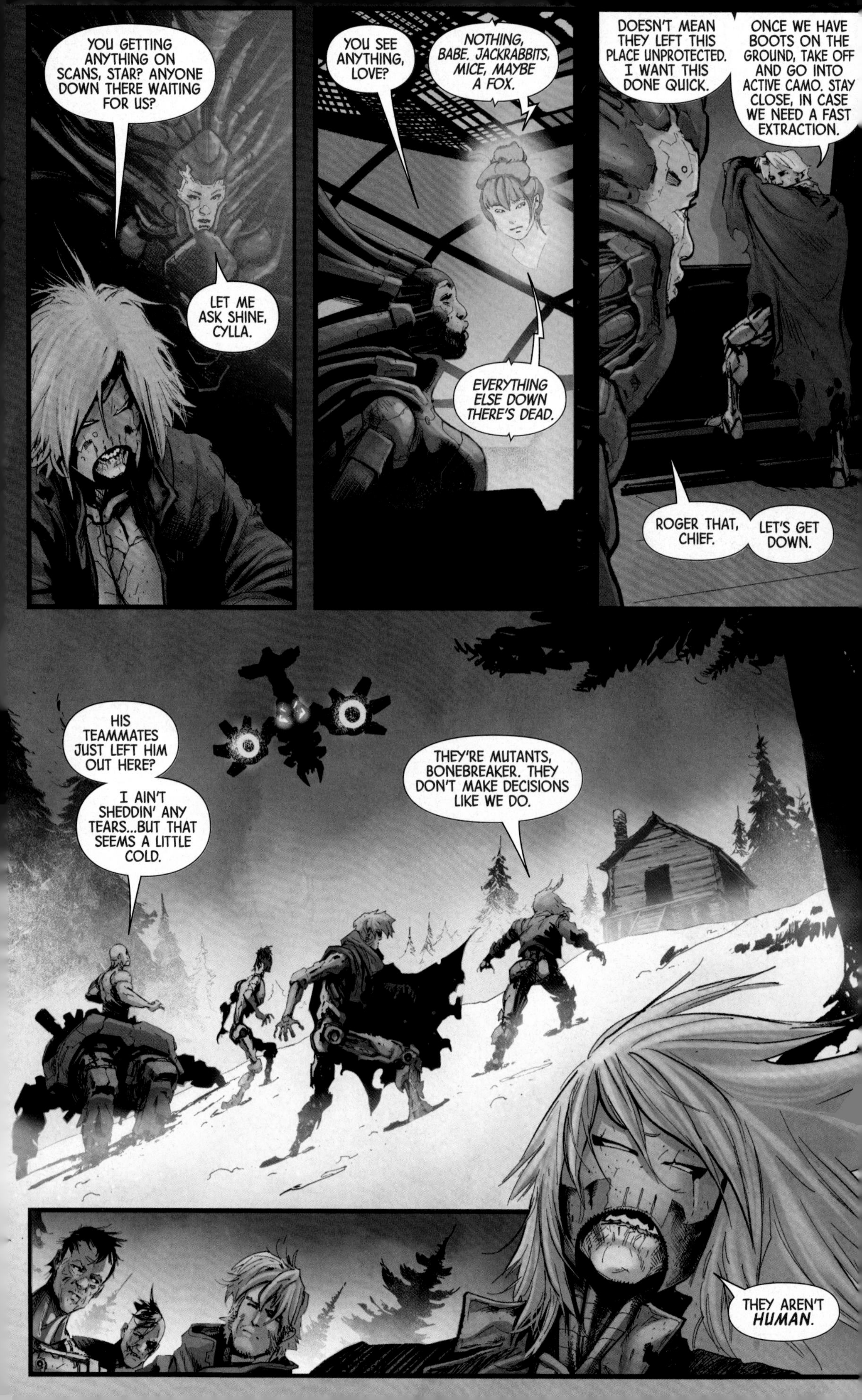
YOU GETTING ANYTHING ON SCANS, STAR? ANYONE DOWN THERE WAITING FOR US?
LET ME ASK SHINE, CYLLA.
YOU SEE ANYTHING, LOVE?
NOTHING, BABE. JACKRABBITS, MICE, MAYBE A FOX.
EVERYTHING ELSE DOWN THERE'S DEAD.
DOESN'T MEAN THEY LEFT THIS PLACE UNPROTECTED. I WANT THIS DONE QUICK.
ONCE WE HAVE BOOTS ON THE GROUND, TAKE OFF AND GO INTO ACTIVE CAMO. STAY CLOSE, IN CASE WE NEED A FAST EXTRACTION.
ROGER THAT, CHIEF.
LET'S GET DOWN.
HIS TEAMMATES JUST LEFT HIM OUT HERE?
I AIN'T SHEDDIN' ANY TEARS...BUT THAT SEEMS A LITTLE COLD.
THEY'RE MUTANTS, BONEBREAKER. THEY DON'T MAKE DECISIONS LIKE WE DO.
THEY AREN'T *HUMAN*.

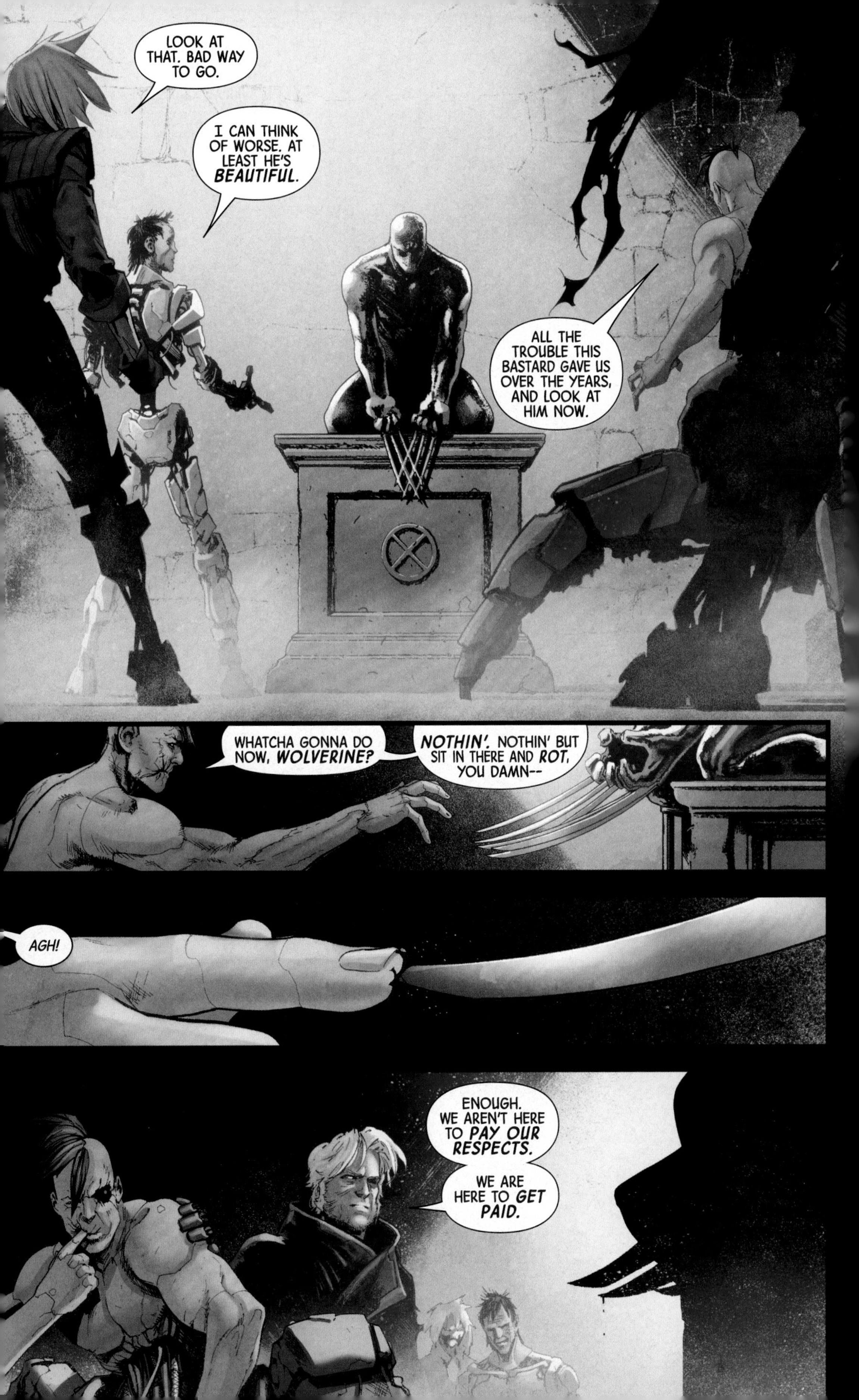
LOOK AT THAT. BAD WAY TO GO.
I CAN THINK OF WORSE. AT LEAST HE'S *BEAUTIFUL*.
ALL THE TROUBLE THIS BASTARD GAVE US OVER THE YEARS, AND LOOK AT HIM NOW.
WHATCHA GONNA DO NOW, *WOLVERINE?*
NOTHIN'. NOTHIN' BUT SIT IN THERE AND *ROT*, YOU DAMN--
AGH!
ENOUGH. WE AREN'T HERE TO *PAY OUR RESPECTS*.
WE ARE HERE TO *GET PAID*.

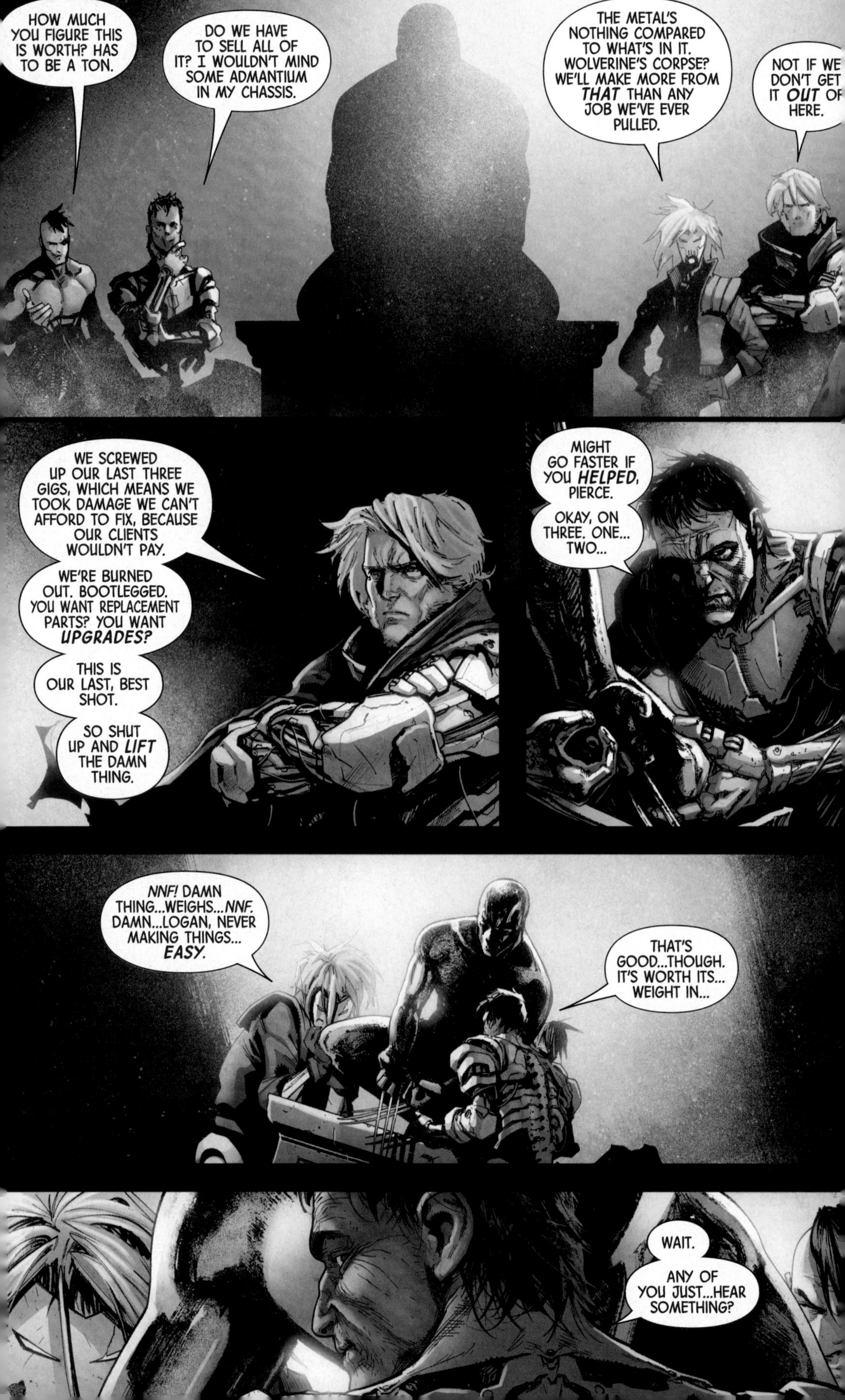

HOW MUCH YOU FIGURE THIS IS WORTH? HAS TO BE A TON.
DO WE HAVE TO SELL ALL OF IT? I WOULDN'T MIND SOME ADMANTIUM IN MY CHASSIS.
THE METAL'S NOTHING COMPARED TO WHAT'S IN IT. WOLVERINE'S CORPSE? WE'LL MAKE MORE FROM THAT THAN ANY JOB WE'VE EVER PULLED.
NOT IF WE DON'T GET IT OUT OF HERE.
WE SCREWED UP OUR LAST THREE GIGS, WHICH MEANS WE TOOK DAMAGE WE CAN'T AFFORD TO FIX, BECAUSE OUR CLIENTS WOULDN'T PAY.
WE'RE BURNED OUT. BOOTLEGGED. YOU WANT REPLACEMENT PARTS? YOU WANT UPGRADES?
THIS IS OUR LAST, BEST SHOT.
SO SHUT UP AND LIFT THE DAMN THING.
MIGHT GO FASTER IF YOU HELPED, PIERCE.
OKAY, ON THREE. ONE... TWO...
NNF! DAMN THING...WEIGHS...NNF. DAMN...LOGAN, NEVER MAKING THINGS... EASY.
THAT'S GOOD...THOUGH. IT'S WORTH ITS... WEIGHT IN...
WAIT.
ANY OF YOU JUST...HEAR SOMETHING?

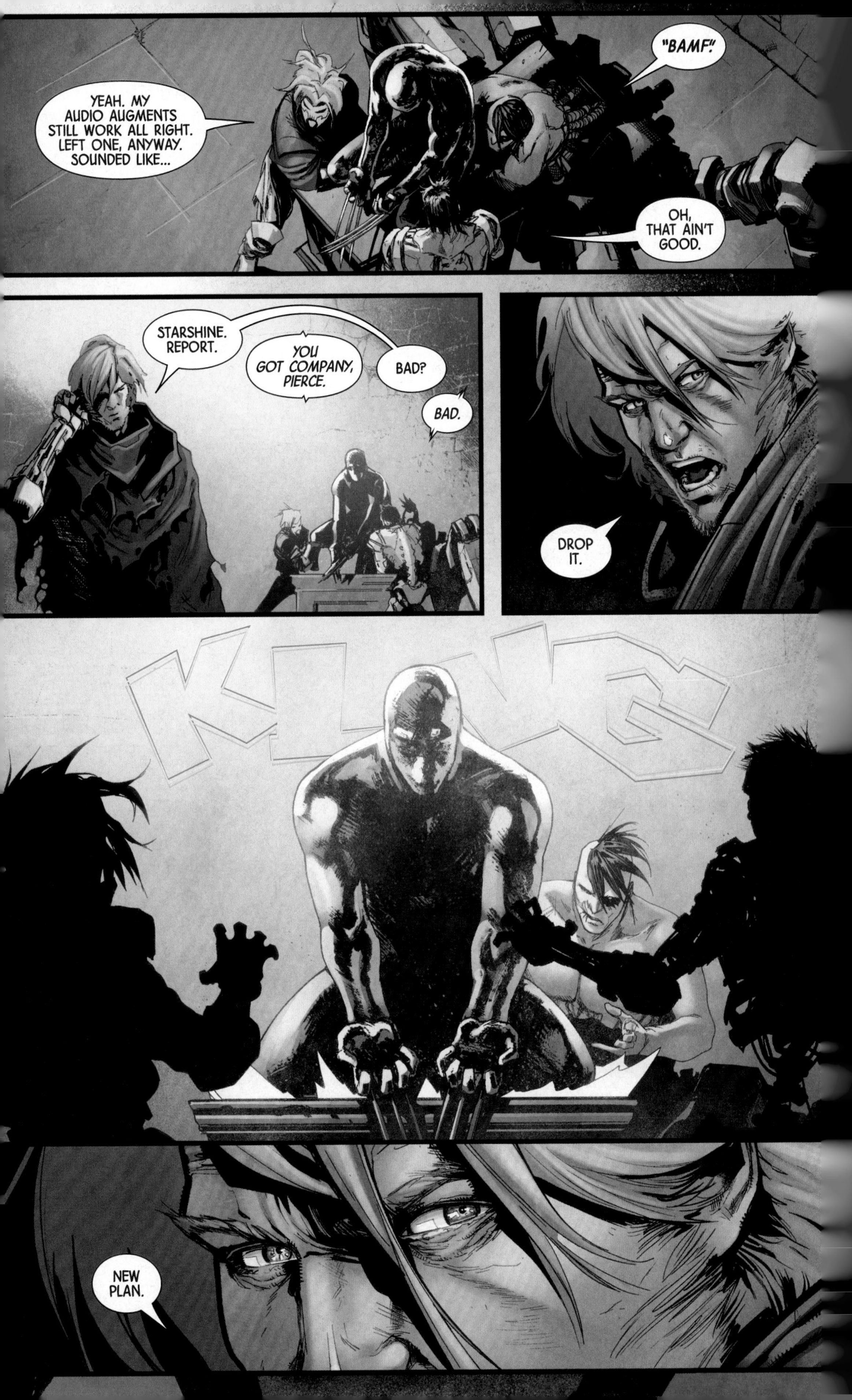
YEAH. MY AUDIO AUGMENTS STILL WORK ALL RIGHT. LEFT ONE, ANYWAY. SOUNDED LIKE...
"BAMF!"
OH, THAT AIN'T GOOD.
STARSHINE. REPORT.
YOU GOT COMPANY, PIERCE.
BAD?
BAD.
DROP IT.
KLANG
NEW PLAN.

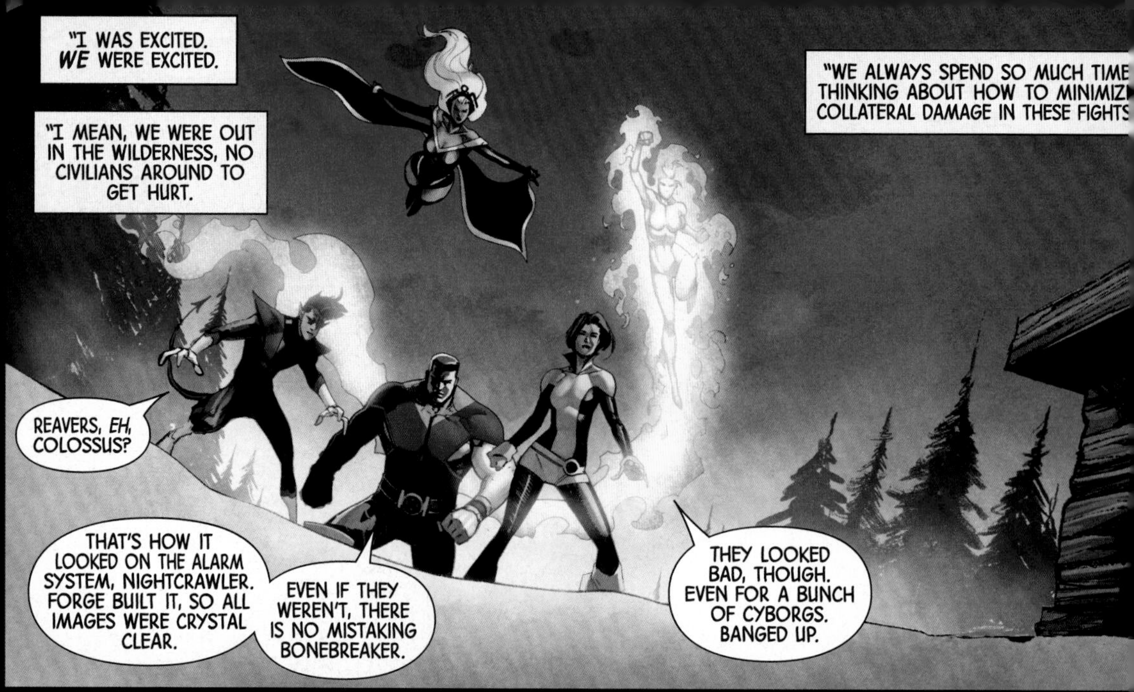
"I WAS EXCITED. *WE* WERE EXCITED.
"I MEAN, WE WERE OUT IN THE WILDERNESS, NO CIVILIANS AROUND TO GET HURT.
"WE ALWAYS SPEND SO MUCH TIME THINKING ABOUT HOW TO MINIMIZ COLLATERAL DAMAGE IN THESE FIGHTS
REAVERS, *EH*, COLOSSUS?
THAT'S HOW IT LOOKED ON THE ALARM SYSTEM, NIGHTCRAWLER. FORGE BUILT IT, SO ALL IMAGES WERE CRYSTAL CLEAR.
EVEN IF THEY WEREN'T, THERE IS NO MISTAKING BONEBREAKER.
THEY LOOKED BAD, THOUGH. EVEN FOR A BUNCH OF CYBORGS. BANGED UP.

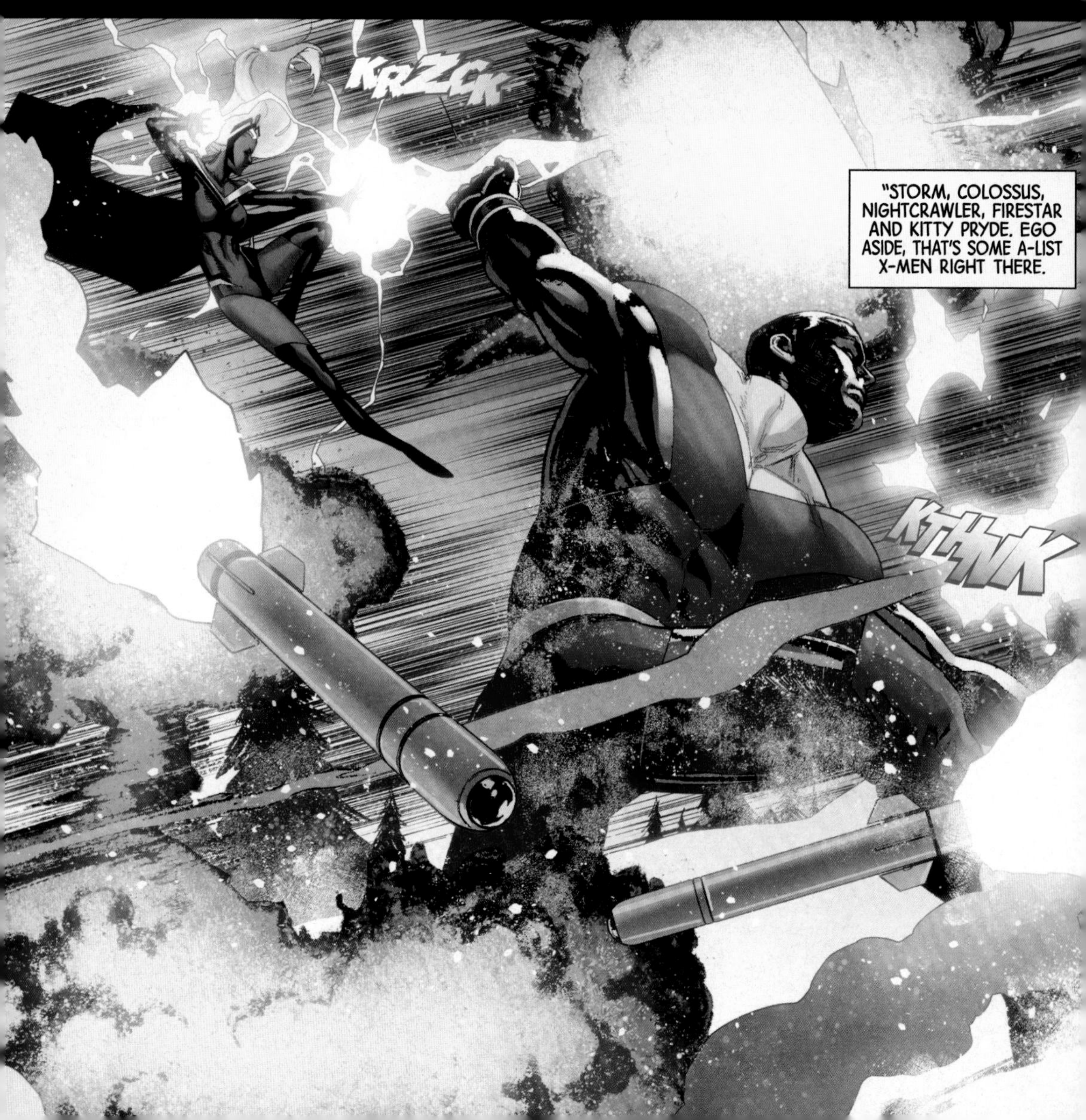
KRZCK
"STORM, COLOSSUS, NIGHTCRAWLER, FIRESTAR AND KITTY PRYDE. EGO ASIDE, THAT'S SOME A-LIST X-MEN RIGHT THERE.
KTHUK

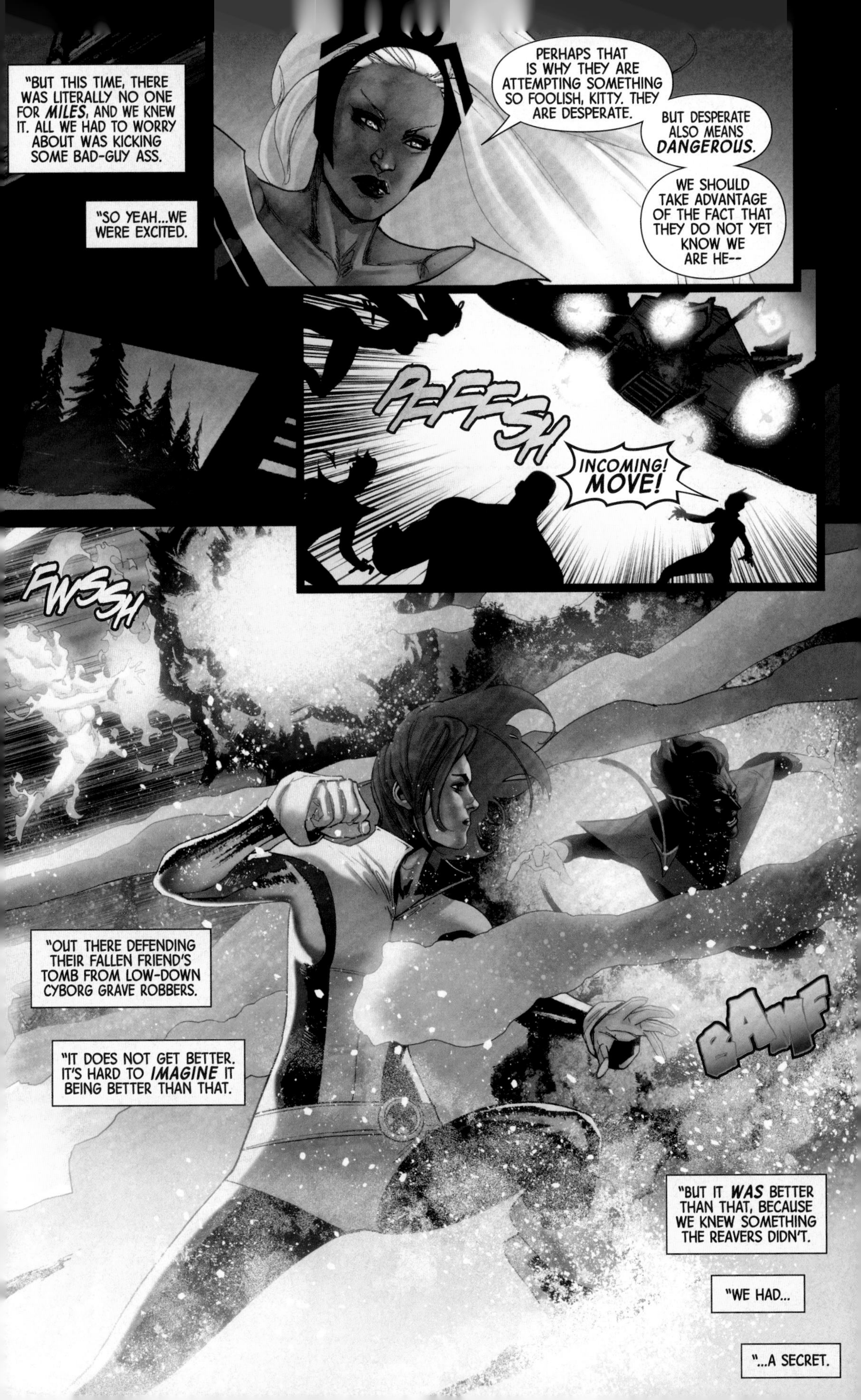
"BUT THIS TIME, THERE WAS LITERALLY NO ONE FOR MILES, AND WE KNEW IT. ALL WE HAD TO WORRY ABOUT WAS KICKING SOME BAD-GUY ASS.
"SO YEAH...WE WERE EXCITED.
PERHAPS THAT IS WHY THEY ARE ATTEMPTING SOMETHING SO FOOLISH, KITTY. THEY ARE DESPERATE.
BUT DESPERATE ALSO MEANS DANGEROUS.
WE SHOULD TAKE ADVANTAGE OF THE FACT THAT THEY DO NOT YET KNOW WE ARE HE--
PEFFSH
INCOMING! MOVE!
FWSSH
"OUT THERE DEFENDING THEIR FALLEN FRIEND'S TOMB FROM LOW-DOWN CYBORG GRAVE ROBBERS.
"IT DOES NOT GET BETTER. IT'S HARD TO IMAGINE IT BEING BETTER THAN THAT.
BAMF
"BUT IT WAS BETTER THAN THAT, BECAUSE WE KNEW SOMETHING THE REAVERS DIDN'T.
"WE HAD...
"...A SECRET.

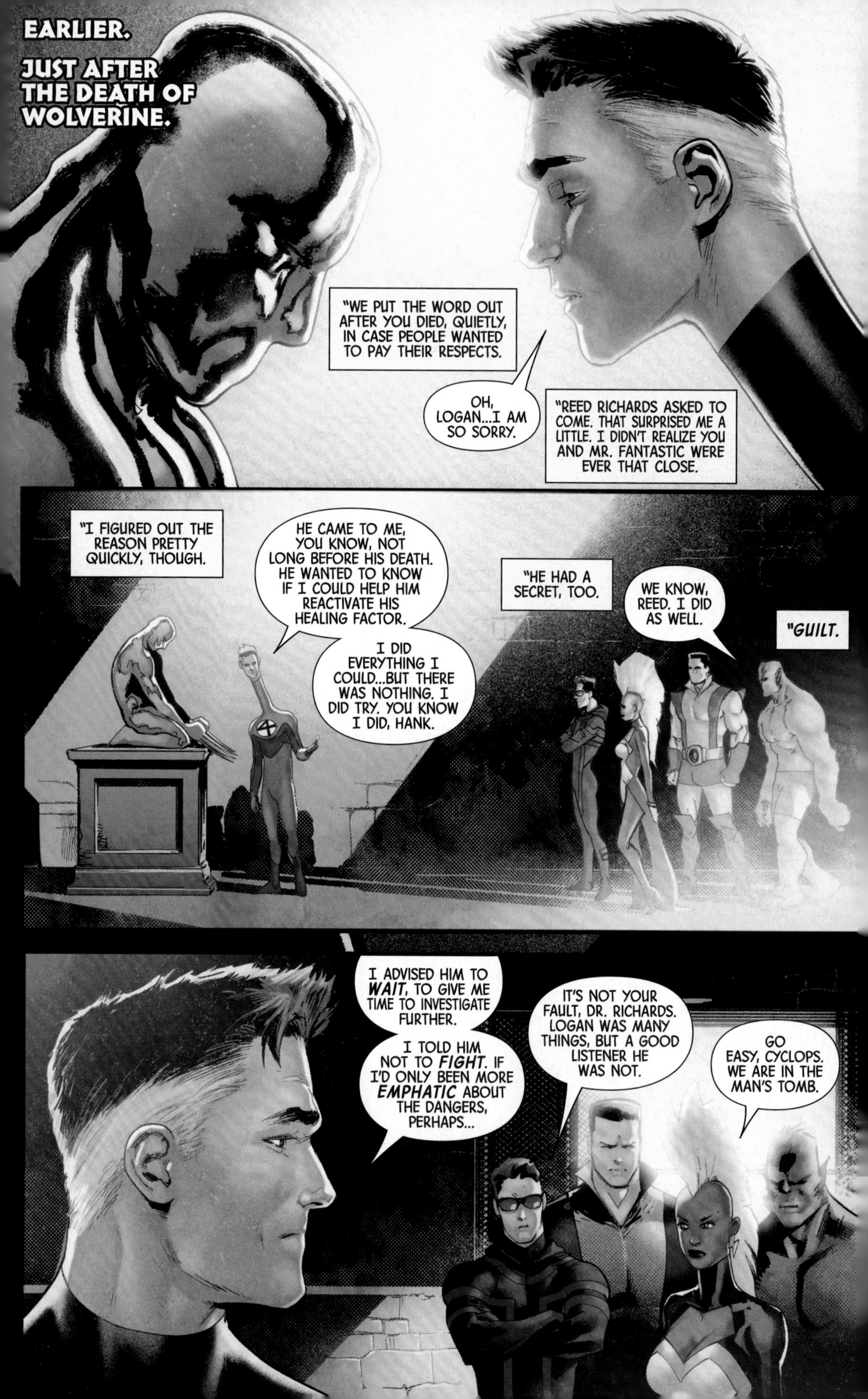
EARLIER.
JUST AFTER THE DEATH OF WOLVERINE.
"WE PUT THE WORD OUT AFTER YOU DIED, QUIETLY, IN CASE PEOPLE WANTED TO PAY THEIR RESPECTS.
OH, LOGAN...I AM SO SORRY.
"REED RICHARDS ASKED TO COME. THAT SURPRISED ME A LITTLE. I DIDN'T REALIZE YOU AND MR. FANTASTIC WERE EVER THAT CLOSE.
"I FIGURED OUT THE REASON PRETTY QUICKLY, THOUGH.
HE CAME TO ME, YOU KNOW, NOT LONG BEFORE HIS DEATH. HE WANTED TO KNOW IF I COULD HELP HIM REACTIVATE HIS HEALING FACTOR.
I DID EVERYTHING I COULD...BUT THERE WAS NOTHING. I DID TRY. YOU KNOW I DID, HANK.
"HE HAD A SECRET, TOO.
WE KNOW, REED. I DID AS WELL.
"GUILT.
I ADVISED HIM TO WAIT, TO GIVE ME TIME TO INVESTIGATE FURTHER.
I TOLD HIM NOT TO FIGHT. IF I'D ONLY BEEN MORE EMPHATIC ABOUT THE DANGERS, PERHAPS...
IT'S NOT YOUR FAULT, DR. RICHARDS. LOGAN WAS MANY THINGS, BUT A GOOD LISTENER HE WAS NOT.
GO EASY, CYCLOPS. WE ARE IN THE MAN'S TOMB.

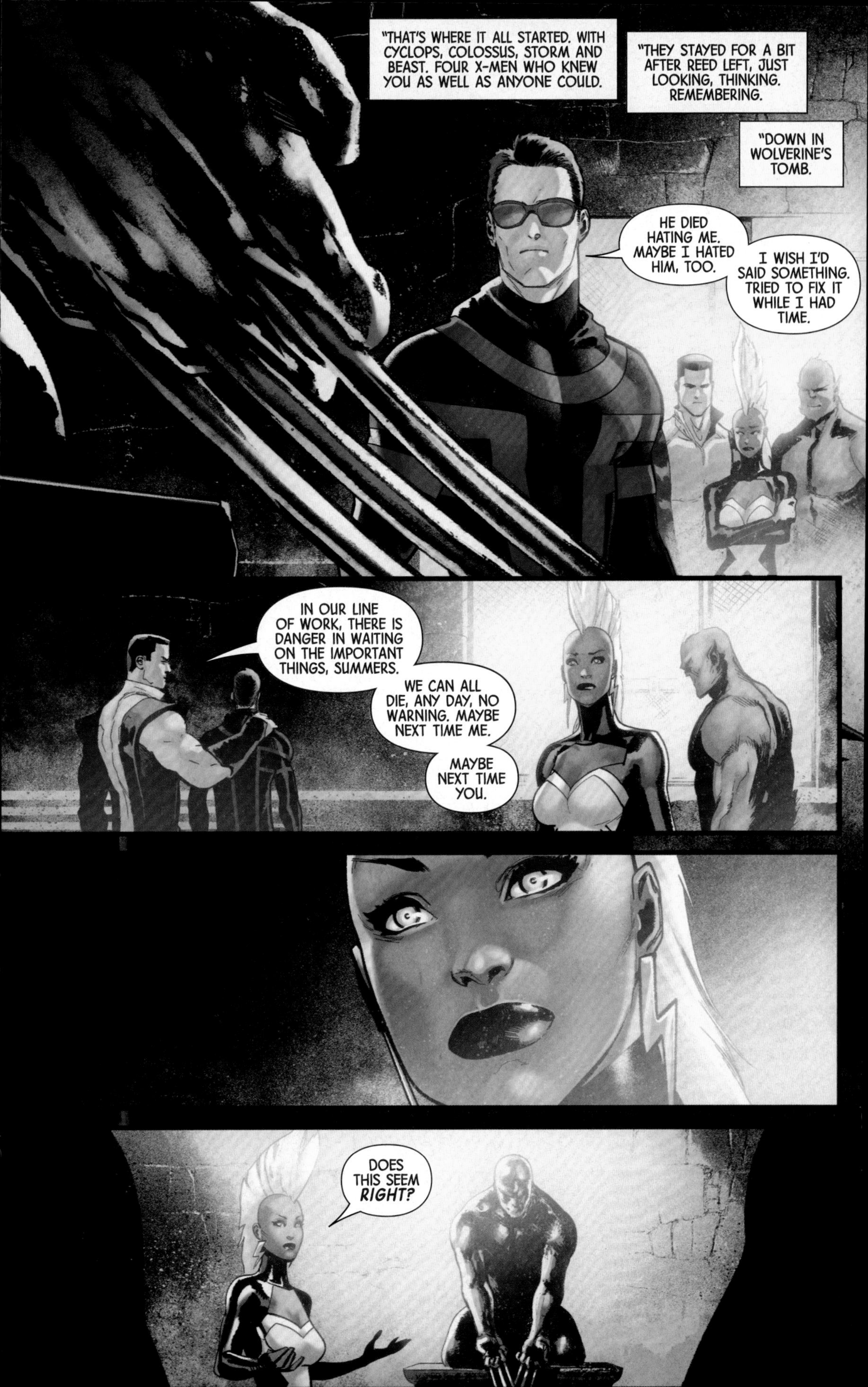
"THAT'S WHERE IT ALL STARTED. WITH CYCLOPS, COLOSSUS, STORM AND BEAST. FOUR X-MEN WHO KNEW YOU AS WELL AS ANYONE COULD.
"THEY STAYED FOR A BIT AFTER REED LEFT, JUST LOOKING, THINKING. REMEMBERING.
"DOWN IN WOLVERINE'S TOMB.
HE DIED HATING ME. MAYBE I HATED HIM, TOO.
I WISH I'D SAID SOMETHING. TRIED TO FIX IT WHILE I HAD TIME.
IN OUR LINE OF WORK, THERE IS DANGER IN WAITING ON THE IMPORTANT THINGS, SUMMERS.
WE CAN ALL DIE, ANY DAY, NO WARNING. MAYBE NEXT TIME ME.
MAYBE NEXT TIME YOU.
DOES THIS SEEM *RIGHT?*

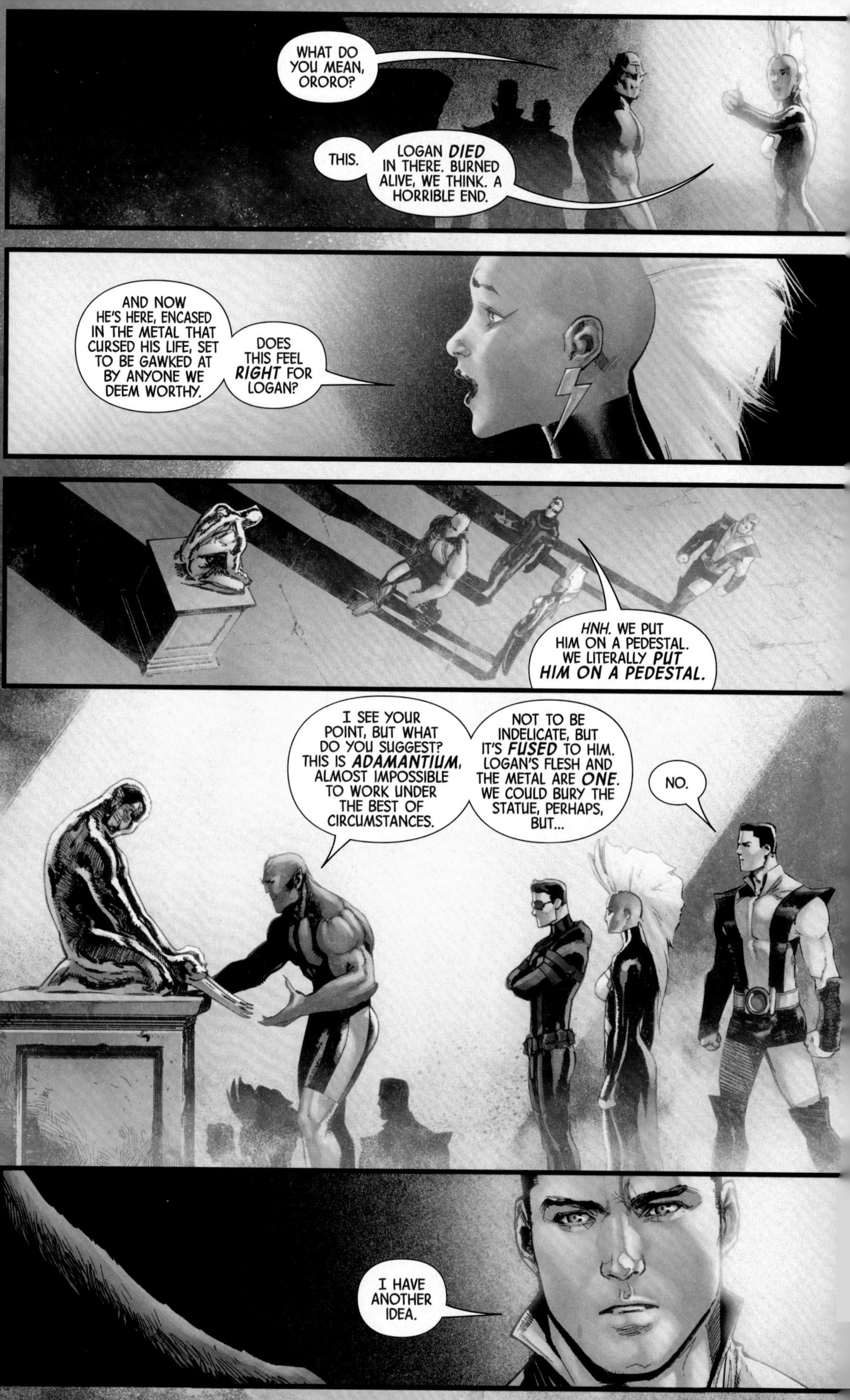
WHAT DO YOU MEAN, ORORO?
THIS.
LOGAN DIED IN THERE. BURNED ALIVE, WE THINK. A HORRIBLE END.
AND NOW HE'S HERE, ENCASED IN THE METAL THAT CURSED HIS LIFE, SET TO BE GAWKED AT BY ANYONE WE DEEM WORTHY.
DOES THIS FEEL RIGHT FOR LOGAN?
HNH. WE PUT HIM ON A PEDESTAL. WE LITERALLY PUT HIM ON A PEDESTAL.
I SEE YOUR POINT, BUT WHAT DO YOU SUGGEST? THIS IS ADAMANTIUM, ALMOST IMPOSSIBLE TO WORK UNDER THE BEST OF CIRCUMSTANCES.
NOT TO BE INDELICATE, BUT IT'S FUSED TO HIM. LOGAN'S FLESH AND THE METAL ARE ONE. WE COULD BURY THE STATUE, PERHAPS, BUT...
NO.
I HAVE ANOTHER IDEA.

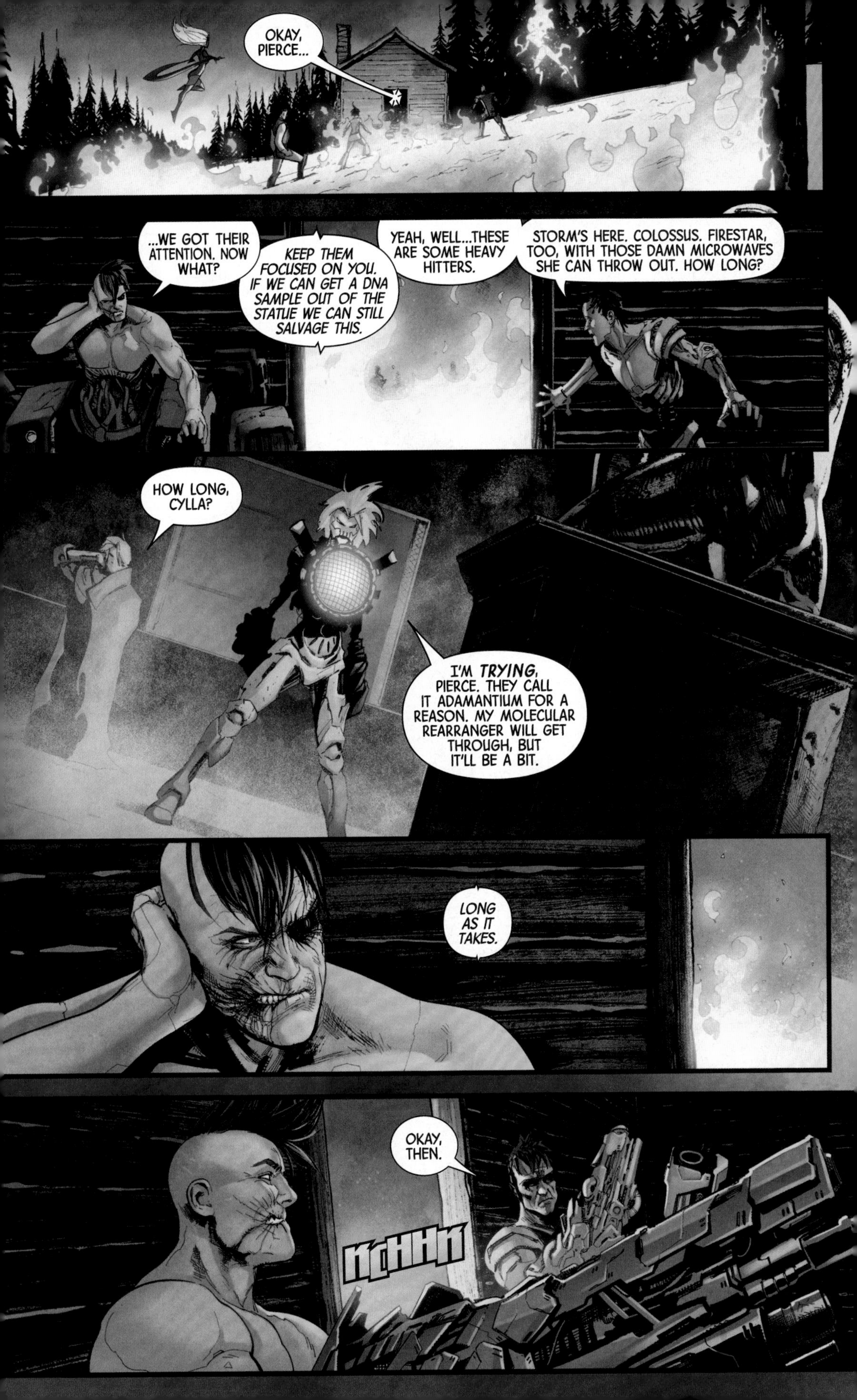
OKAY, PIERCE...
...WE GOT THEIR ATTENTION. NOW WHAT?
KEEP THEM FOCUSED ON YOU. IF WE CAN GET A DNA SAMPLE OUT OF THE STATUE WE CAN STILL SALVAGE THIS.
YEAH, WELL...THESE ARE SOME HEAVY HITTERS.
STORM'S HERE. COLOSSUS. FIRESTAR, TOO, WITH THOSE DAMN MICROWAVES SHE CAN THROW OUT. HOW LONG?
HOW LONG, CYLLA?
I'M TRYING, PIERCE. THEY CALL IT ADAMANTIUM FOR A REASON. MY MOLECULAR REARRANGER WILL GET THROUGH, BUT IT'LL BE A BIT.
LONG AS IT TAKES.
OKAY, THEN.
KCHHK

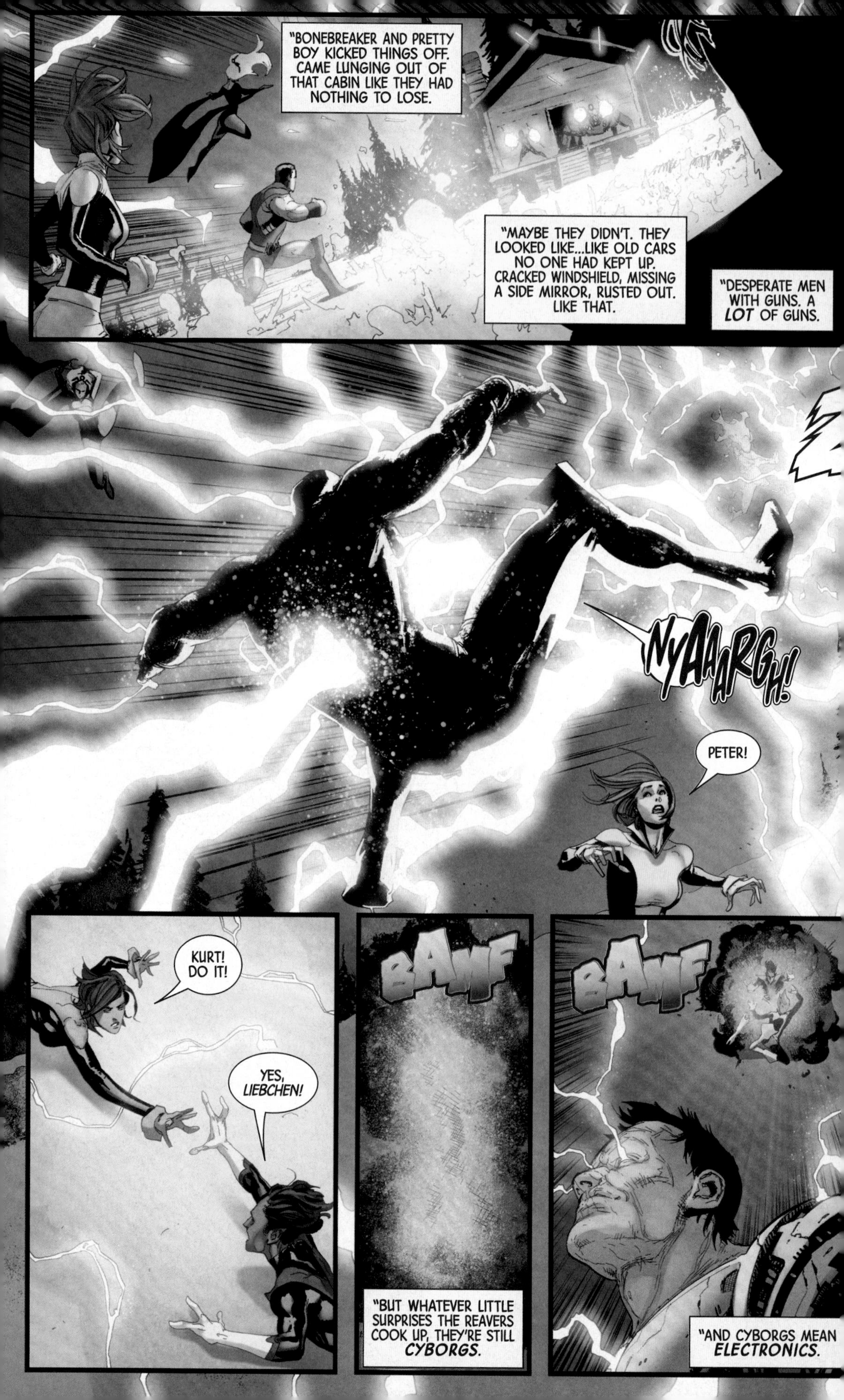
"BONEBREAKER AND PRETTY BOY KICKED THINGS OFF. CAME LUNGING OUT OF THAT CABIN LIKE THEY HAD NOTHING TO LOSE.
"MAYBE THEY DIDN'T. THEY LOOKED LIKE...LIKE OLD CARS NO ONE HAD KEPT UP. CRACKED WINDSHIELD, MISSING A SIDE MIRROR, RUSTED OUT. LIKE THAT.
"DESPERATE MEN WITH GUNS. A *LOT* OF GUNS.
NYAAARGH!
PETER!
KURT! DO IT!
YES, LIEBCHEN!
BAMF
"BUT WHATEVER LITTLE SURPRISES THE REAVERS COOK UP, THEY'RE STILL *CYBORGS*.
BAMF
"AND CYBORGS MEAN *ELECTRONICS*.

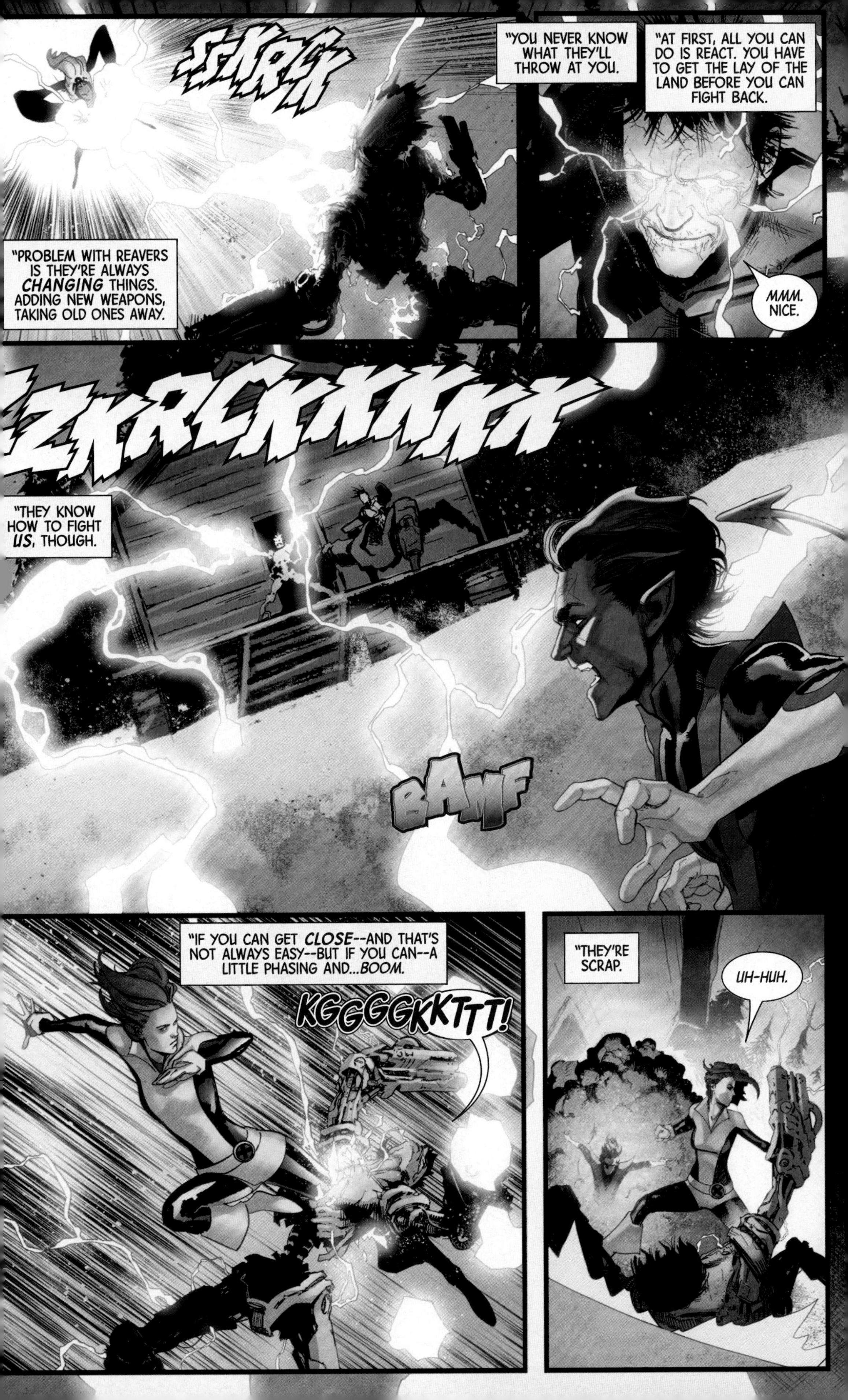

SKRAK
"YOU NEVER KNOW WHAT THEY'LL THROW AT YOU.
"AT FIRST, ALL YOU CAN DO IS REACT. YOU HAVE TO GET THE LAY OF THE LAND BEFORE YOU CAN FIGHT BACK.
"PROBLEM WITH REAVERS IS THEY'RE ALWAYS CHANGING THINGS. ADDING NEW WEAPONS, TAKING OLD ONES AWAY.
MMM. NICE.
ZKRCKKKKK
"THEY KNOW HOW TO FIGHT US, THOUGH.
BAMF
"IF YOU CAN GET CLOSE--AND THAT'S NOT ALWAYS EASY--BUT IF YOU CAN--A LITTLE PHASING AND...BOOM.
KGGGGKKTTT!
"THEY'RE SCRAP.
UH-HUH.

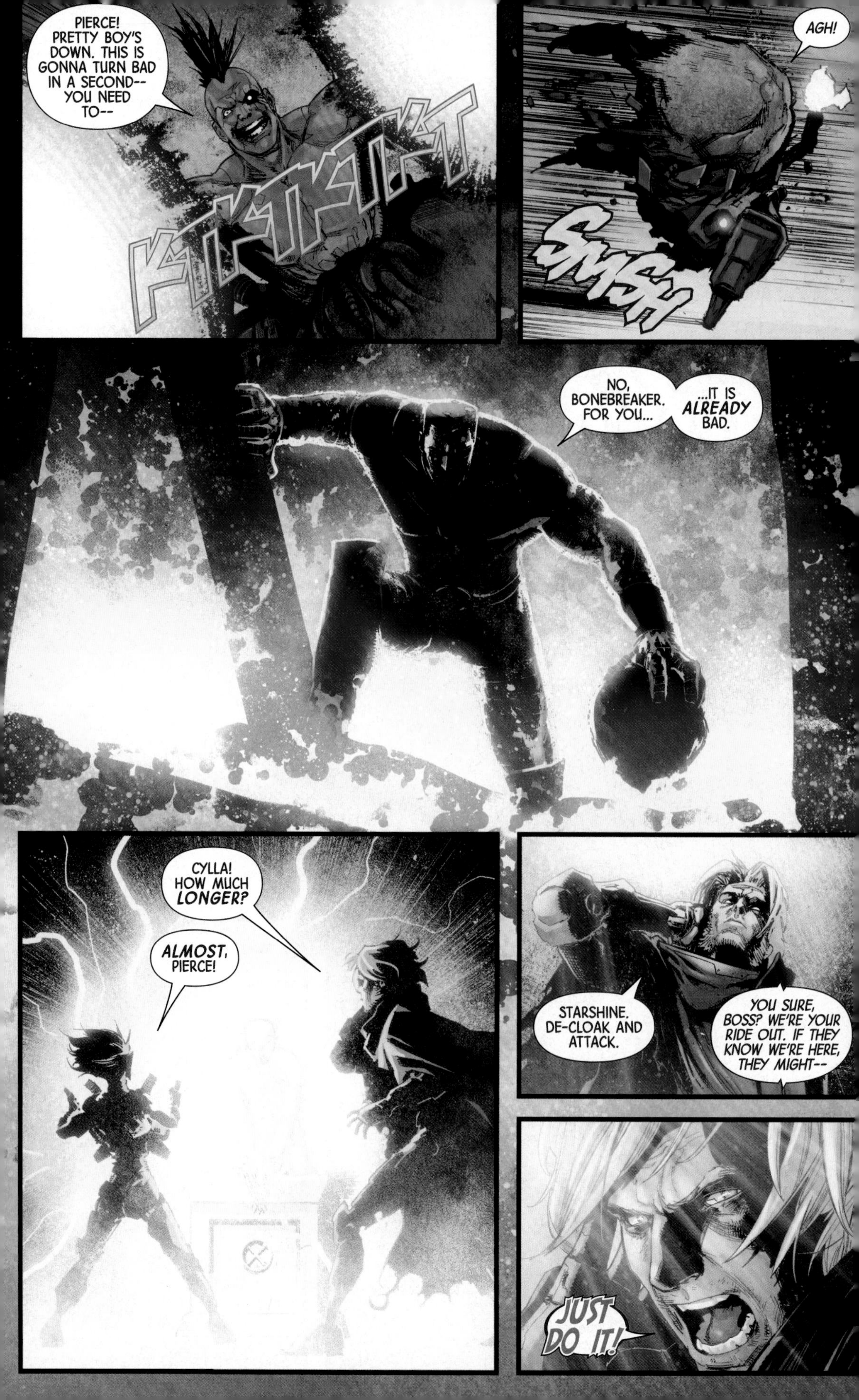
PIERCE! PRETTY BOY'S DOWN. THIS IS GONNA TURN BAD IN A SECOND-- YOU NEED TO--
KTKTKTKT
AGH!
SMSH
NO, BONEBREAKER. FOR YOU...
...IT IS ALREADY BAD.
CYLLA! HOW MUCH LONGER?
ALMOST, PIERCE!
STARSHINE. DE-CLOAK AND ATTACK.
YOU SURE, BOSS? WE'RE YOUR RIDE OUT. IF THEY KNOW WE'RE HERE, THEY MIGHT--
JUST DO IT!

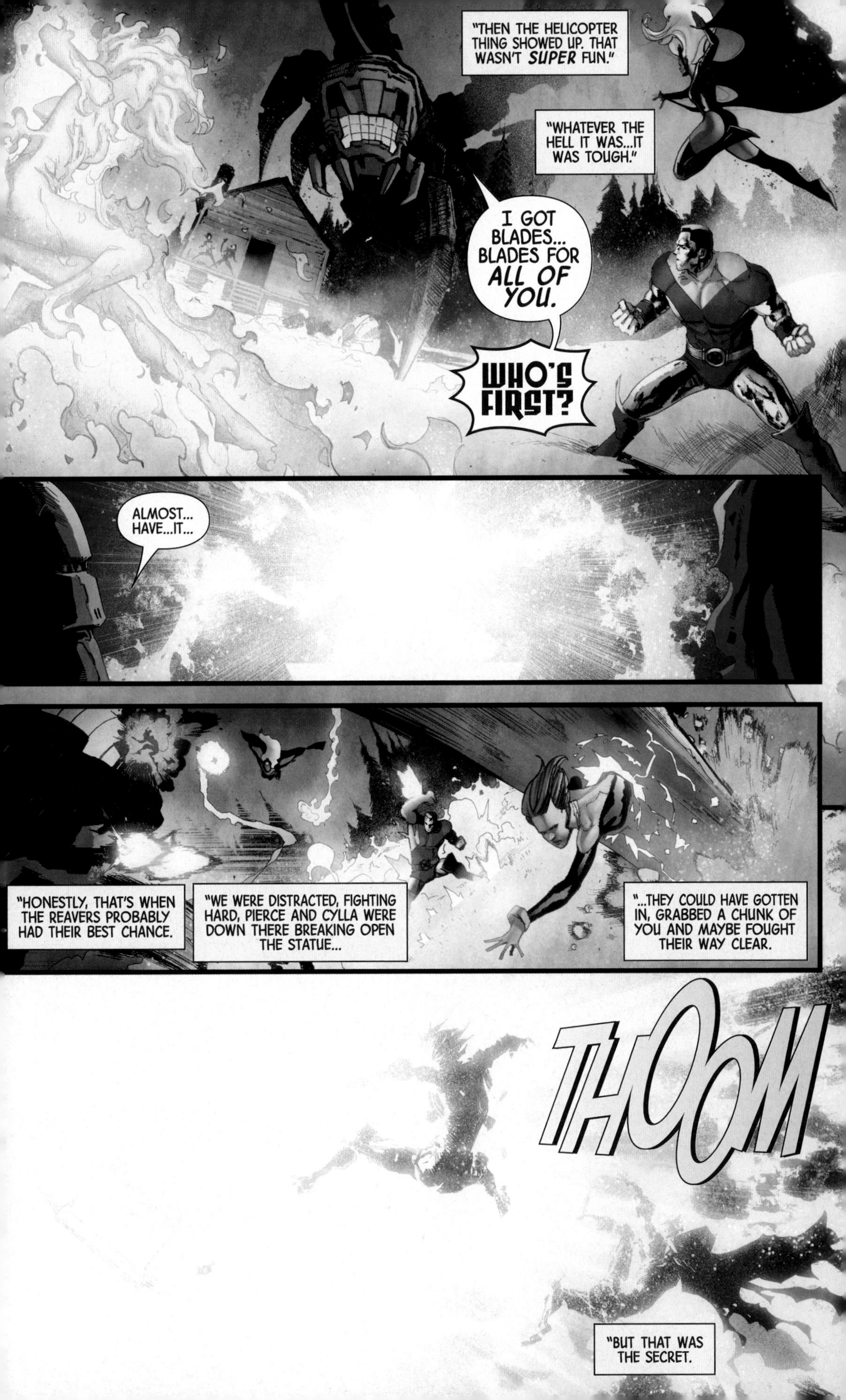
"THEN THE HELICOPTER THING SHOWED UP. THAT WASN'T *SUPER* FUN."
"WHATEVER THE HELL IT WAS...IT WAS TOUGH."
I GOT BLADES... BLADES FOR **ALL OF YOU.**
WHO'S FIRST?
ALMOST... HAVE...IT...
"HONESTLY, THAT'S WHEN THE REAVERS PROBABLY HAD THEIR BEST CHANCE.
"WE WERE DISTRACTED, FIGHTING HARD, PIERCE AND CYLLA WERE DOWN THERE BREAKING OPEN THE STATUE...
"...THEY COULD HAVE GOTTEN IN, GRABBED A CHUNK OF YOU AND MAYBE FOUGHT THEIR WAY CLEAR.
THOOM
"BUT THAT WAS THE SECRET.

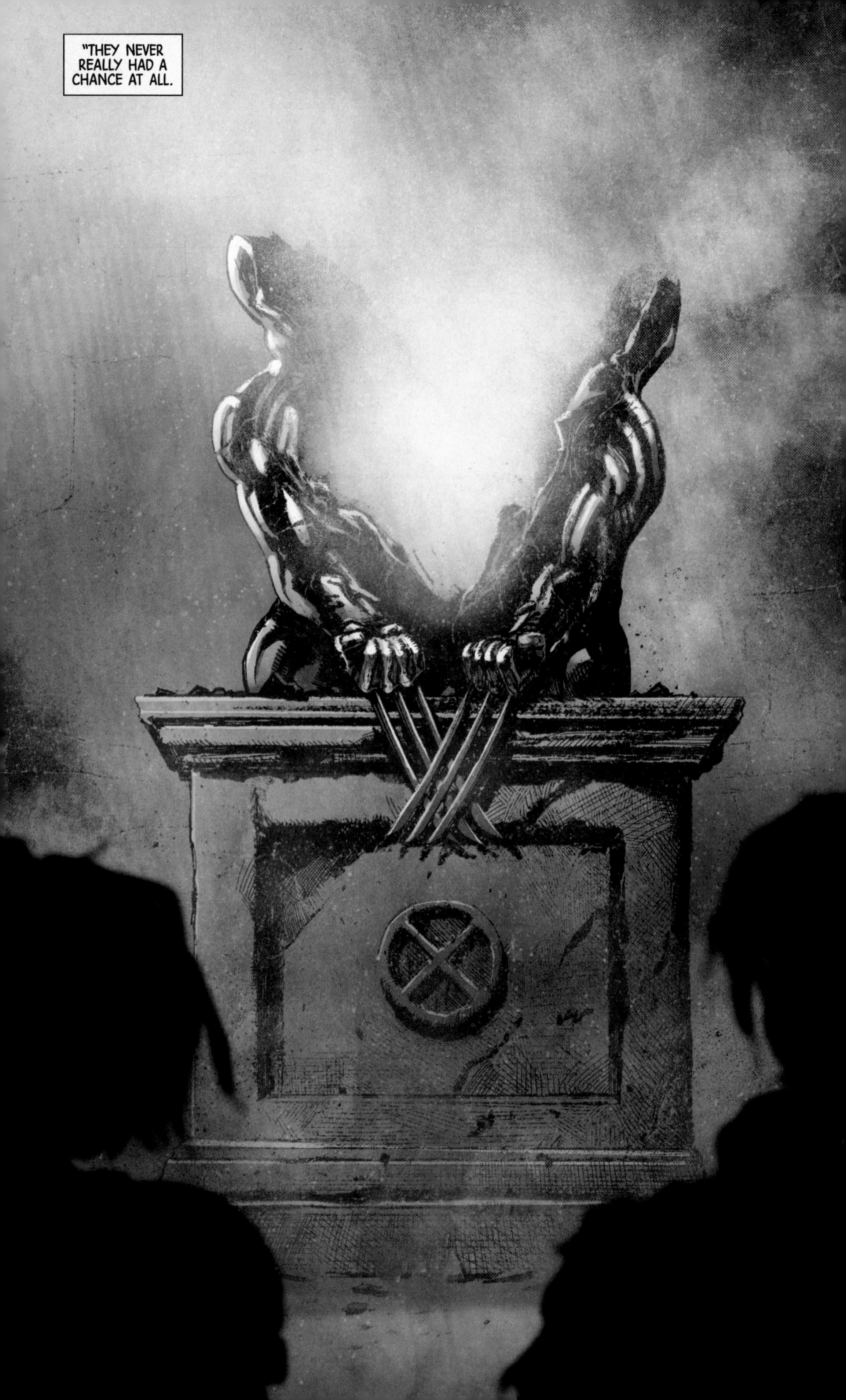
"THEY NEVER REALLY HAD A CHANCE AT ALL.

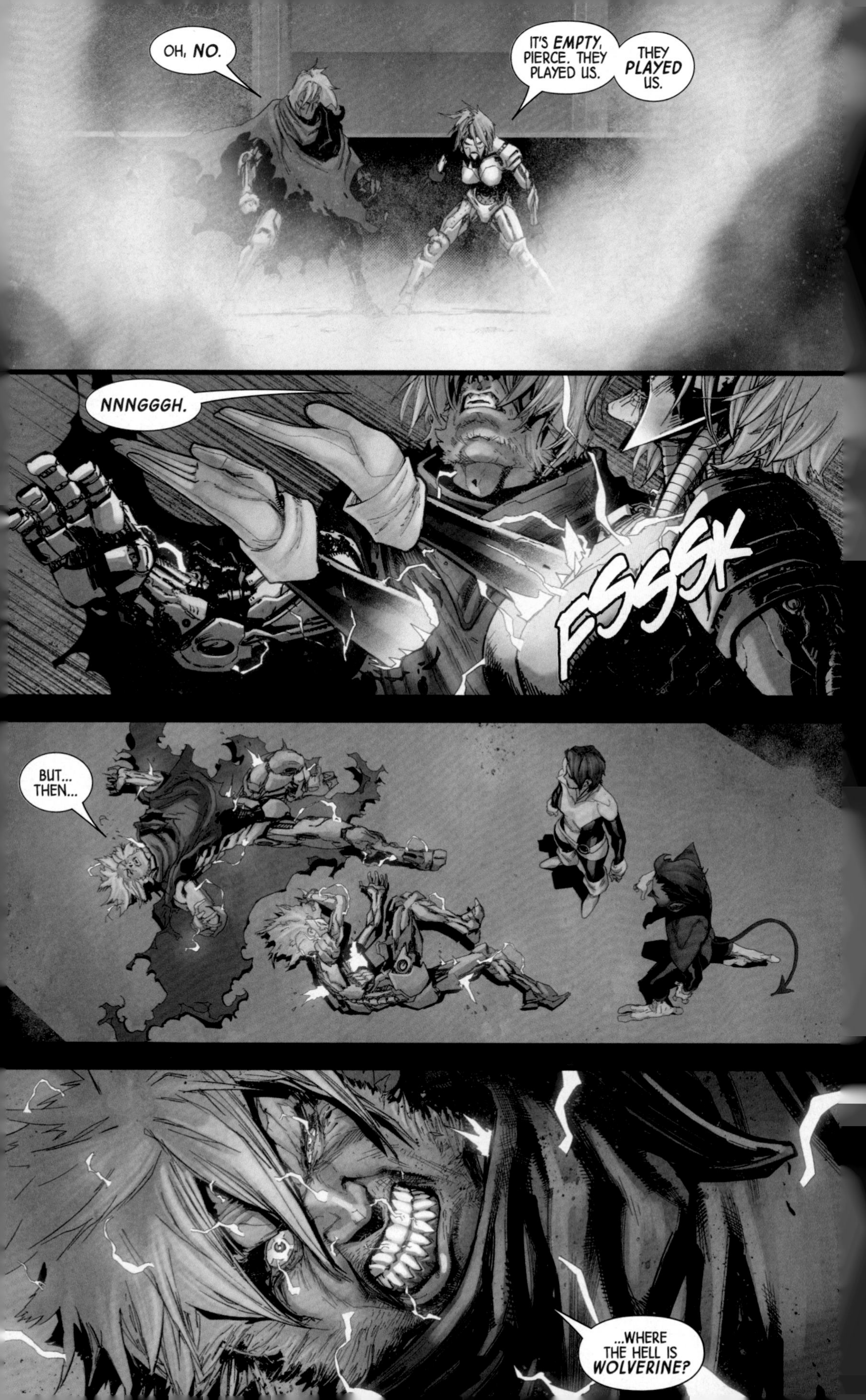
OH, NO.
IT'S EMPTY, PIERCE. THEY PLAYED US.
THEY PLAYED US.
NNNGGGH.
FSSSK
BUT... THEN...
...WHERE THE HELL IS WOLVERINE?

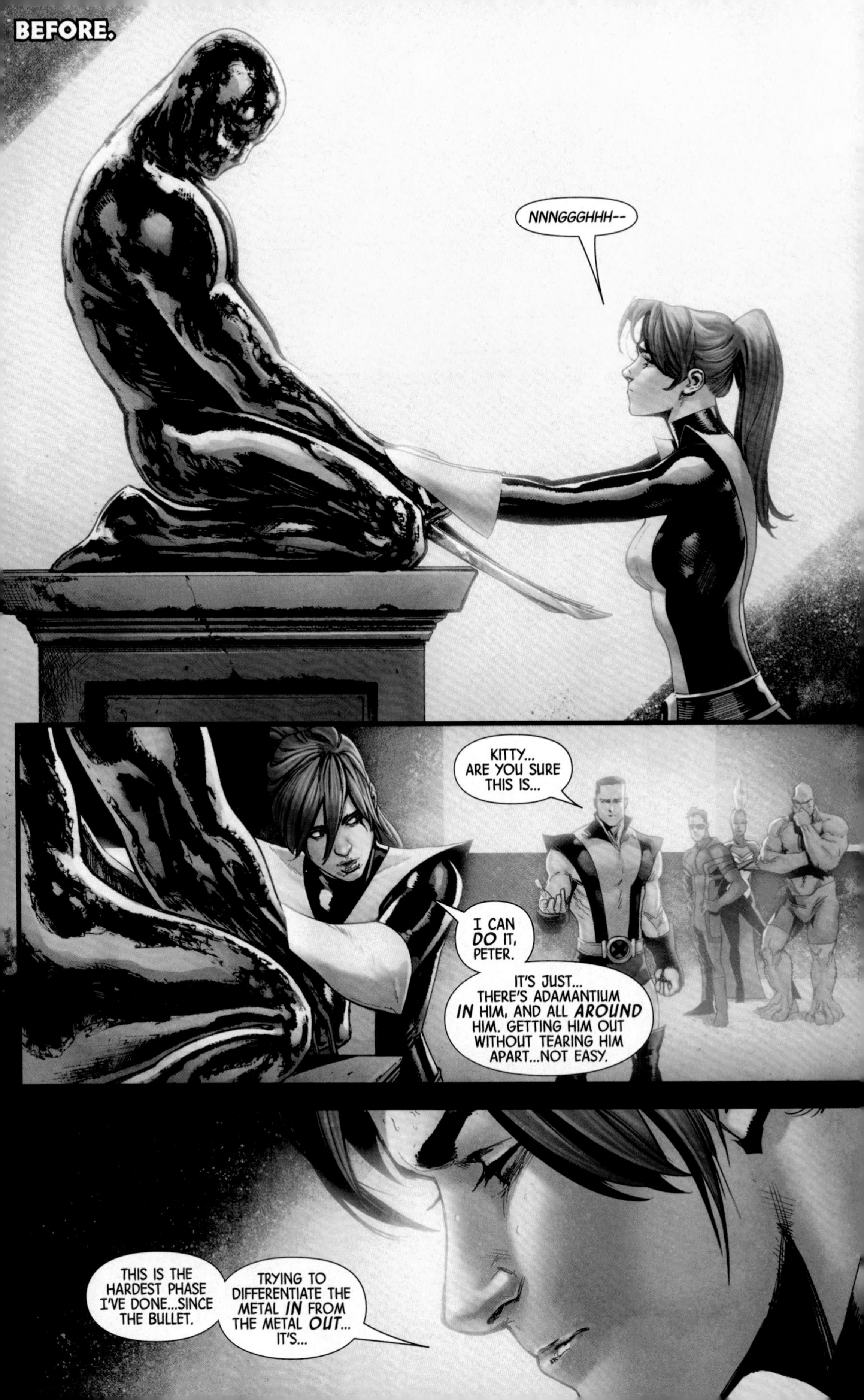
BEFORE.
NNNGGGHHH--
KITTY... ARE YOU SURE THIS IS...
I CAN DO IT, PETER.
IT'S JUST... THERE'S ADAMANTIUM IN HIM, AND ALL AROUND HIM. GETTING HIM OUT WITHOUT TEARING HIM APART...NOT EASY.
THIS IS THE HARDEST PHASE I'VE DONE...SINCE THE BULLET.
TRYING TO DIFFERENTIATE THE METAL IN FROM THE METAL OUT... IT'S...

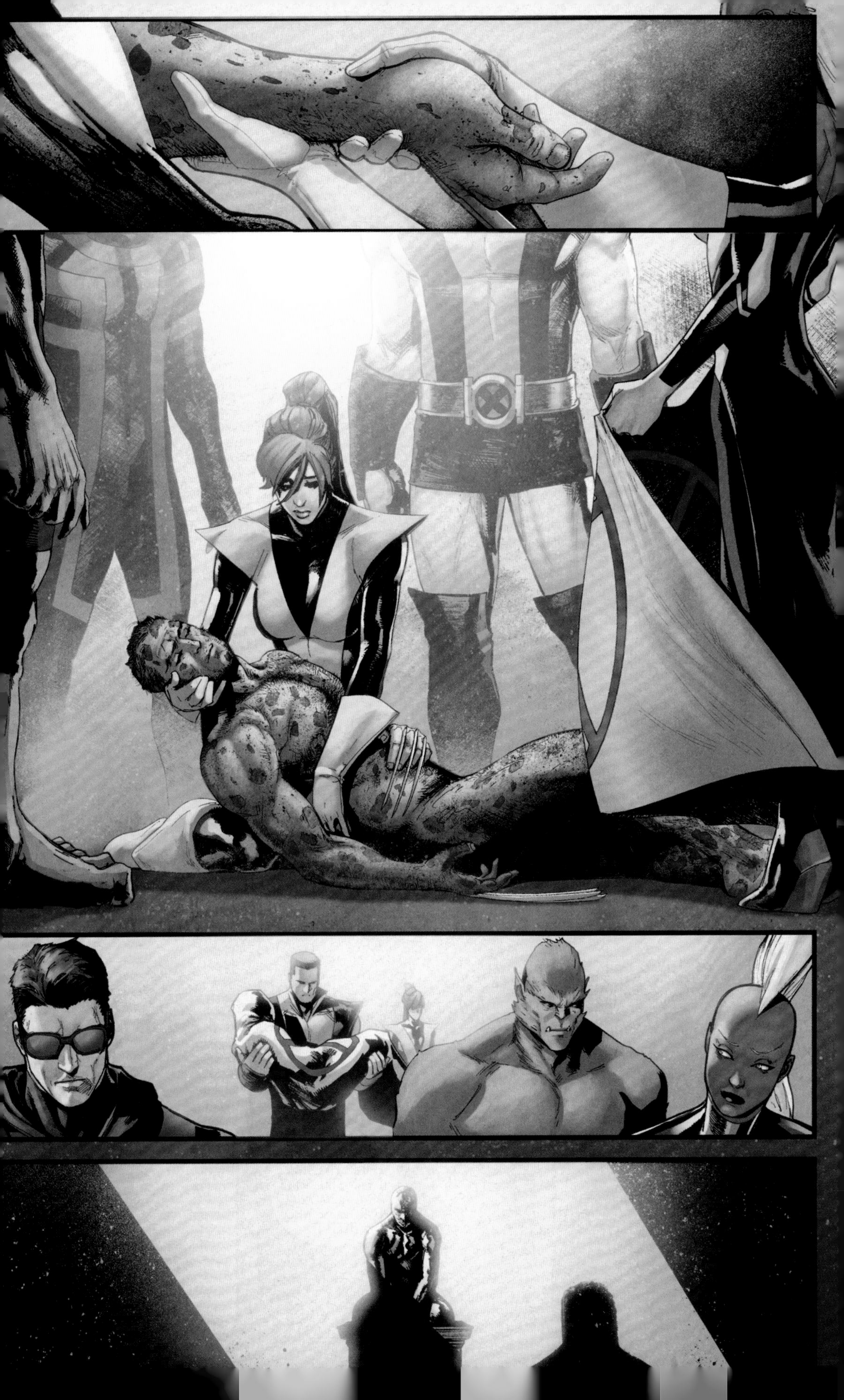

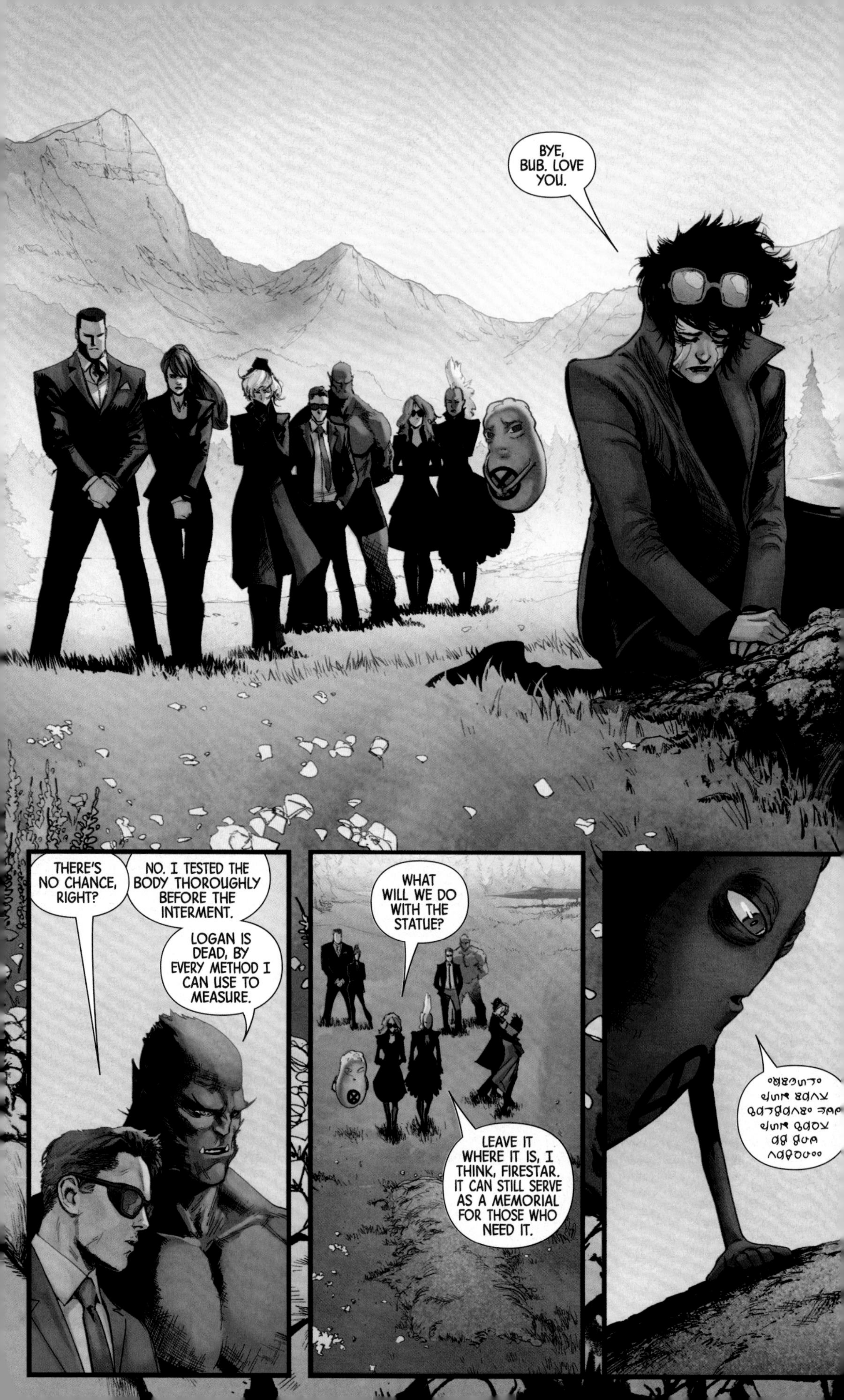
BYE, BUB. LOVE YOU.
THERE'S NO CHANCE, RIGHT?
NO. I TESTED THE BODY THOROUGHLY BEFORE THE INTERMENT.
LOGAN IS DEAD, BY EVERY METHOD I CAN USE TO MEASURE.
WHAT WILL WE DO WITH THE STATUE?
LEAVE IT WHERE IT IS, I THINK, FIRESTAR. IT CAN STILL SERVE AS A MEMORIAL FOR THOSE WHO NEED IT.

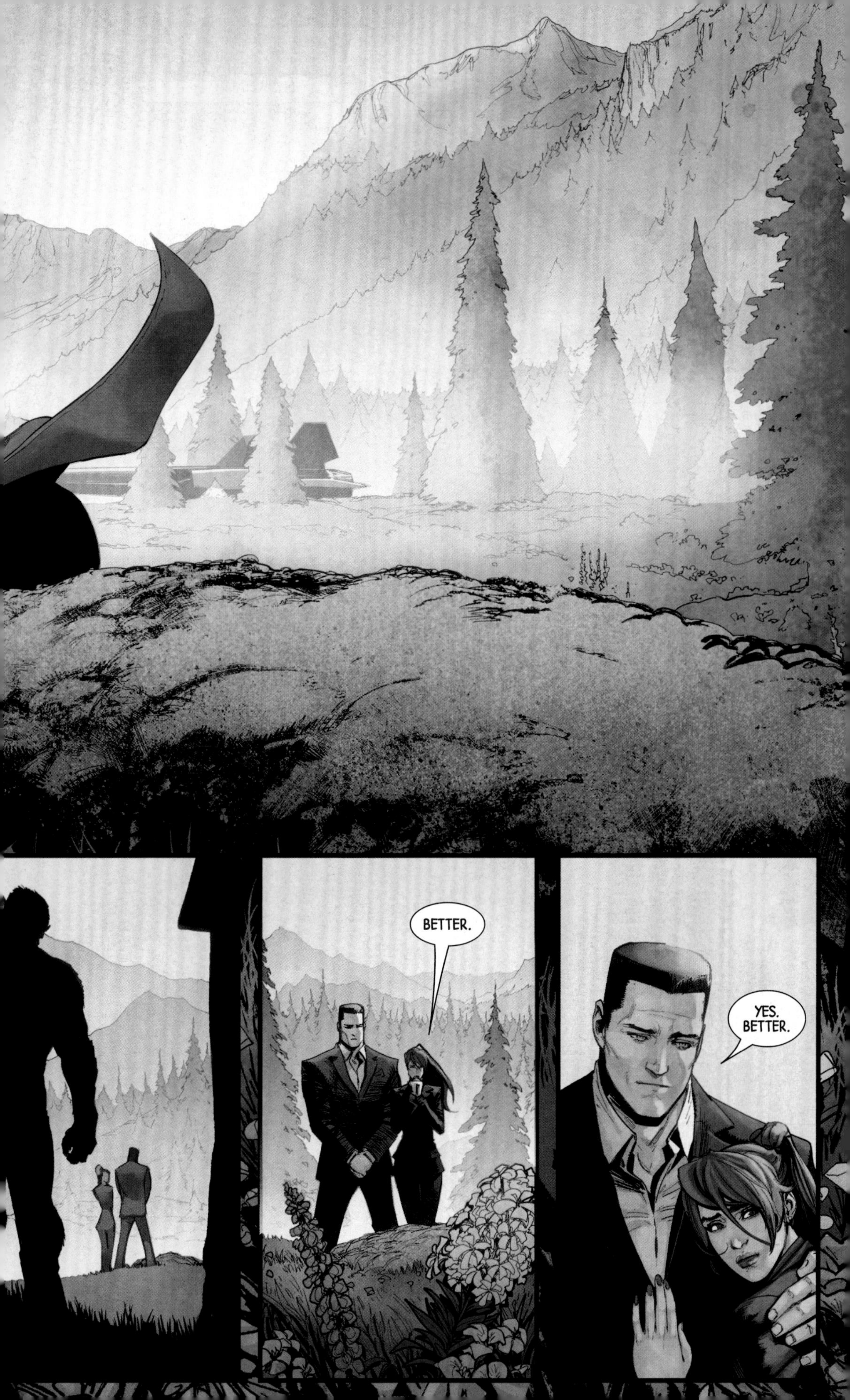
BETTER.
YES. BETTER.

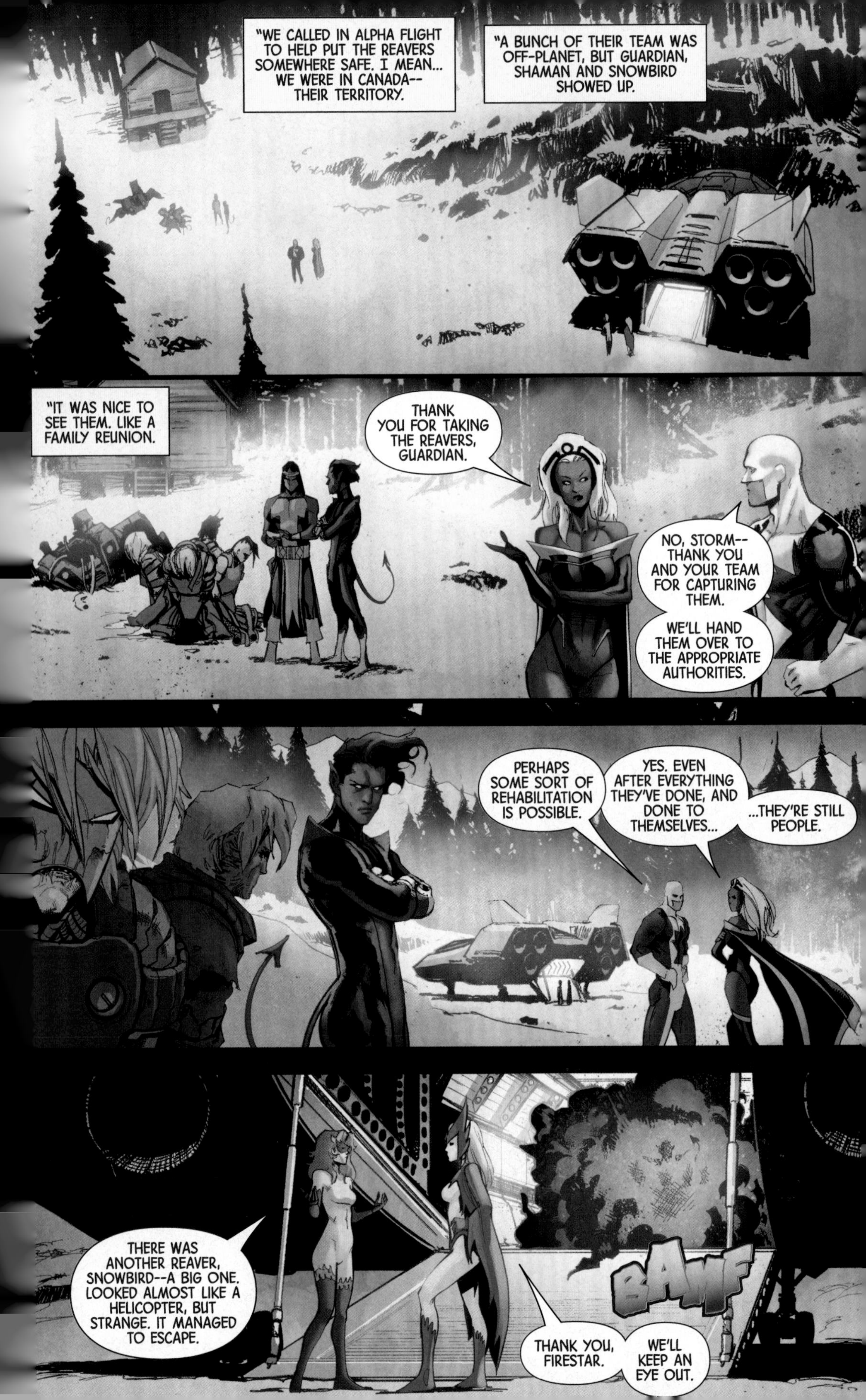
"WE CALLED IN ALPHA FLIGHT TO HELP PUT THE REAVERS SOMEWHERE SAFE. I MEAN... WE WERE IN CANADA-- THEIR TERRITORY.
"A BUNCH OF THEIR TEAM WAS OFF-PLANET, BUT GUARDIAN, SHAMAN AND SNOWBIRD SHOWED UP.
"IT WAS NICE TO SEE THEM. LIKE A FAMILY REUNION.
THANK YOU FOR TAKING THE REAVERS, GUARDIAN.
NO, STORM-- THANK YOU AND YOUR TEAM FOR CAPTURING THEM.
WE'LL HAND THEM OVER TO THE APPROPRIATE AUTHORITIES.
PERHAPS SOME SORT OF REHABILITATION IS POSSIBLE.
YES. EVEN AFTER EVERYTHING THEY'VE DONE, AND DONE TO THEMSELVES...
...THEY'RE STILL PEOPLE.
BAMF
THERE WAS ANOTHER REAVER, SNOWBIRD--A BIG ONE. LOOKED ALMOST LIKE A HELICOPTER, BUT STRANGE. IT MANAGED TO ESCAPE.
THANK YOU, FIRESTAR.
WE'LL KEEP AN EYE OUT.

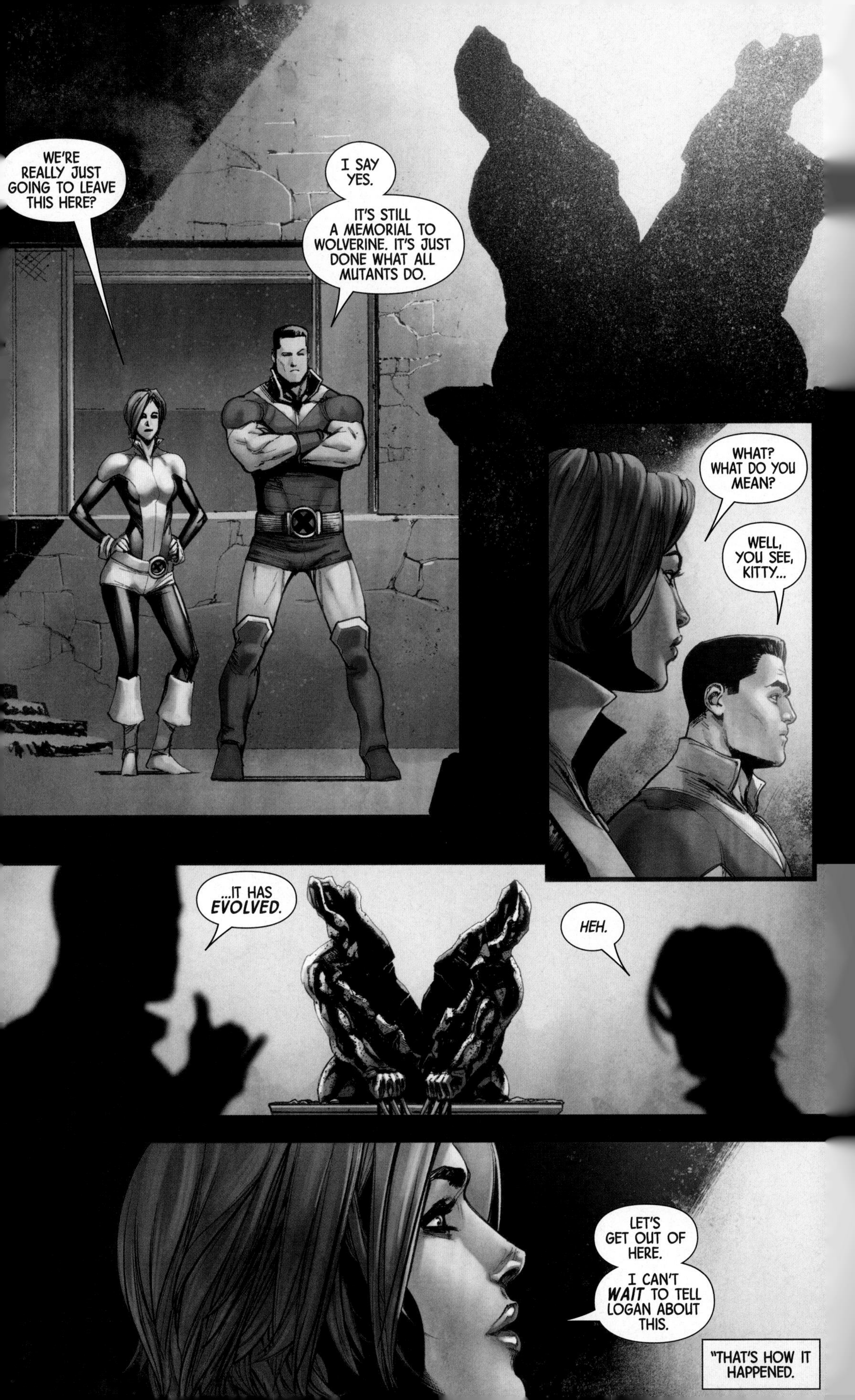
WE'RE REALLY JUST GOING TO LEAVE THIS HERE?
I SAY YES.
IT'S STILL A MEMORIAL TO WOLVERINE. IT'S JUST DONE WHAT ALL MUTANTS DO.
WHAT? WHAT DO YOU MEAN?
WELL, YOU SEE, KITTY...
...IT HAS *EVOLVED*.
HEH.
LET'S GET OUT OF HERE.
I CAN'T *WAIT* TO TELL LOGAN ABOUT THIS.
"THAT'S HOW IT HAPPENED.

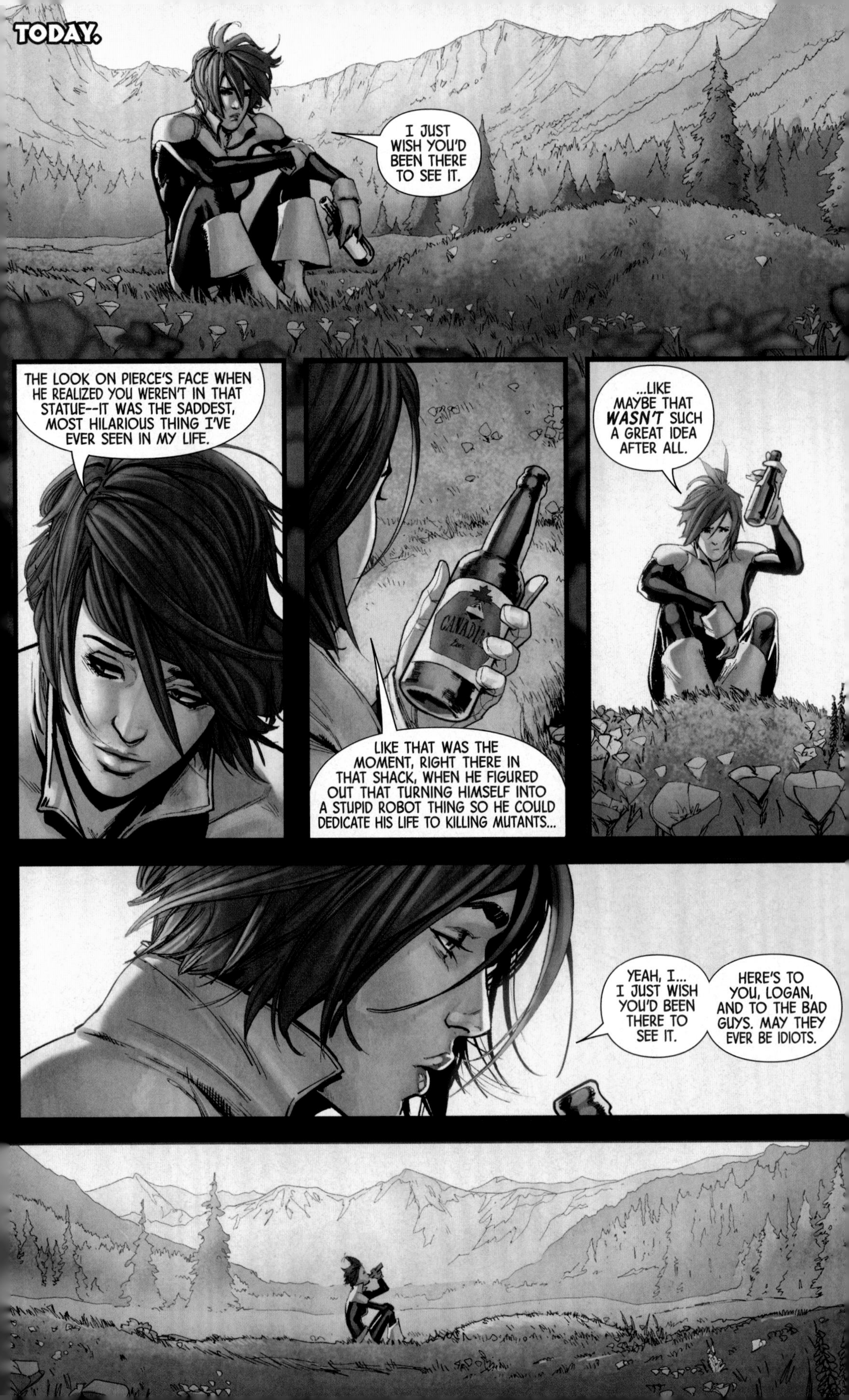

TODAY.
I JUST WISH YOU'D BEEN THERE TO SEE IT.
THE LOOK ON PIERCE'S FACE WHEN HE REALIZED YOU WEREN'T IN THAT STATUE--IT WAS THE SADDEST, MOST HILARIOUS THING I'VE EVER SEEN IN MY LIFE.
LIKE THAT WAS THE MOMENT, RIGHT THERE IN THAT SHACK, WHEN HE FIGURED OUT THAT TURNING HIMSELF INTO A STUPID ROBOT THING SO HE COULD DEDICATE HIS LIFE TO KILLING MUTANTS...
CANADIAN
...LIKE MAYBE THAT *WASN'T* SUCH A GREAT IDEA AFTER ALL.
YEAH, I... I JUST WISH YOU'D BEEN THERE TO SEE IT.
HERE'S TO YOU, LOGAN, AND TO THE BAD GUYS. MAY THEY EVER BE IDIOTS.

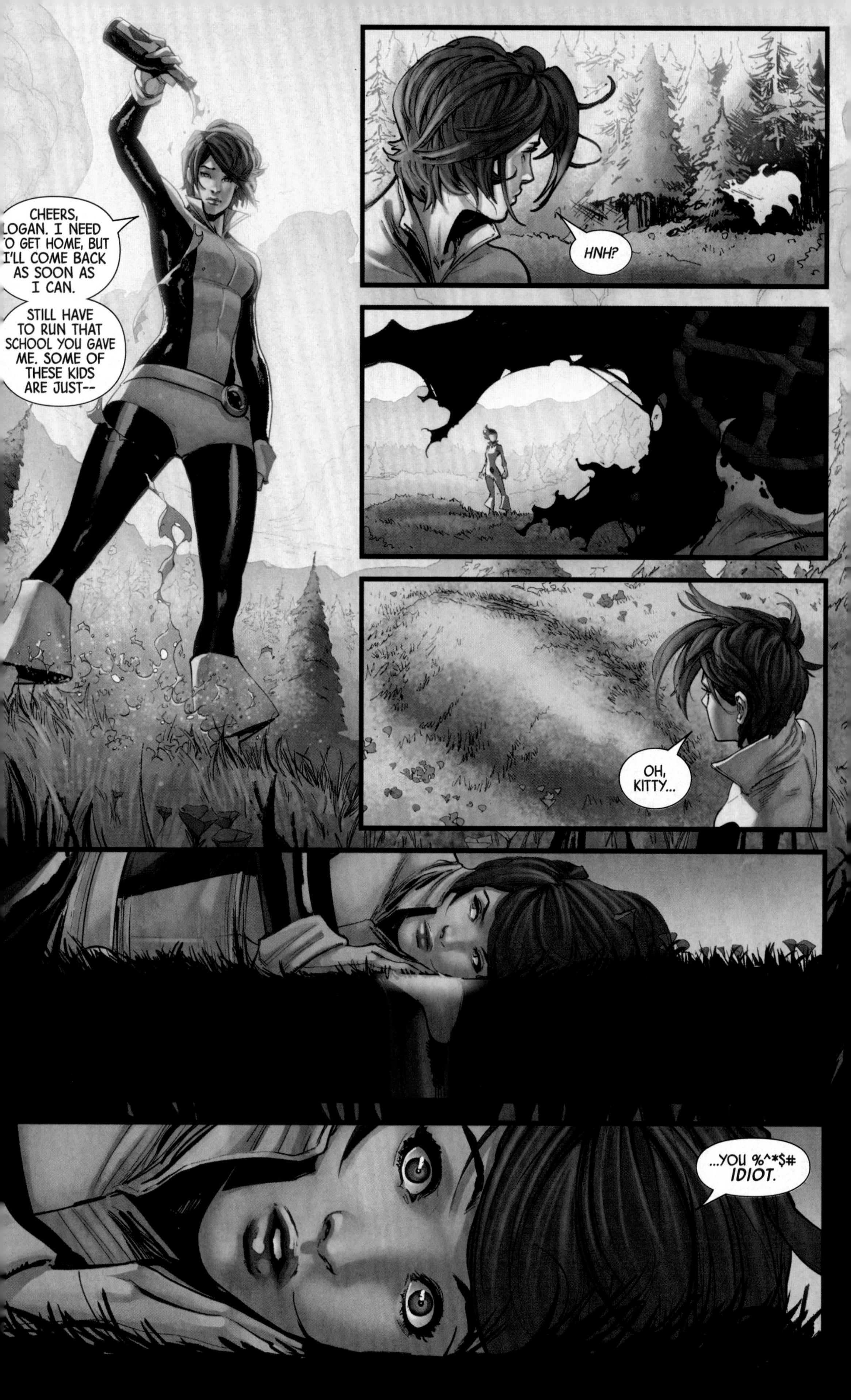

CHEERS, LOGAN. I NEED TO GET HOME, BUT I'LL COME BACK AS SOON AS I CAN.
STILL HAVE TO RUN THAT SCHOOL YOU GAVE ME. SOME OF THESE KIDS ARE JUST--
HNH?
OH, KITTY...
...YOU %^*$# IDIOT.

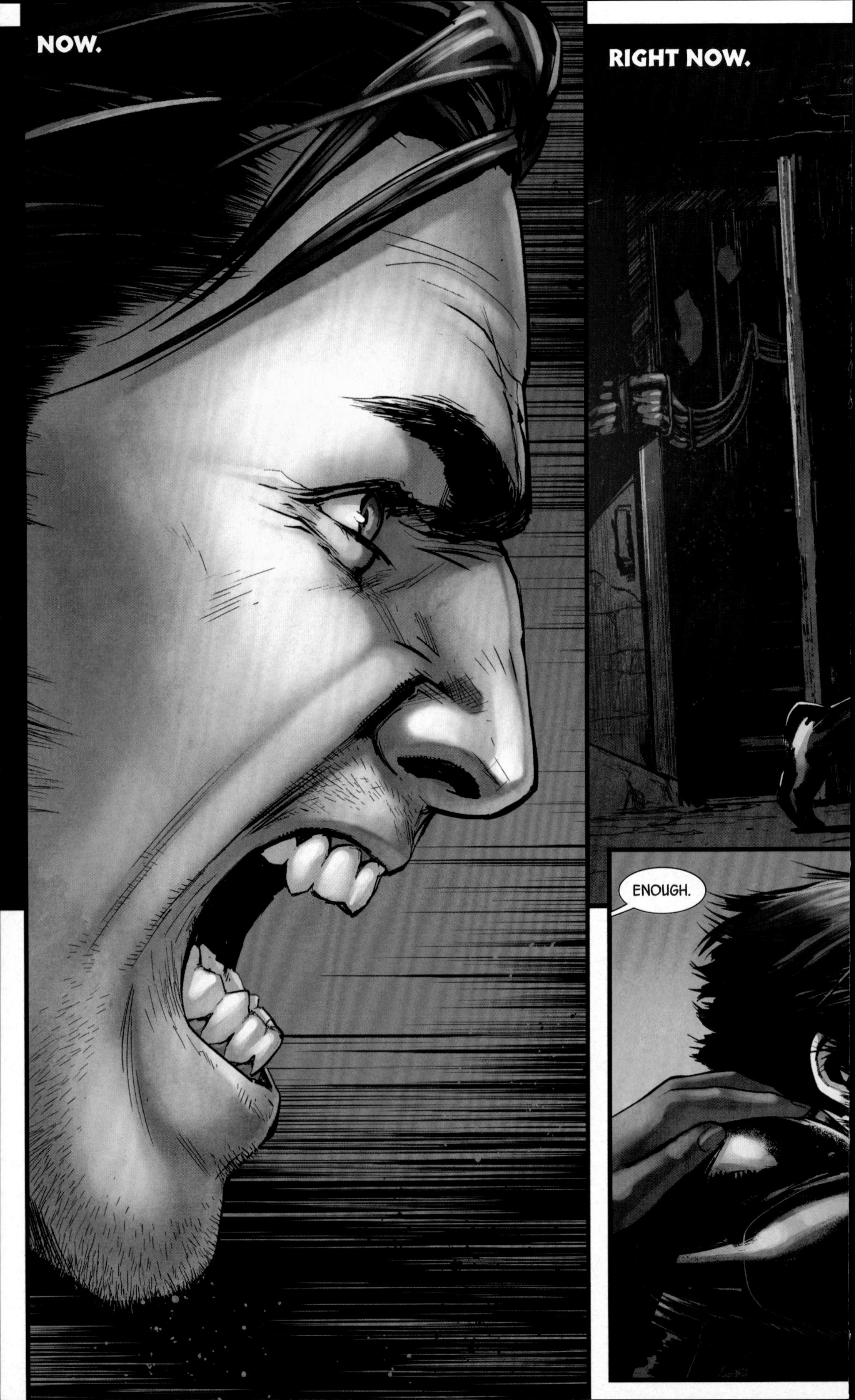
NOW.
RIGHT NOW.
ENOUGH.

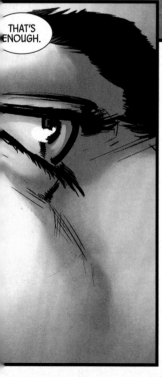

THAT'S ENOUGH.

SNIKT

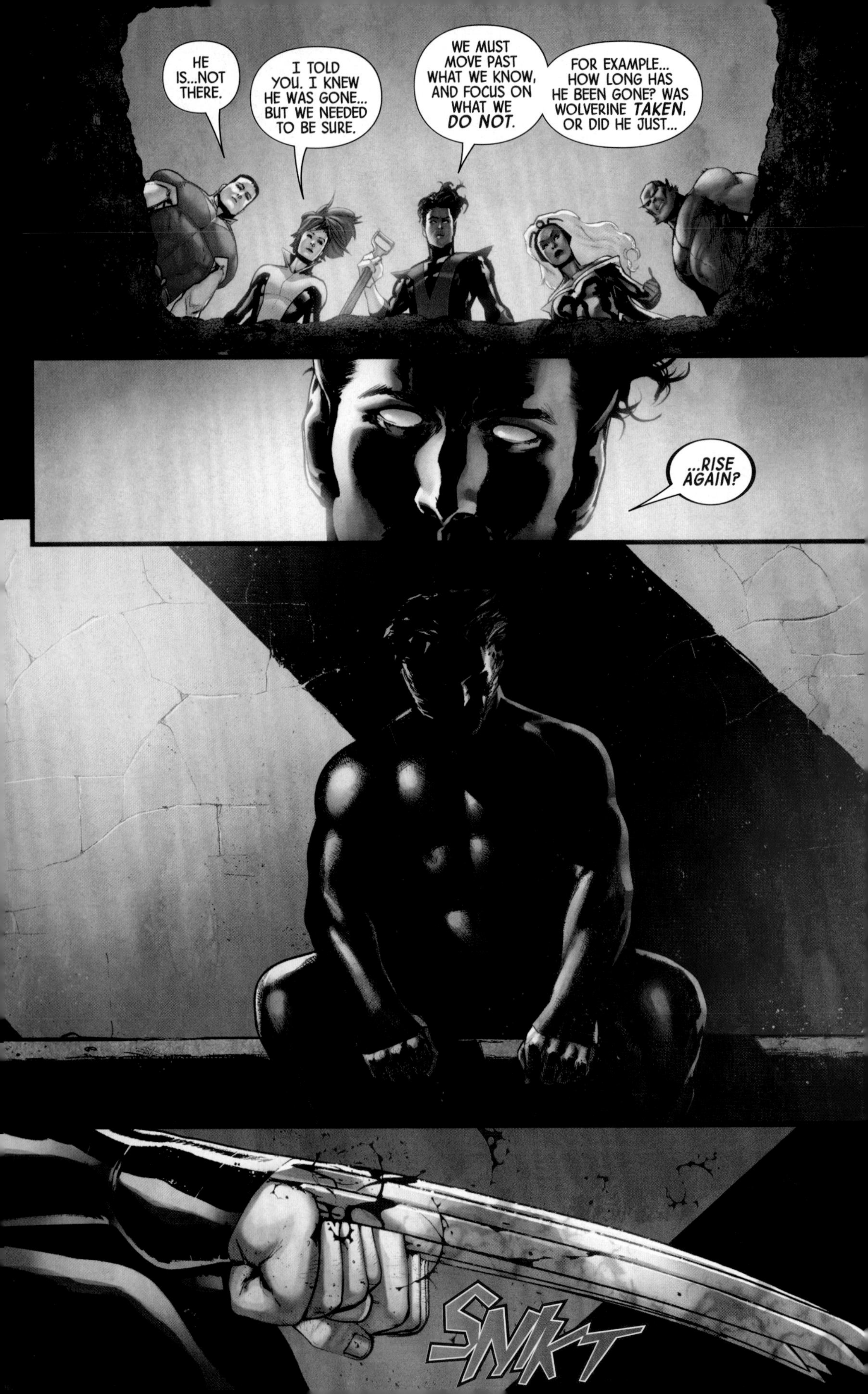
HE IS...NOT THERE.
I TOLD YOU. I KNEW HE WAS GONE... BUT WE NEEDED TO BE SURE.
WE MUST MOVE PAST WHAT WE KNOW, AND FOCUS ON WHAT WE *DO NOT*.
FOR EXAMPLE... HOW LONG HAS HE BEEN GONE? WAS WOLVERINE *TAKEN*, OR DID HE JUST...
...RISE AGAIN?
SNIKT

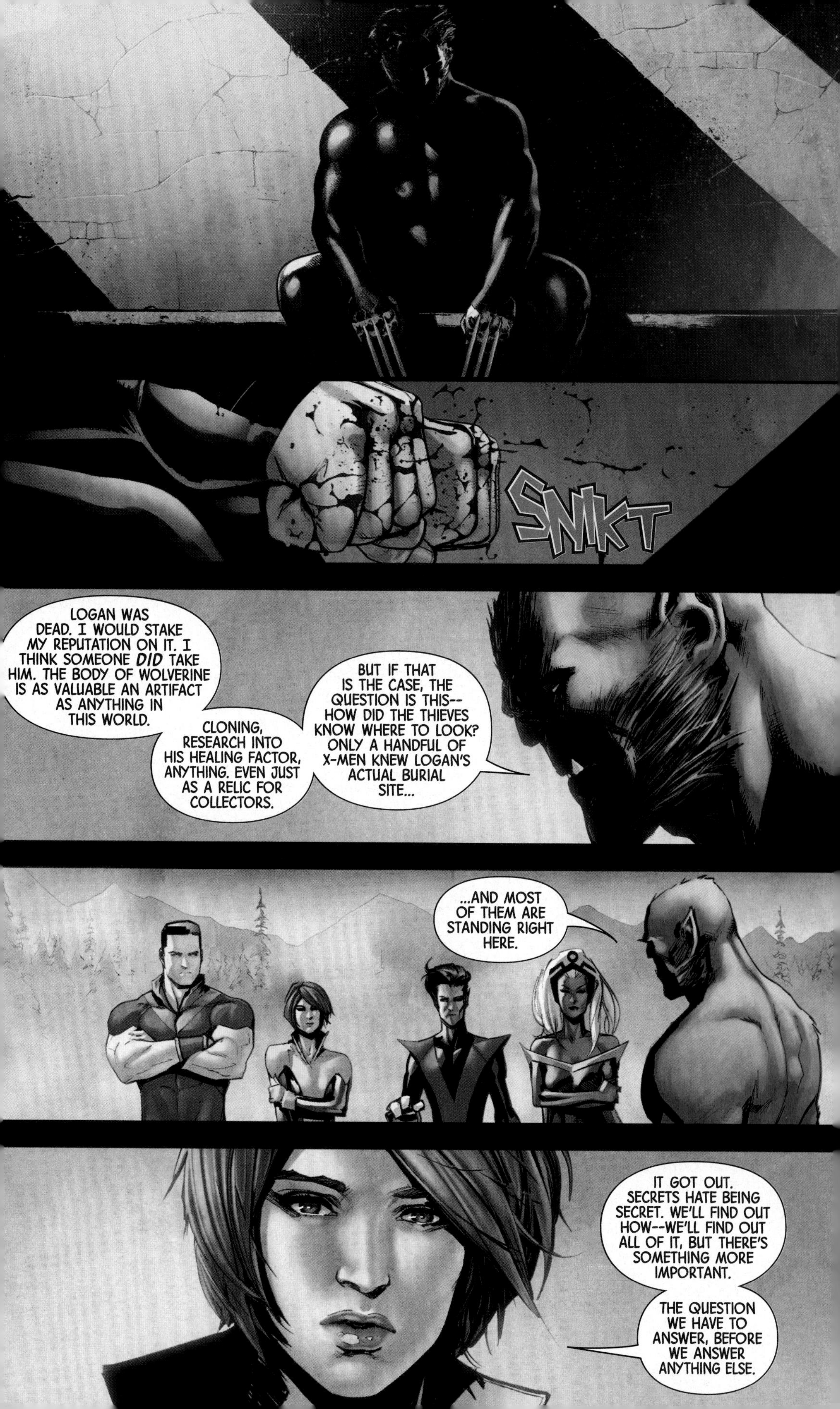
SNIKT
LOGAN WAS DEAD. I WOULD STAKE MY REPUTATION ON IT. I THINK SOMEONE *DID* TAKE HIM. THE BODY OF WOLVERINE IS AS VALUABLE AN ARTIFACT AS ANYTHING IN THIS WORLD.
CLONING, RESEARCH INTO HIS HEALING FACTOR, ANYTHING. EVEN JUST AS A RELIC FOR COLLECTORS.
BUT IF THAT IS THE CASE, THE QUESTION IS THIS--HOW DID THE THIEVES KNOW WHERE TO LOOK? ONLY A HANDFUL OF X-MEN KNEW LOGAN'S ACTUAL BURIAL SITE...
...AND MOST OF THEM ARE STANDING RIGHT HERE.
IT GOT OUT. SECRETS HATE BEING SECRET. WE'LL FIND OUT HOW--WE'LL FIND OUT ALL OF IT, BUT THERE'S SOMETHING MORE IMPORTANT.
THE QUESTION WE HAVE TO ANSWER, BEFORE WE ANSWER ANYTHING ELSE.

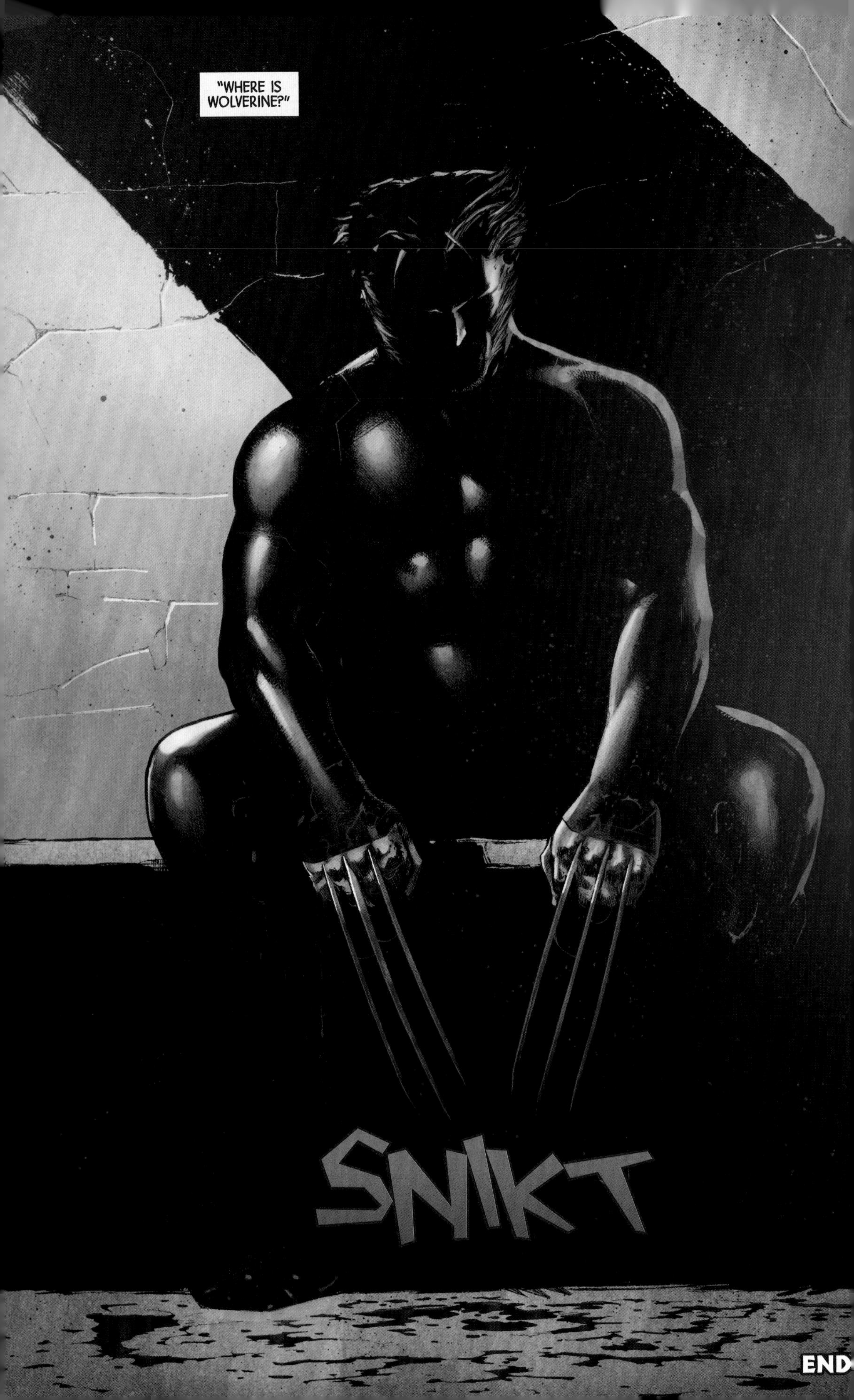
"WHERE IS WOLVERINE?"
SNIKT
END

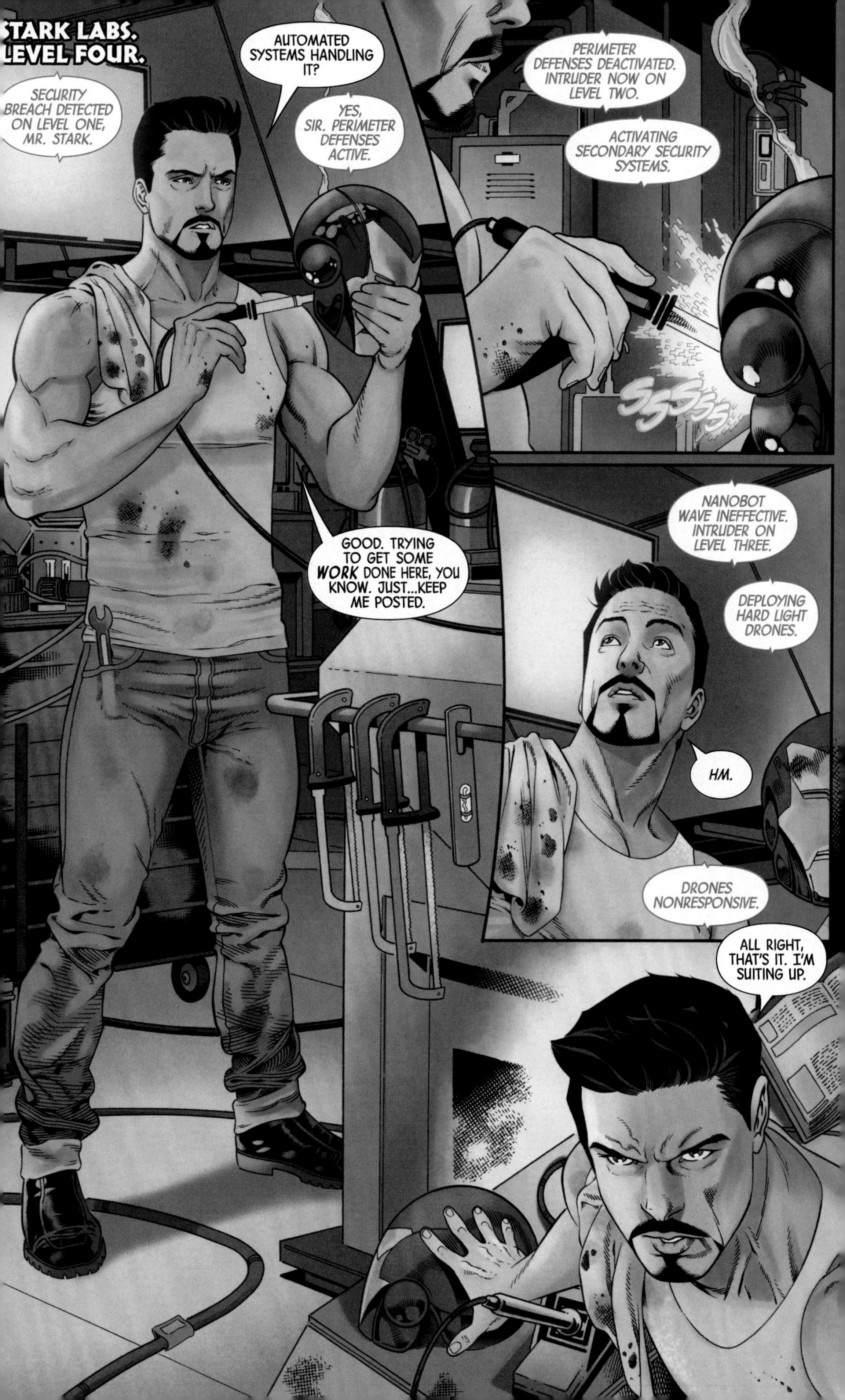
STARK LABS. LEVEL FOUR.
SECURITY BREACH DETECTED ON LEVEL ONE, MR. STARK.
AUTOMATED SYSTEMS HANDLING IT?
YES, SIR. PERIMETER DEFENSES ACTIVE.
GOOD. TRYING TO GET SOME WORK DONE HERE, YOU KNOW. JUST...KEEP ME POSTED.
PERIMETER DEFENSES DEACTIVATED. INTRUDER NOW ON LEVEL TWO.
ACTIVATING SECONDARY SECURITY SYSTEMS.
SSSSS
NANOBOT WAVE INEFFECTIVE. INTRUDER ON LEVEL THREE.
DEPLOYING HARD LIGHT DRONES.
HM.
DRONES NONRESPONSIVE.
ALL RIGHT, THAT'S IT. I'M SUITING UP.

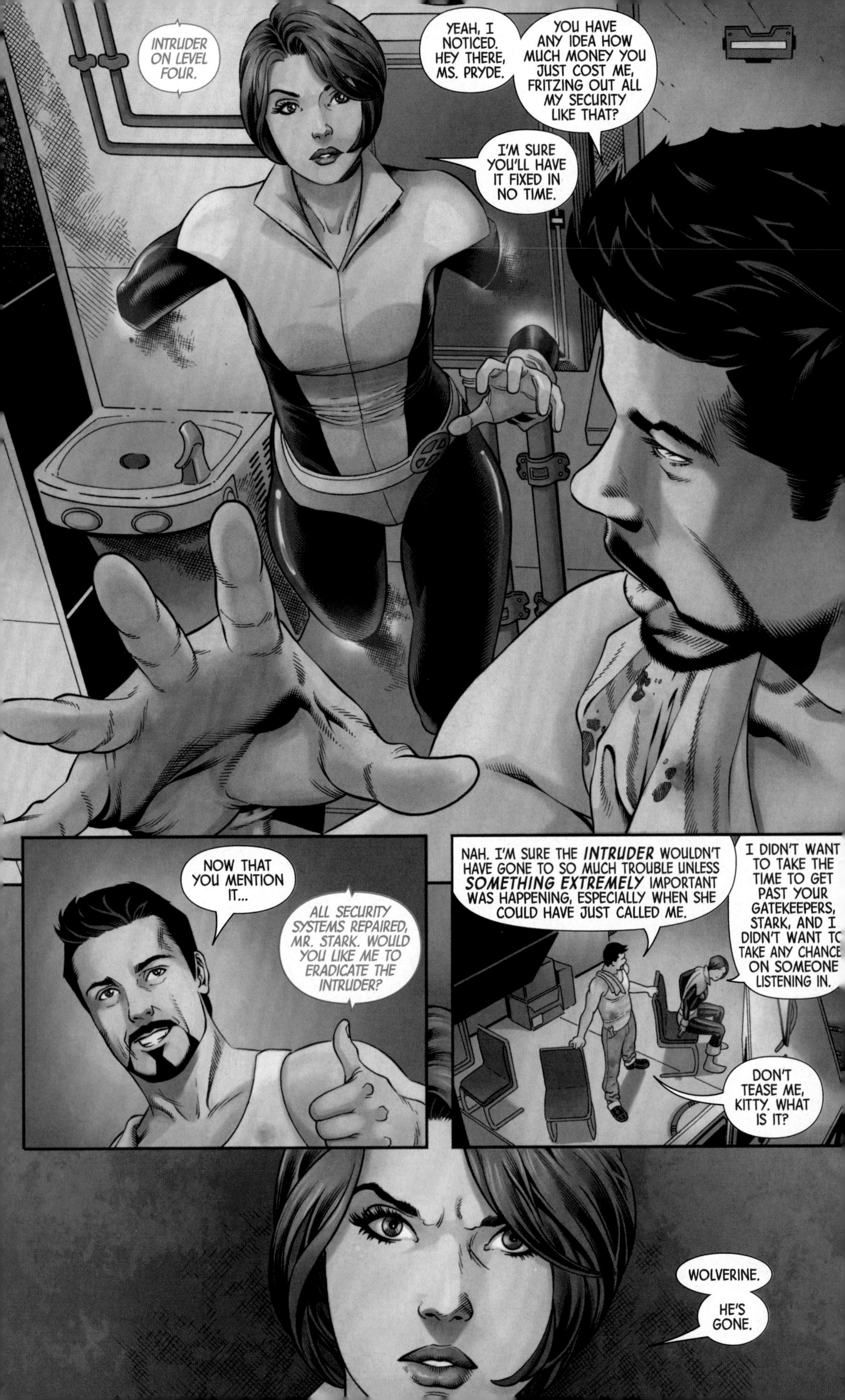
INTRUDER ON LEVEL FOUR.
YEAH, I NOTICED. HEY THERE, MS. PRYDE.
YOU HAVE ANY IDEA HOW MUCH MONEY YOU JUST COST ME, FRITZING OUT ALL MY SECURITY LIKE THAT?
I'M SURE YOU'LL HAVE IT FIXED IN NO TIME.
NOW THAT YOU MENTION IT...
ALL SECURITY SYSTEMS REPAIRED, MR. STARK. WOULD YOU LIKE ME TO ERADICATE THE INTRUDER?
NAH. I'M SURE THE *INTRUDER* WOULDN'T HAVE GONE TO SO MUCH TROUBLE UNLESS *SOMETHING EXTREMELY* IMPORTANT WAS HAPPENING, ESPECIALLY WHEN SHE COULD HAVE JUST CALLED ME.
I DIDN'T WANT TO TAKE THE TIME TO GET PAST YOUR GATEKEEPERS, STARK, AND I DIDN'T WANT TO TAKE ANY CHANCE ON SOMEONE LISTENING IN.
DON'T TEASE ME, KITTY. WHAT IS IT?
WOLVERINE.
HE'S GONE.

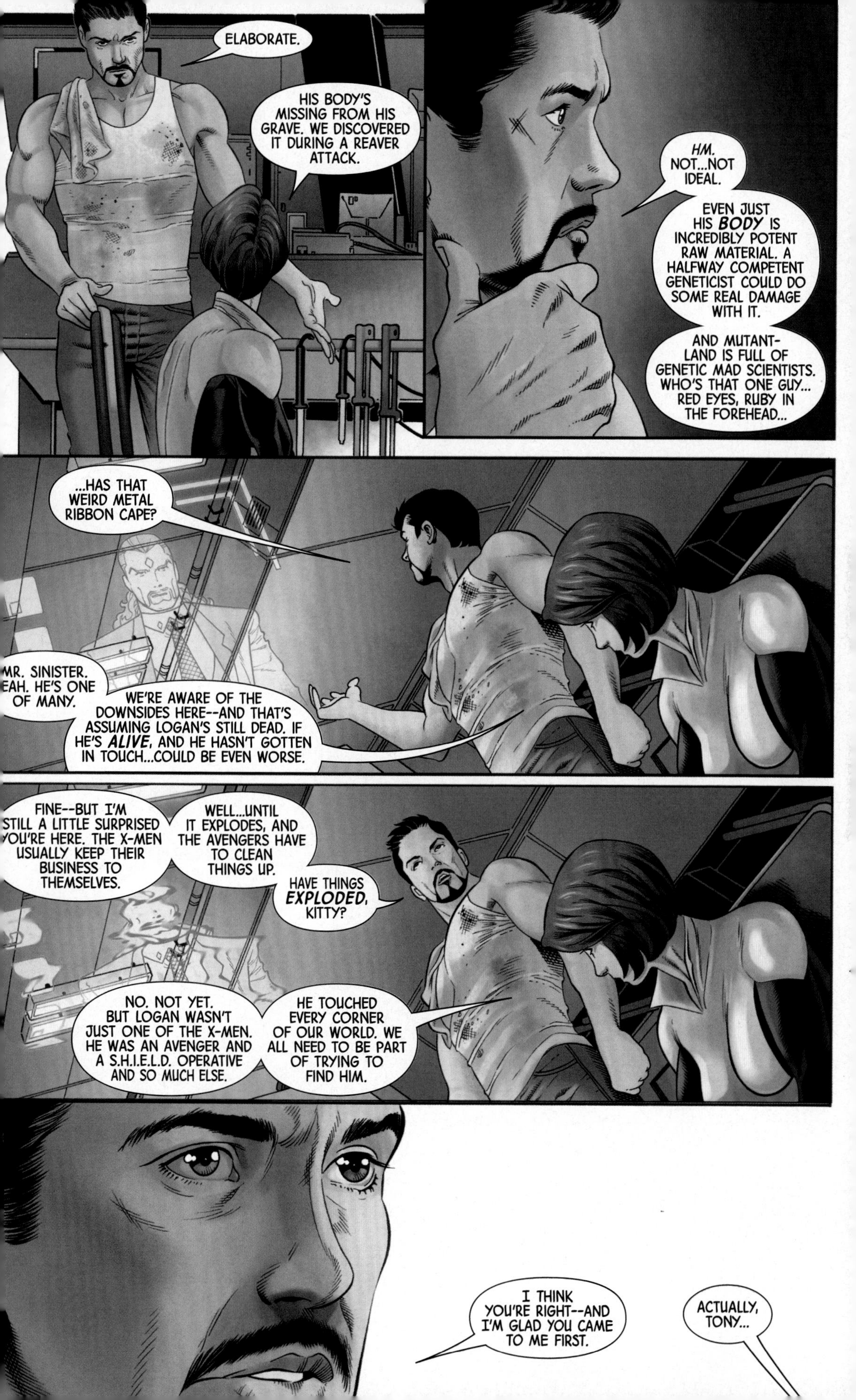
ELABORATE.
HIS BODY'S MISSING FROM HIS GRAVE. WE DISCOVERED IT DURING A REAVER ATTACK.
HM. NOT...NOT IDEAL.
EVEN JUST HIS BODY IS INCREDIBLY POTENT RAW MATERIAL. A HALFWAY COMPETENT GENETICIST COULD DO SOME REAL DAMAGE WITH IT.
AND MUTANT-LAND IS FULL OF GENETIC MAD SCIENTISTS. WHO'S THAT ONE GUY... RED EYES, RUBY IN THE FOREHEAD...
...HAS THAT WEIRD METAL RIBBON CAPE?
MR. SINISTER. EAH. HE'S ONE OF MANY.
WE'RE AWARE OF THE DOWNSIDES HERE--AND THAT'S ASSUMING LOGAN'S STILL DEAD. IF HE'S ALIVE, AND HE HASN'T GOTTEN IN TOUCH...COULD BE EVEN WORSE.
FINE--BUT I'M STILL A LITTLE SURPRISED YOU'RE HERE. THE X-MEN USUALLY KEEP THEIR BUSINESS TO THEMSELVES.
WELL...UNTIL IT EXPLODES, AND THE AVENGERS HAVE TO CLEAN THINGS UP.
HAVE THINGS EXPLODED, KITTY?
NO. NOT YET. BUT LOGAN WASN'T JUST ONE OF THE X-MEN. HE WAS AN AVENGER AND A S.H.I.E.L.D. OPERATIVE AND SO MUCH ELSE.
HE TOUCHED EVERY CORNER OF OUR WORLD. WE ALL NEED TO BE PART OF TRYING TO FIND HIM.
I THINK YOU'RE RIGHT--AND I'M GLAD YOU CAME TO ME FIRST.
ACTUALLY, TONY...

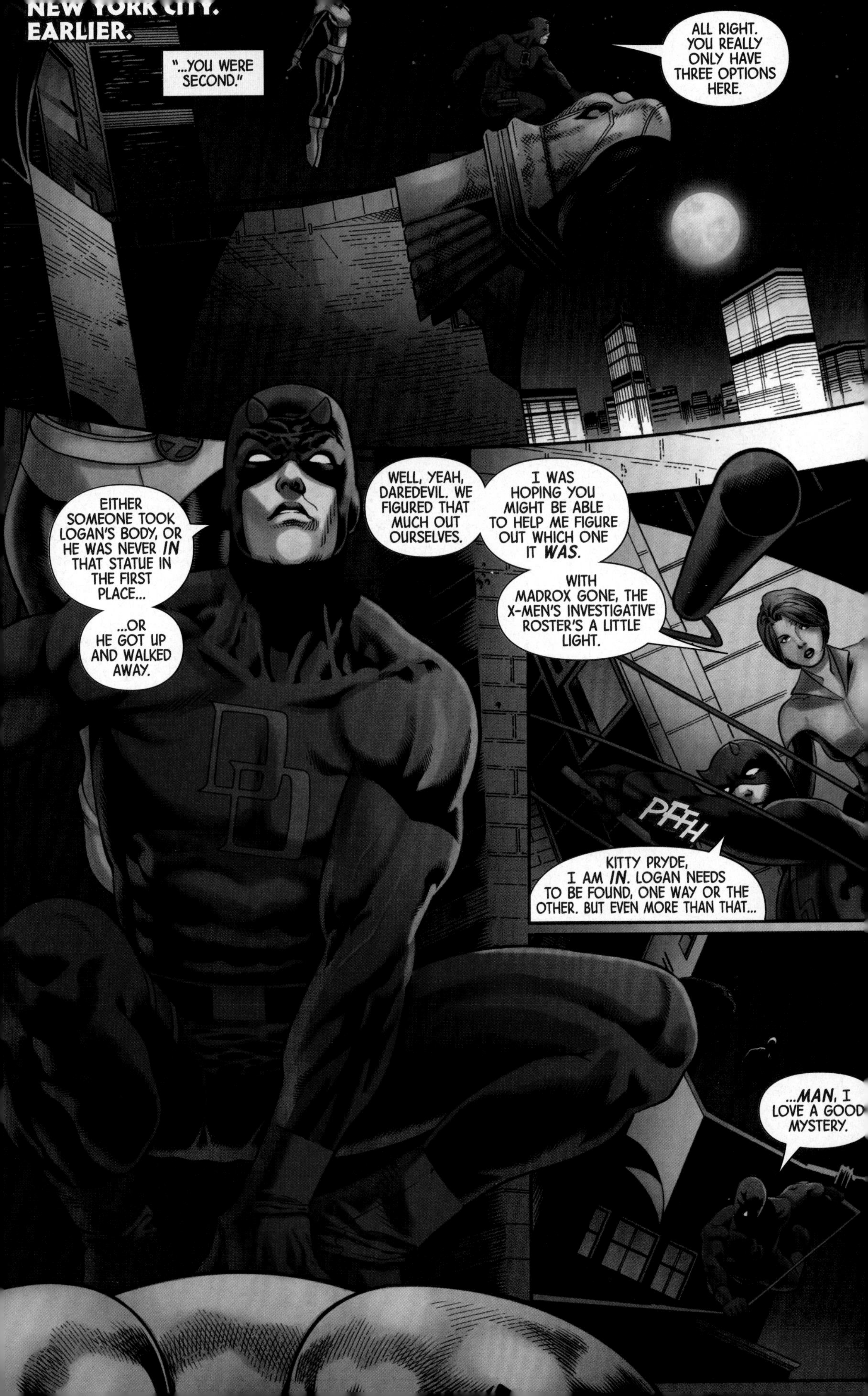
NEW YORK CITY. EARLIER.
"...YOU WERE SECOND."
ALL RIGHT. YOU REALLY ONLY HAVE THREE OPTIONS HERE.
EITHER SOMEONE TOOK LOGAN'S BODY, OR HE WAS NEVER IN THAT STATUE IN THE FIRST PLACE...
...OR HE GOT UP AND WALKED AWAY.
WELL, YEAH, DAREDEVIL. WE FIGURED THAT MUCH OUT OURSELVES.
I WAS HOPING YOU MIGHT BE ABLE TO HELP ME FIGURE OUT WHICH ONE IT WAS.
WITH MADROX GONE, THE X-MEN'S INVESTIGATIVE ROSTER'S A LITTLE LIGHT.
PFFH
KITTY PRYDE, I AM IN. LOGAN NEEDS TO BE FOUND, ONE WAY OR THE OTHER. BUT EVEN MORE THAN THAT...
...MAN, I LOVE A GOOD MYSTERY.

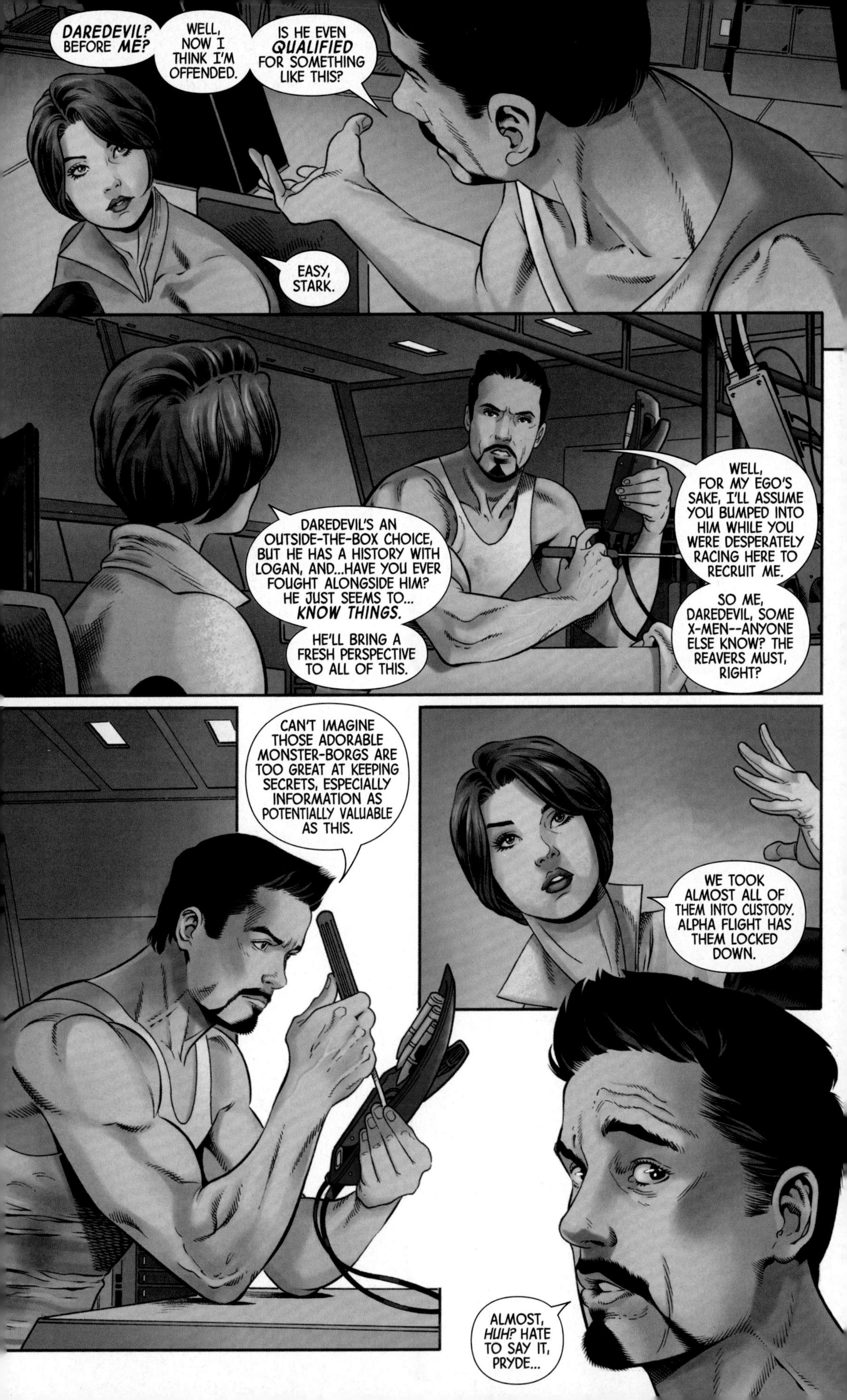
DAREDEVIL? BEFORE ME?
WELL, NOW I THINK I'M OFFENDED.
IS HE EVEN QUALIFIED FOR SOMETHING LIKE THIS?
EASY, STARK.
DAREDEVIL'S AN OUTSIDE-THE-BOX CHOICE, BUT HE HAS A HISTORY WITH LOGAN, AND...HAVE YOU EVER FOUGHT ALONGSIDE HIM? HE JUST SEEMS TO... KNOW THINGS.
HE'LL BRING A FRESH PERSPECTIVE TO ALL OF THIS.
WELL, FOR MY EGO'S SAKE, I'LL ASSUME YOU BUMPED INTO HIM WHILE YOU WERE DESPERATELY RACING HERE TO RECRUIT ME.
SO ME, DAREDEVIL, SOME X-MEN--ANYONE ELSE KNOW? THE REAVERS MUST, RIGHT?
CAN'T IMAGINE THOSE ADORABLE MONSTER-BORGS ARE TOO GREAT AT KEEPING SECRETS, ESPECIALLY INFORMATION AS POTENTIALLY VALUABLE AS THIS.
WE TOOK ALMOST ALL OF THEM INTO CUSTODY. ALPHA FLIGHT HAS THEM LOCKED DOWN.
ALMOST, HUH? HATE TO SAY IT, PRYDE...

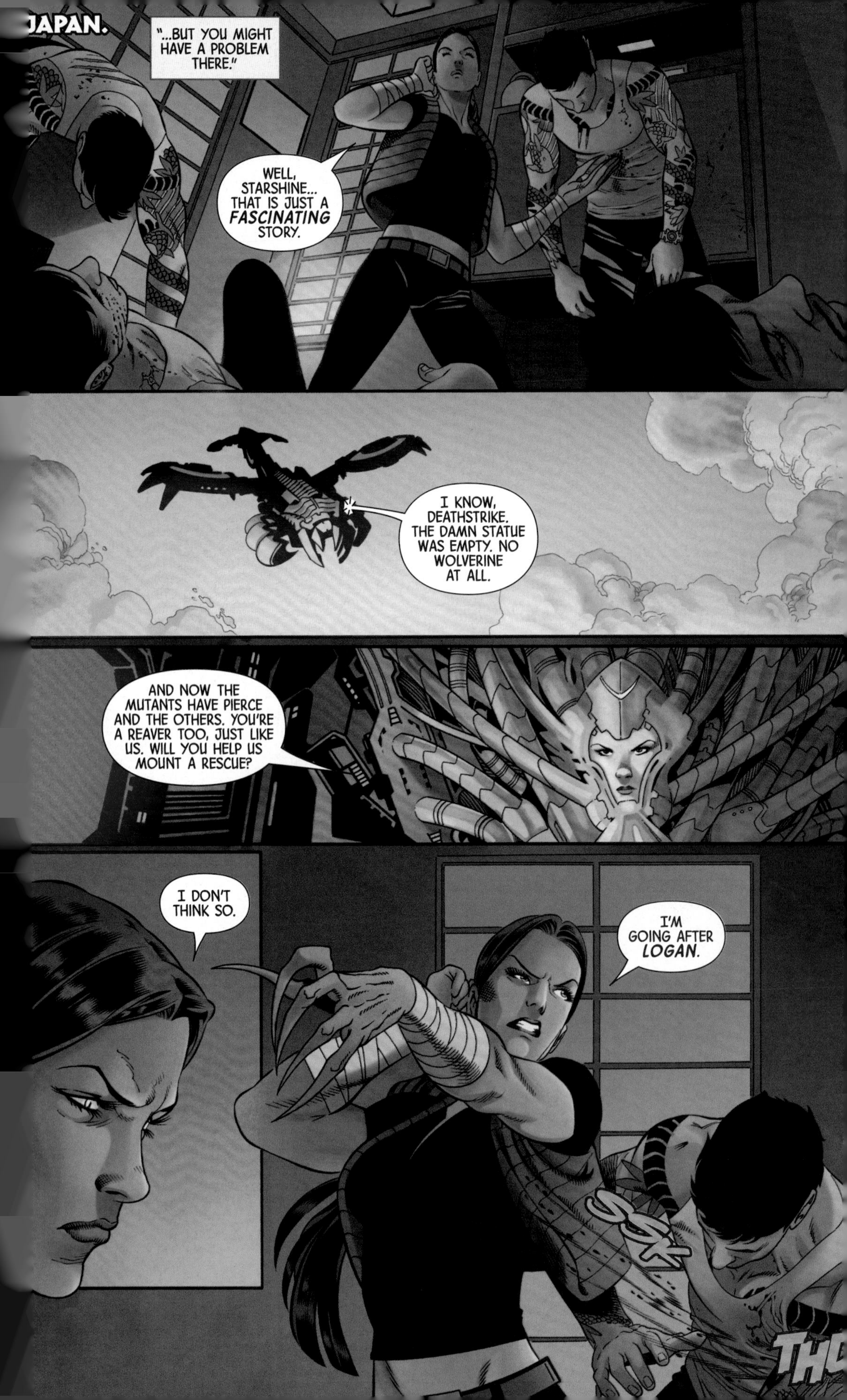
JAPAN.
"...BUT YOU MIGHT HAVE A PROBLEM THERE."
WELL, STARSHINE... THAT IS JUST A FASCINATING STORY.
I KNOW, DEATHSTRIKE. THE DAMN STATUE WAS EMPTY. NO WOLVERINE AT ALL.
AND NOW THE MUTANTS HAVE PIERCE AND THE OTHERS. YOU'RE A REAVER TOO, JUST LIKE US. WILL YOU HELP US MOUNT A RESCUE?
I DON'T THINK SO.
I'M GOING AFTER LOGAN.
SSK

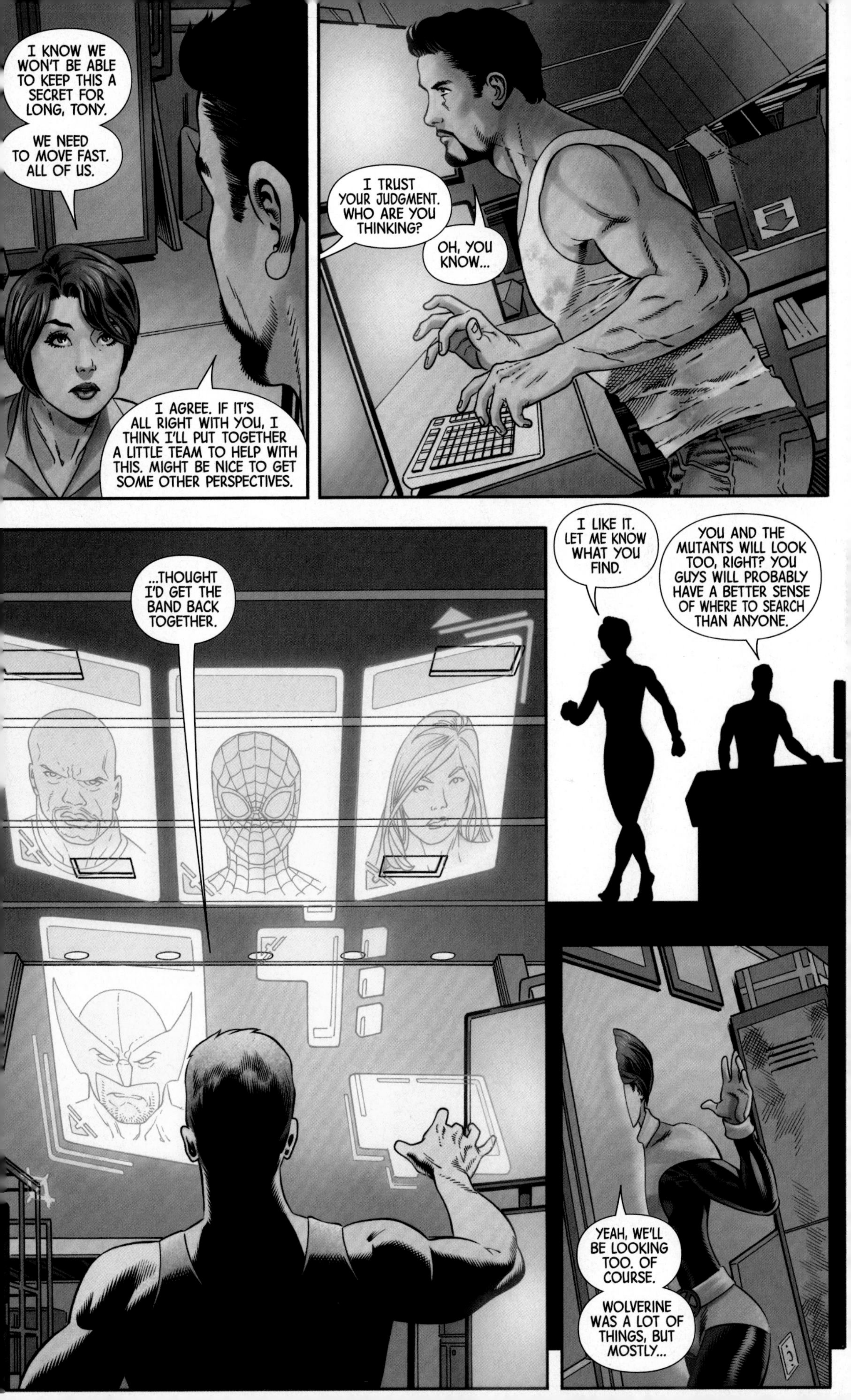
I KNOW WE WON'T BE ABLE TO KEEP THIS A SECRET FOR LONG, TONY.
WE NEED TO MOVE FAST. ALL OF US.
I AGREE. IF IT'S ALL RIGHT WITH YOU, I THINK I'LL PUT TOGETHER A LITTLE TEAM TO HELP WITH THIS. MIGHT BE NICE TO GET SOME OTHER PERSPECTIVES.
I TRUST YOUR JUDGMENT. WHO ARE YOU THINKING?
OH, YOU KNOW...
...THOUGHT I'D GET THE BAND BACK TOGETHER.
I LIKE IT. LET ME KNOW WHAT YOU FIND.
YOU AND THE MUTANTS WILL LOOK TOO, RIGHT? YOU GUYS WILL PROBABLY HAVE A BETTER SENSE OF WHERE TO SEARCH THAN ANYONE.
YEAH, WE'LL BE LOOKING TOO. OF COURSE.
WOLVERINE WAS A LOT OF THINGS, BUT MOSTLY...

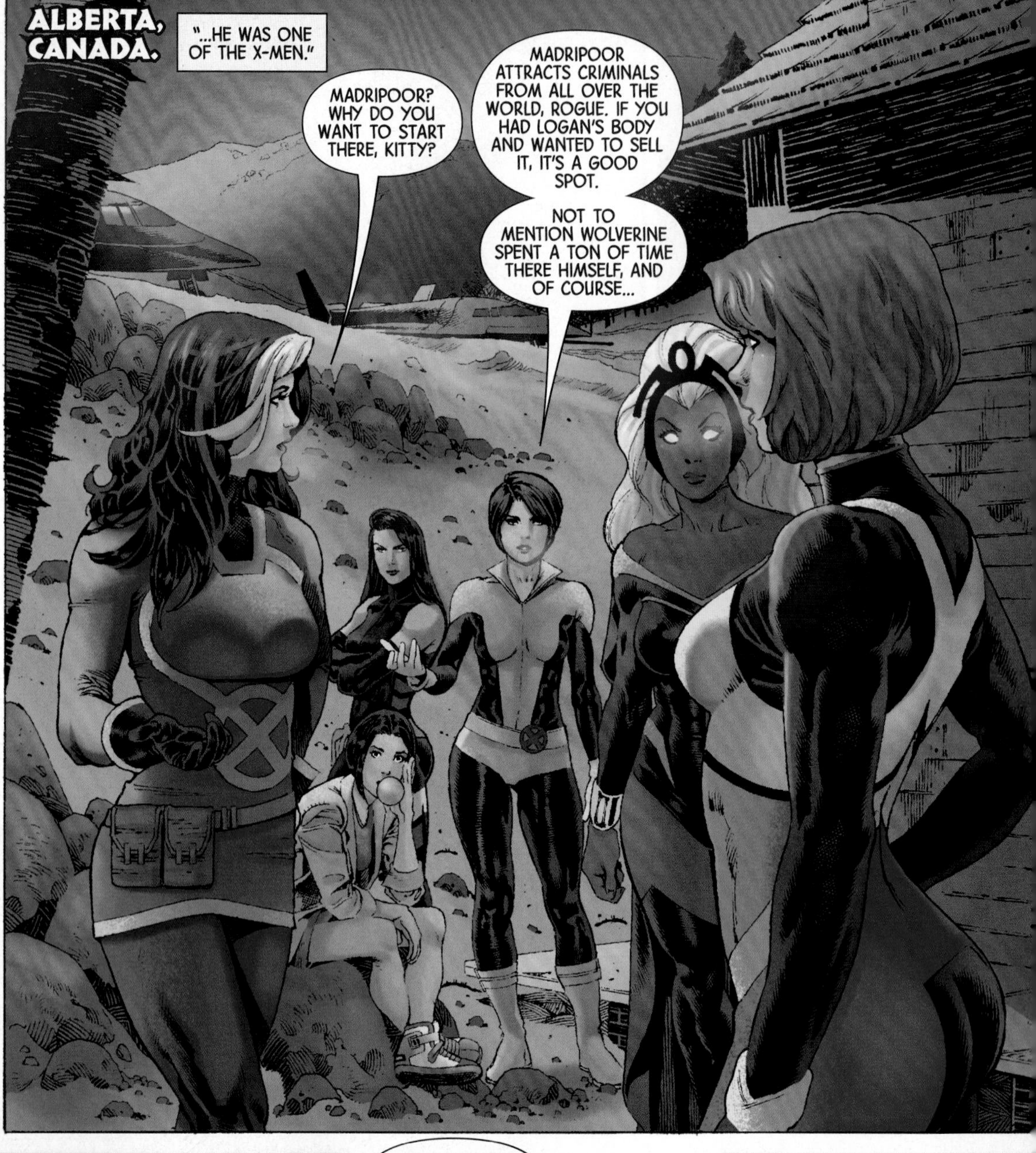
ALBERTA, CANADA.
"...HE WAS ONE OF THE X-MEN."
MADRIPOOR? WHY DO YOU WANT TO START THERE, KITTY?
MADRIPOOR ATTRACTS CRIMINALS FROM ALL OVER THE WORLD, ROGUE. IF YOU HAD LOGAN'S BODY AND WANTED TO SELL IT, IT'S A GOOD SPOT.
NOT TO MENTION WOLVERINE SPENT A TON OF TIME THERE HIMSELF, AND OF COURSE...

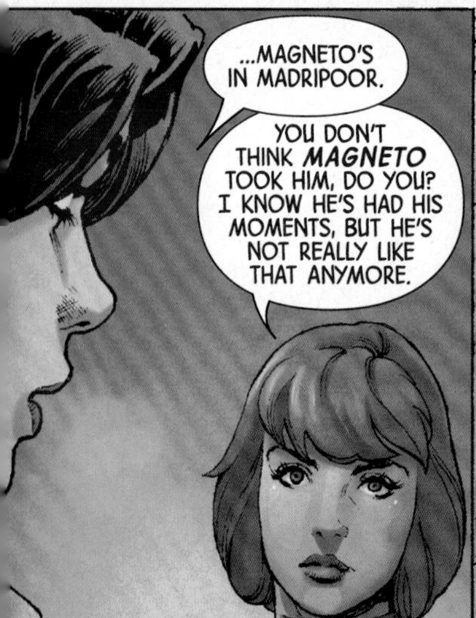
...MAGNETO'S IN MADRIPOOR.
YOU DON'T THINK MAGNETO TOOK HIM, DO YOU? I KNOW HE'S HAD HIS MOMENTS, BUT HE'S NOT REALLY LIKE THAT ANYMORE.

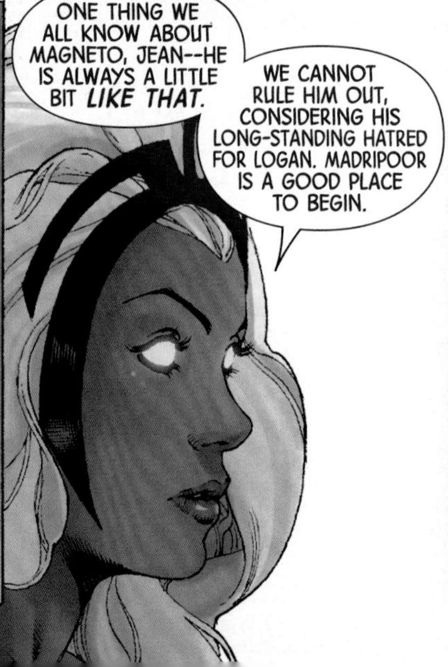
ONE THING WE ALL KNOW ABOUT MAGNETO, JEAN--HE IS ALWAYS A LITTLE BIT LIKE THAT.
WE CANNOT RULE HIM OUT, CONSIDERING HIS LONG-STANDING HATRED FOR LOGAN. MADRIPOOR IS A GOOD PLACE TO BEGIN.

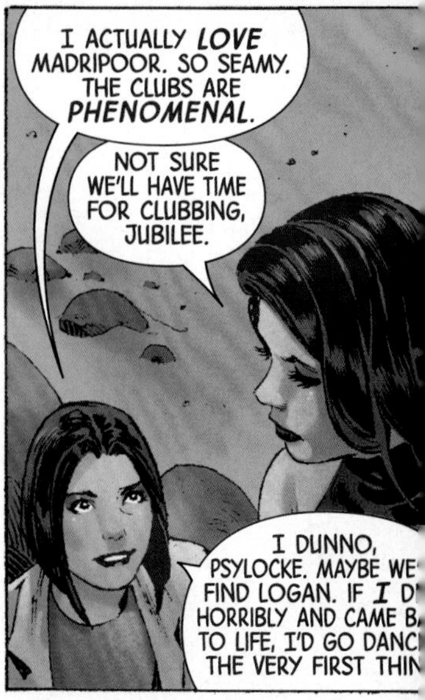
I ACTUALLY LOVE MADRIPOOR. SO SEAMY. THE CLUBS ARE PHENOMENAL.
NOT SURE WE'LL HAVE TIME FOR CLUBBING, JUBILEE.
I DUNNO, PSYLOCKE. MAYBE WE FIND LOGAN. IF I D HORRIBLY AND CAME B TO LIFE, I'D GO DANC THE VERY FIRST THIN

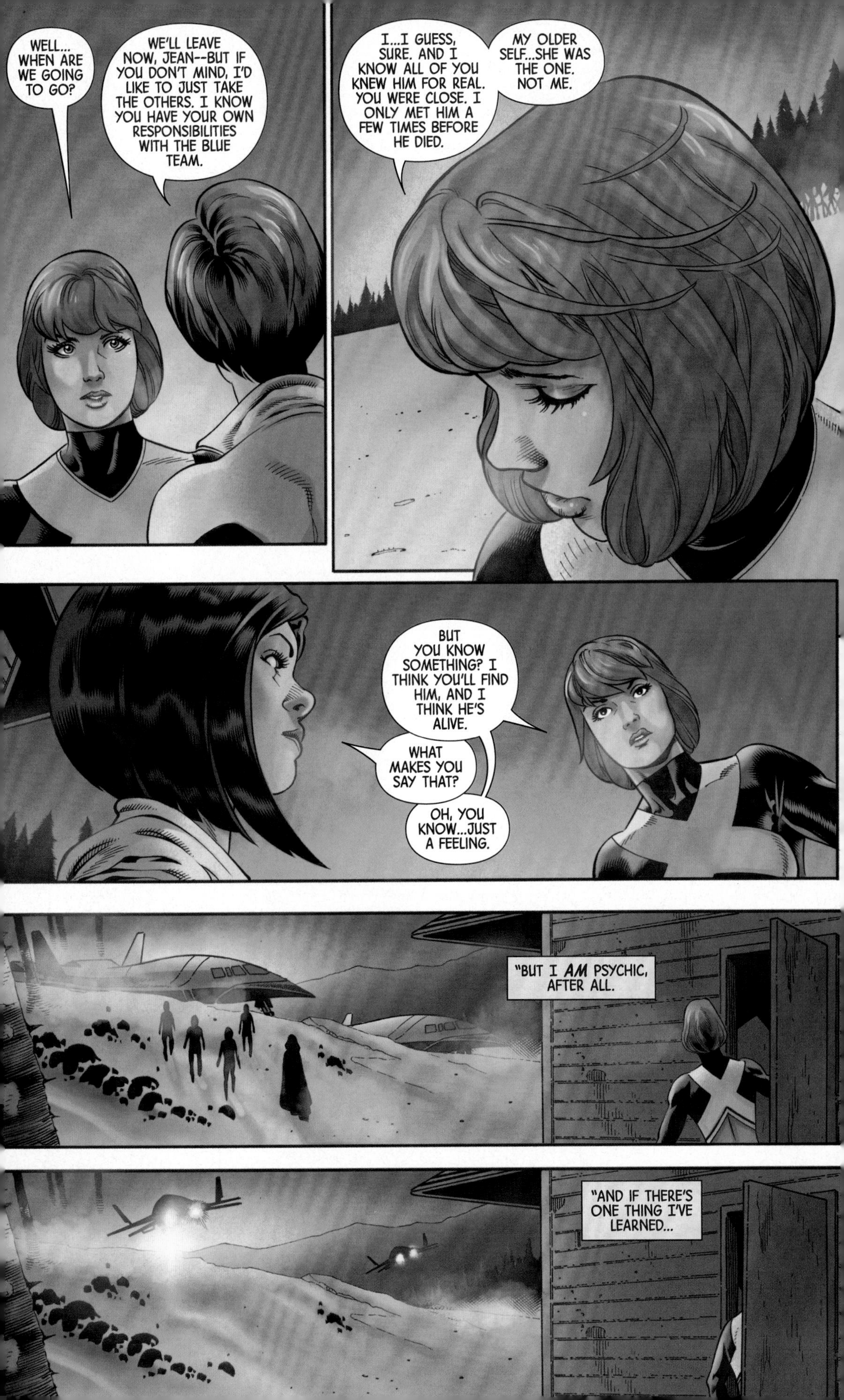
WELL... WHEN ARE WE GOING TO GO?
WE'LL LEAVE NOW, JEAN--BUT IF YOU DON'T MIND, I'D LIKE TO JUST TAKE THE OTHERS. I KNOW YOU HAVE YOUR OWN RESPONSIBILITIES WITH THE BLUE TEAM.
I...I GUESS, SURE. AND I KNOW ALL OF YOU KNEW HIM FOR REAL. YOU WERE CLOSE. I ONLY MET HIM A FEW TIMES BEFORE HE DIED.
MY OLDER SELF...SHE WAS THE ONE. NOT ME.
BUT YOU KNOW SOMETHING? I THINK YOU'LL FIND HIM, AND I THINK HE'S ALIVE.
WHAT MAKES YOU SAY THAT?
OH, YOU KNOW...JUST A FEELING.
"BUT I *AM* PSYCHIC, AFTER ALL.
"AND IF THERE'S ONE THING I'VE LEARNED...

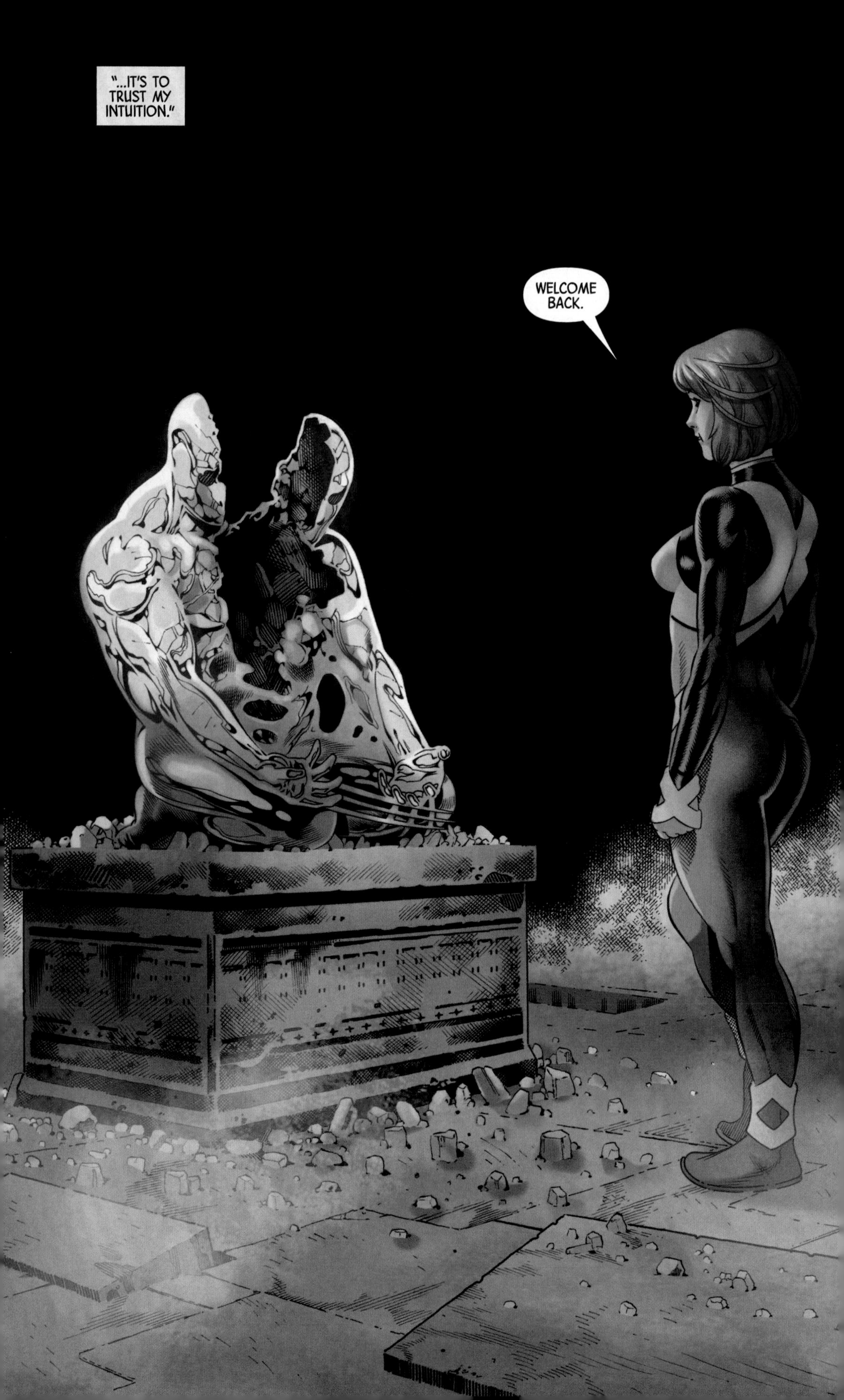
"...IT'S TO TRUST MY INTUITION."
WELCOME BACK.

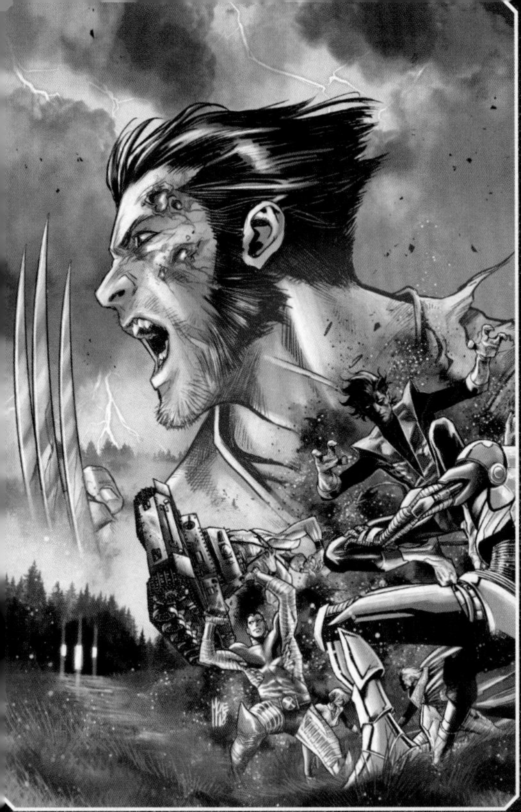

Marco Checchetto
HUNT FOR WOLVERINE #1 VARIANT

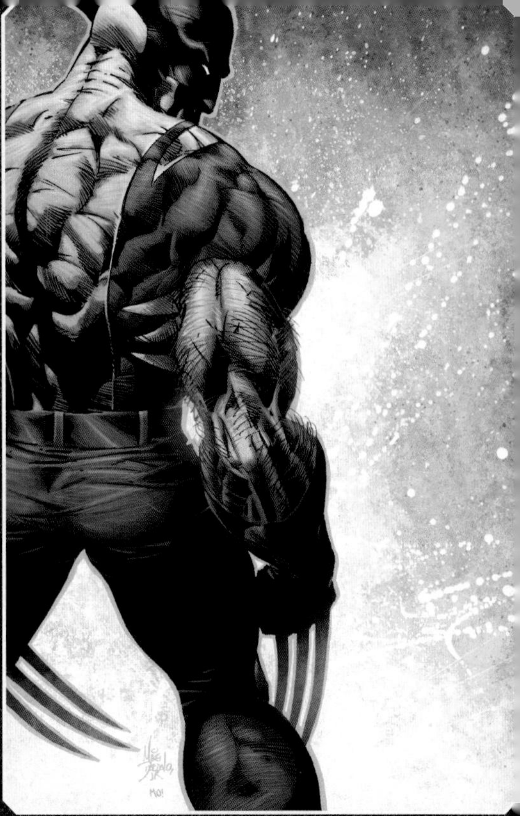

Mike Deodato Jr. & Morry Hollowell
HUNT FOR WOLVERINE #1 VARIANT

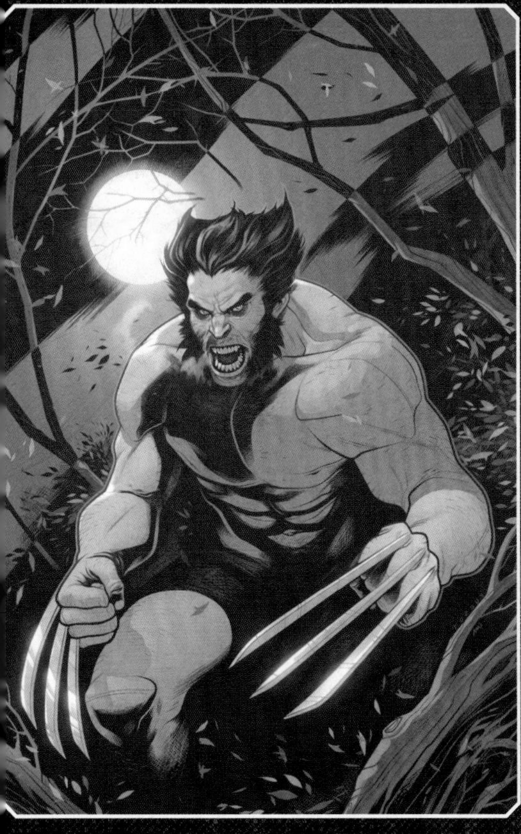

Elizabeth Torque & Nolan Woodard
HUNT FOR WOLVERINE #1 VARIANT

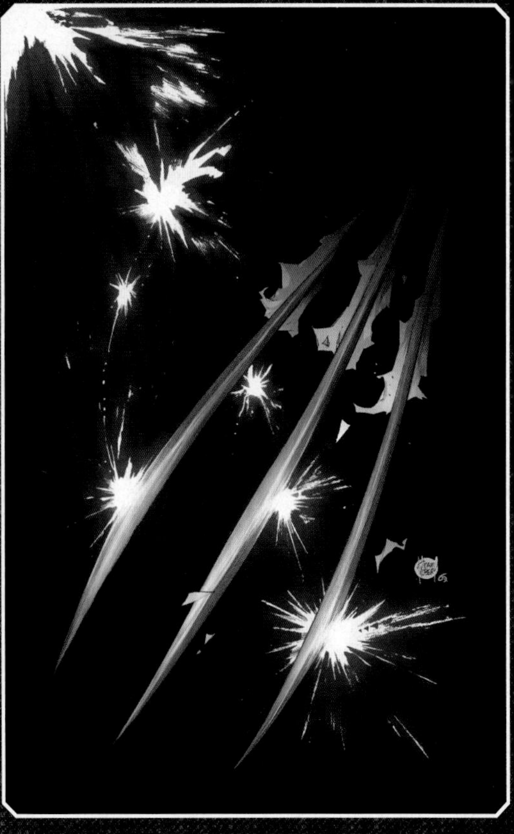

Adam Kubert & Dan Brown
HUNT FOR WOLVERINE #1 TEASER VARIANT

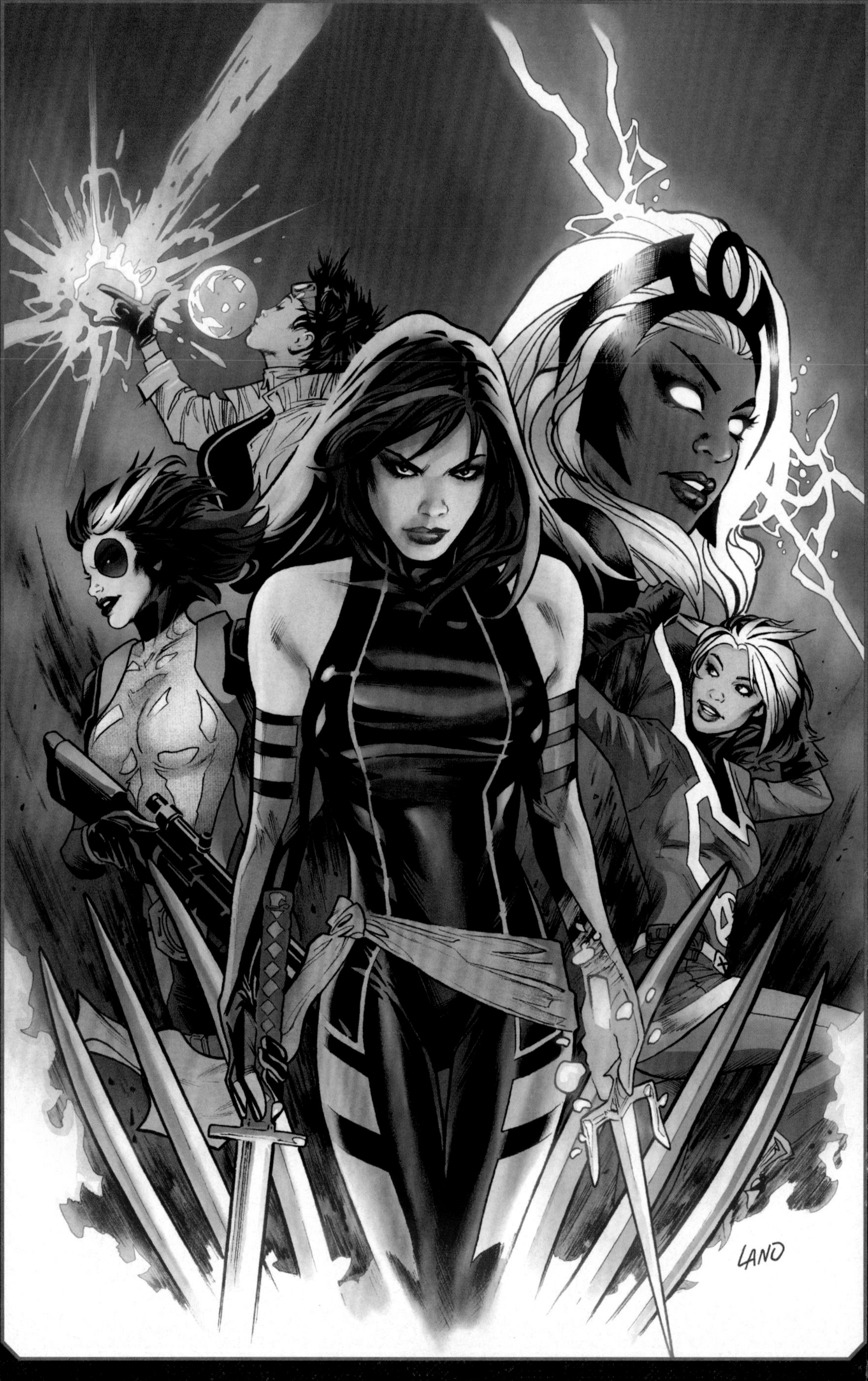
LAND

MYSTERY IN MADRIPOOR 1

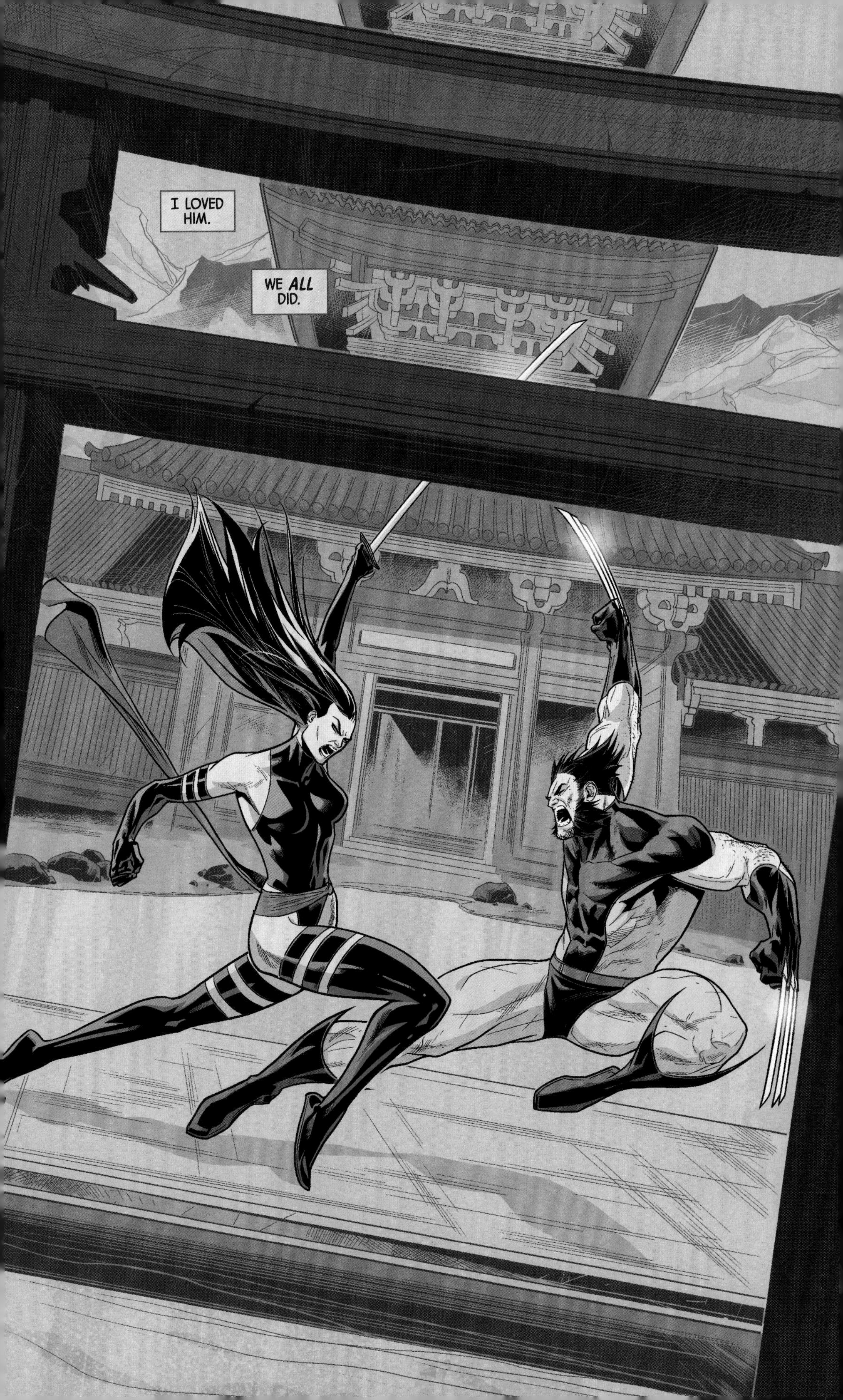

I LOVED HIM.
WE ALL DID.

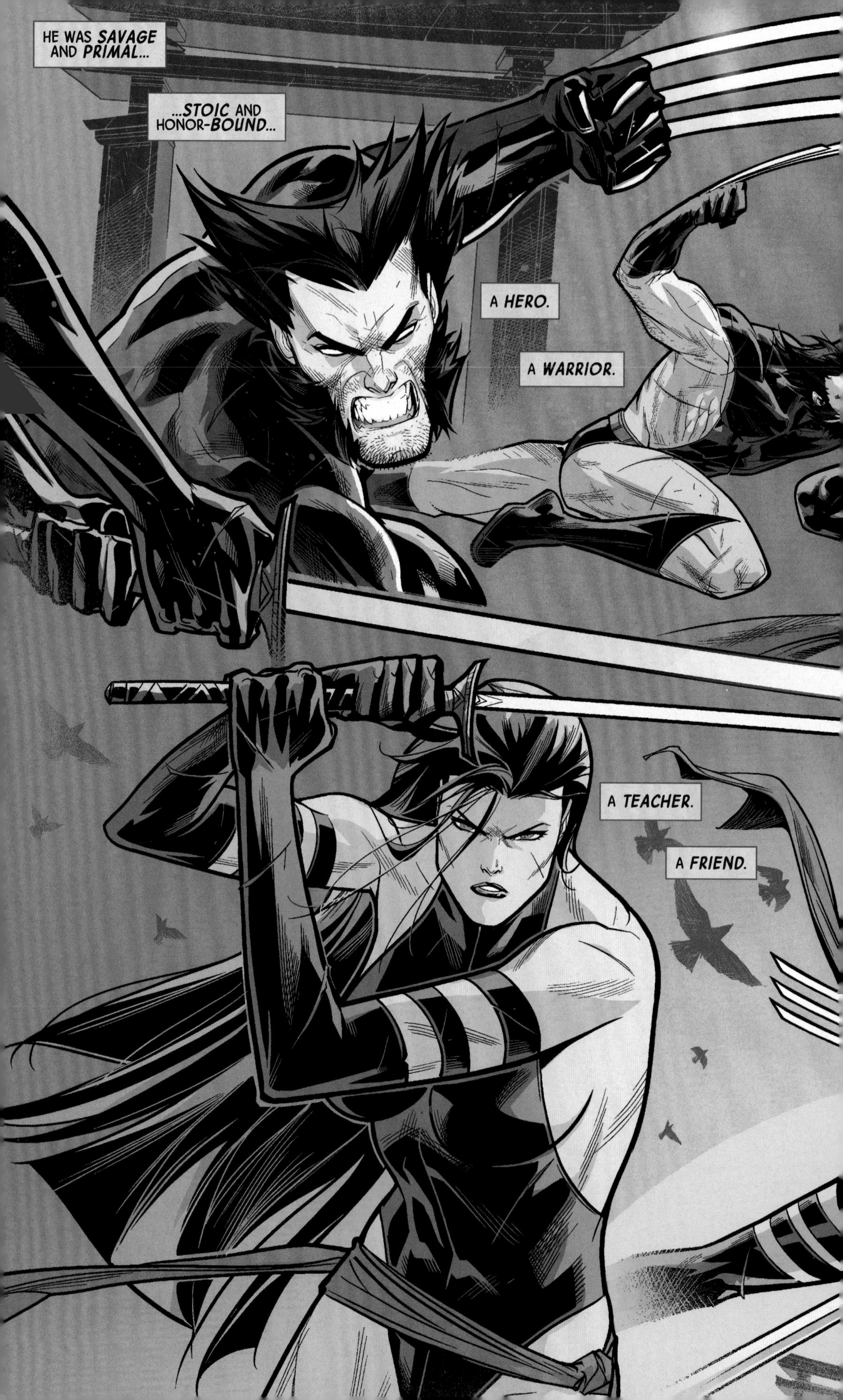
HE WAS SAVAGE AND PRIMAL...
...STOIC AND HONOR-BOUND...
A HERO.
A WARRIOR.
A TEACHER.
A FRIEND.

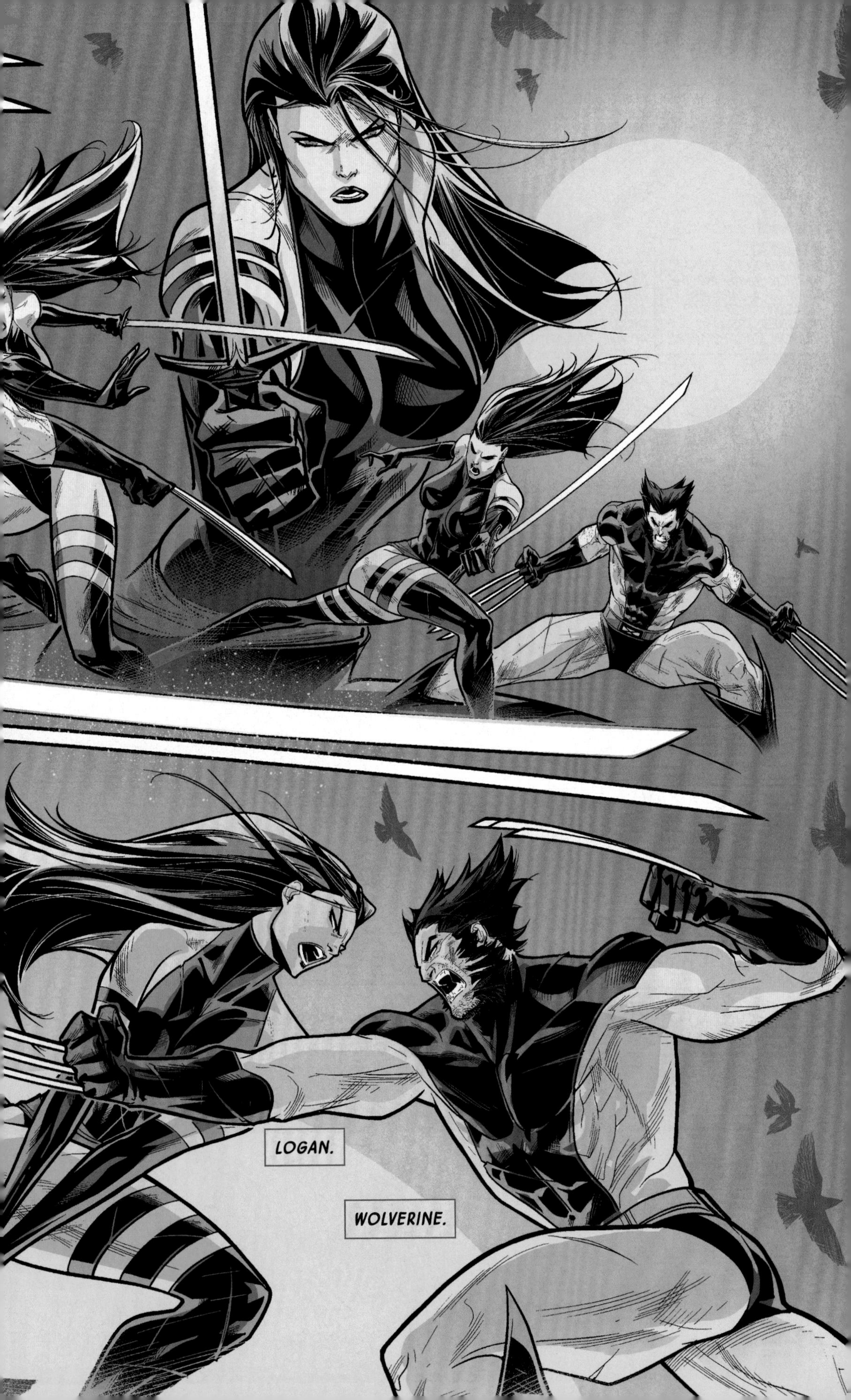
LOGAN.
WOLVERINE.

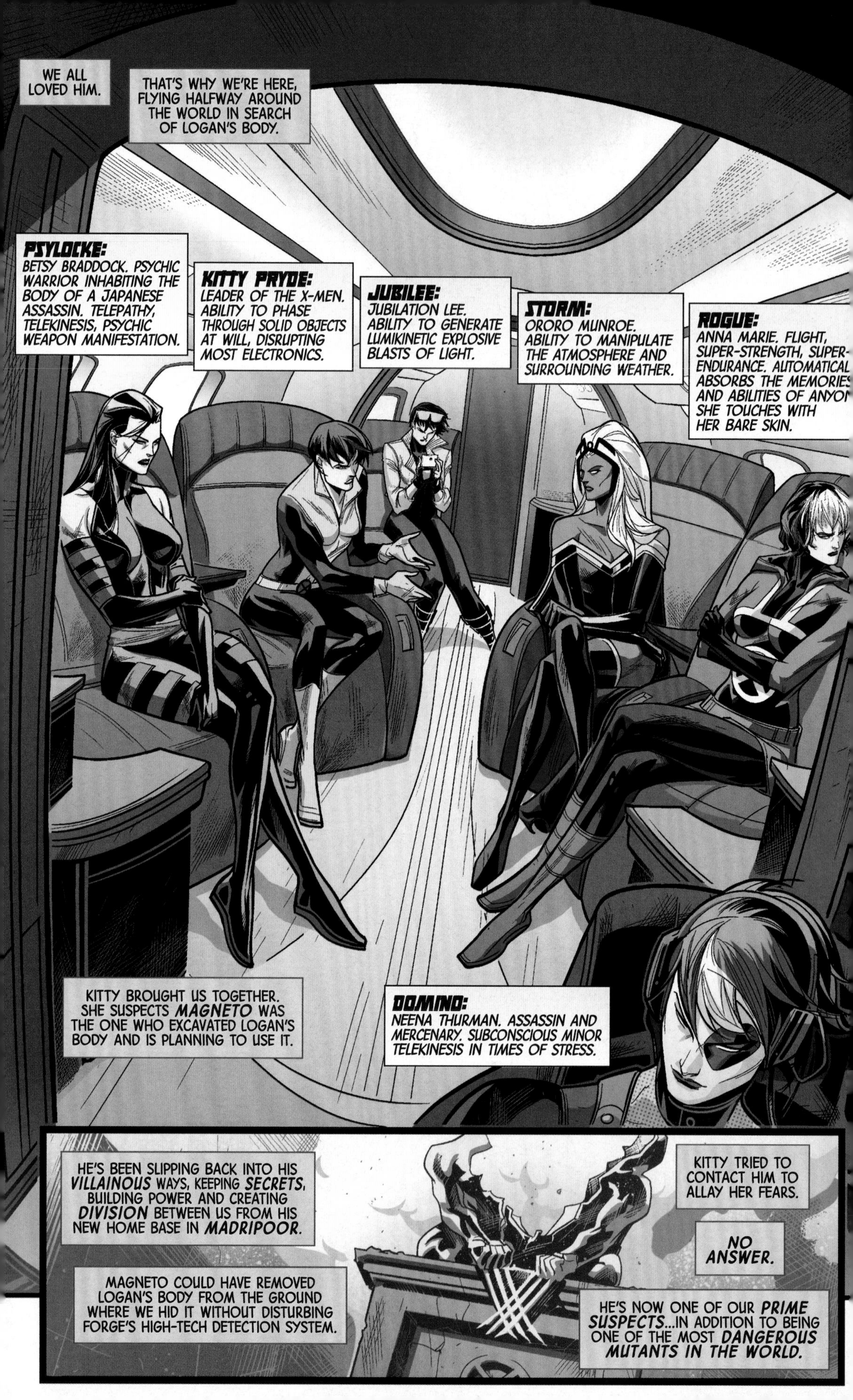
WE ALL LOVED HIM.
THAT'S WHY WE'RE HERE, FLYING HALFWAY AROUND THE WORLD IN SEARCH OF LOGAN'S BODY.
PSYLOCKE: BETSY BRADDOCK. PSYCHIC WARRIOR INHABITING THE BODY OF A JAPANESE ASSASSIN. TELEPATHY, TELEKINESIS, PSYCHIC WEAPON MANIFESTATION.
KITTY PRYDE: LEADER OF THE X-MEN. ABILITY TO PHASE THROUGH SOLID OBJECTS AT WILL, DISRUPTING MOST ELECTRONICS.
JUBILEE: JUBILATION LEE. ABILITY TO GENERATE LUMIKINETIC EXPLOSIVE BLASTS OF LIGHT.
STORM: ORORO MUNROE. ABILITY TO MANIPULATE THE ATMOSPHERE AND SURROUNDING WEATHER.
ROGUE: ANNA MARIE. FLIGHT, SUPER-STRENGTH, SUPER-ENDURANCE. AUTOMATICAL ABSORBS THE MEMORIES AND ABILITIES OF ANYON SHE TOUCHES WITH HER BARE SKIN.
KITTY BROUGHT US TOGETHER. SHE SUSPECTS MAGNETO WAS THE ONE WHO EXCAVATED LOGAN'S BODY AND IS PLANNING TO USE IT.
DOMINO: NEENA THURMAN. ASSASSIN AND MERCENARY. SUBCONSCIOUS MINOR TELEKINESIS IN TIMES OF STRESS.
HE'S BEEN SLIPPING BACK INTO HIS VILLAINOUS WAYS, KEEPING SECRETS, BUILDING POWER AND CREATING DIVISION BETWEEN US FROM HIS NEW HOME BASE IN MADRIPOOR.
MAGNETO COULD HAVE REMOVED LOGAN'S BODY FROM THE GROUND WHERE WE HID IT WITHOUT DISTURBING FORGE'S HIGH-TECH DETECTION SYSTEM.
KITTY TRIED TO CONTACT HIM TO ALLAY HER FEARS.
NO ANSWER.
HE'S NOW ONE OF OUR PRIME SUSPECTS...IN ADDITION TO BEING ONE OF THE MOST DANGEROUS MUTANTS IN THE WORLD.

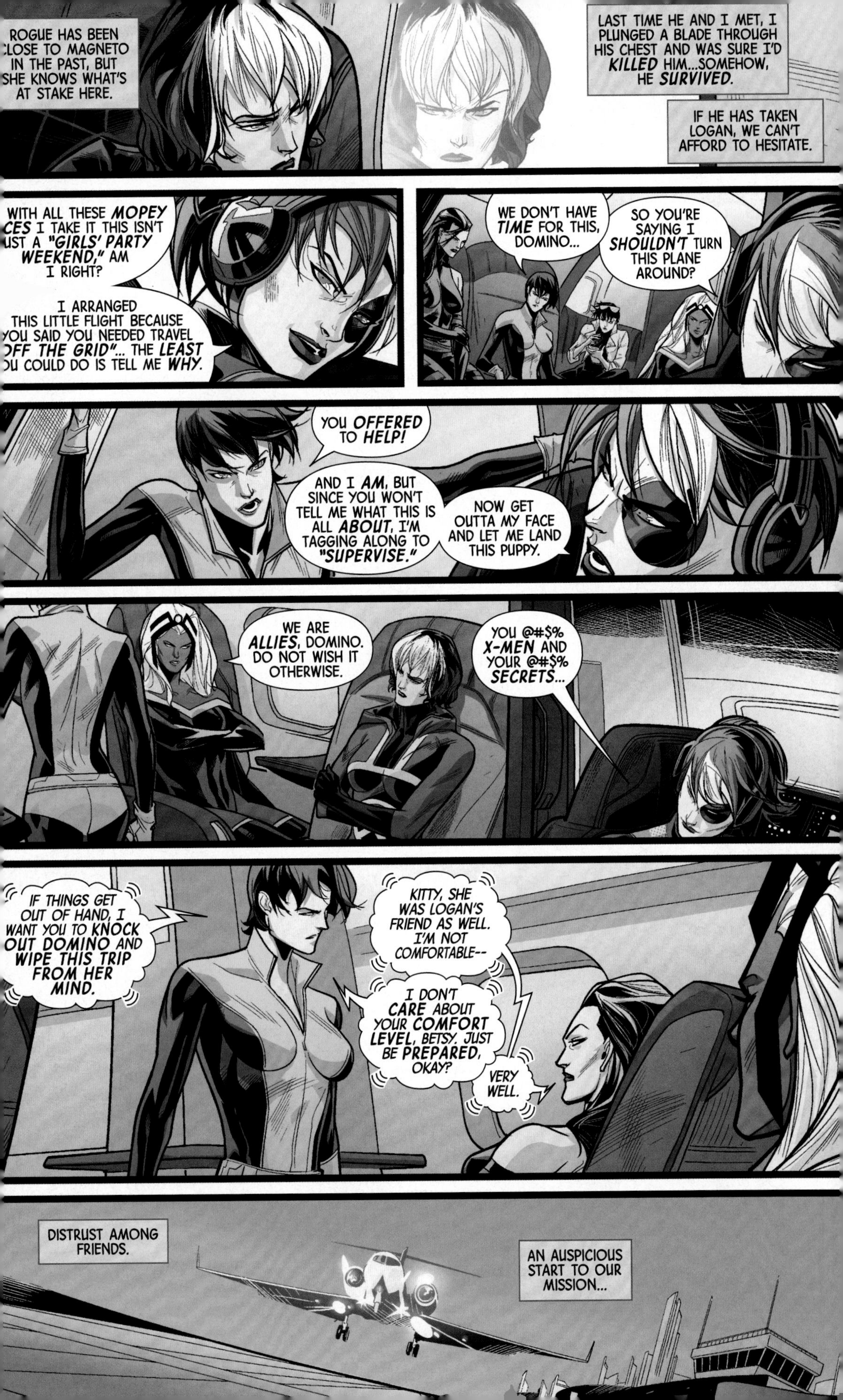
ROGUE HAS BEEN CLOSE TO MAGNETO IN THE PAST, BUT SHE KNOWS WHAT'S AT STAKE HERE.
LAST TIME HE AND I MET, I PLUNGED A BLADE THROUGH HIS CHEST AND WAS SURE I'D KILLED HIM...SOMEHOW, HE SURVIVED.
IF HE HAS TAKEN LOGAN, WE CAN'T AFFORD TO HESITATE.
WITH ALL THESE MOPEY CES I TAKE IT THIS ISN'T UST A "GIRLS' PARTY WEEKEND," AM I RIGHT?
I ARRANGED THIS LITTLE FLIGHT BECAUSE YOU SAID YOU NEEDED TRAVEL OFF THE GRID"... THE LEAST OU COULD DO IS TELL ME WHY.
WE DON'T HAVE TIME FOR THIS, DOMINO...
SO YOU'RE SAYING I SHOULDN'T TURN THIS PLANE AROUND?
YOU OFFERED TO HELP!
AND I AM, BUT SINCE YOU WON'T TELL ME WHAT THIS IS ALL ABOUT, I'M TAGGING ALONG TO "SUPERVISE."
NOW GET OUTTA MY FACE AND LET ME LAND THIS PUPPY.
WE ARE ALLIES, DOMINO. DO NOT WISH IT OTHERWISE.
YOU @#$% X-MEN AND YOUR @#$% SECRETS...
IF THINGS GET OUT OF HAND, I WANT YOU TO KNOCK OUT DOMINO AND WIPE THIS TRIP FROM HER MIND.
KITTY, SHE WAS LOGAN'S FRIEND AS WELL. I'M NOT COMFORTABLE--
I DON'T CARE ABOUT YOUR COMFORT LEVEL, BETSY. JUST BE PREPARED, OKAY?
VERY WELL.
DISTRUST AMONG FRIENDS.
AN AUSPICIOUS START TO OUR MISSION...

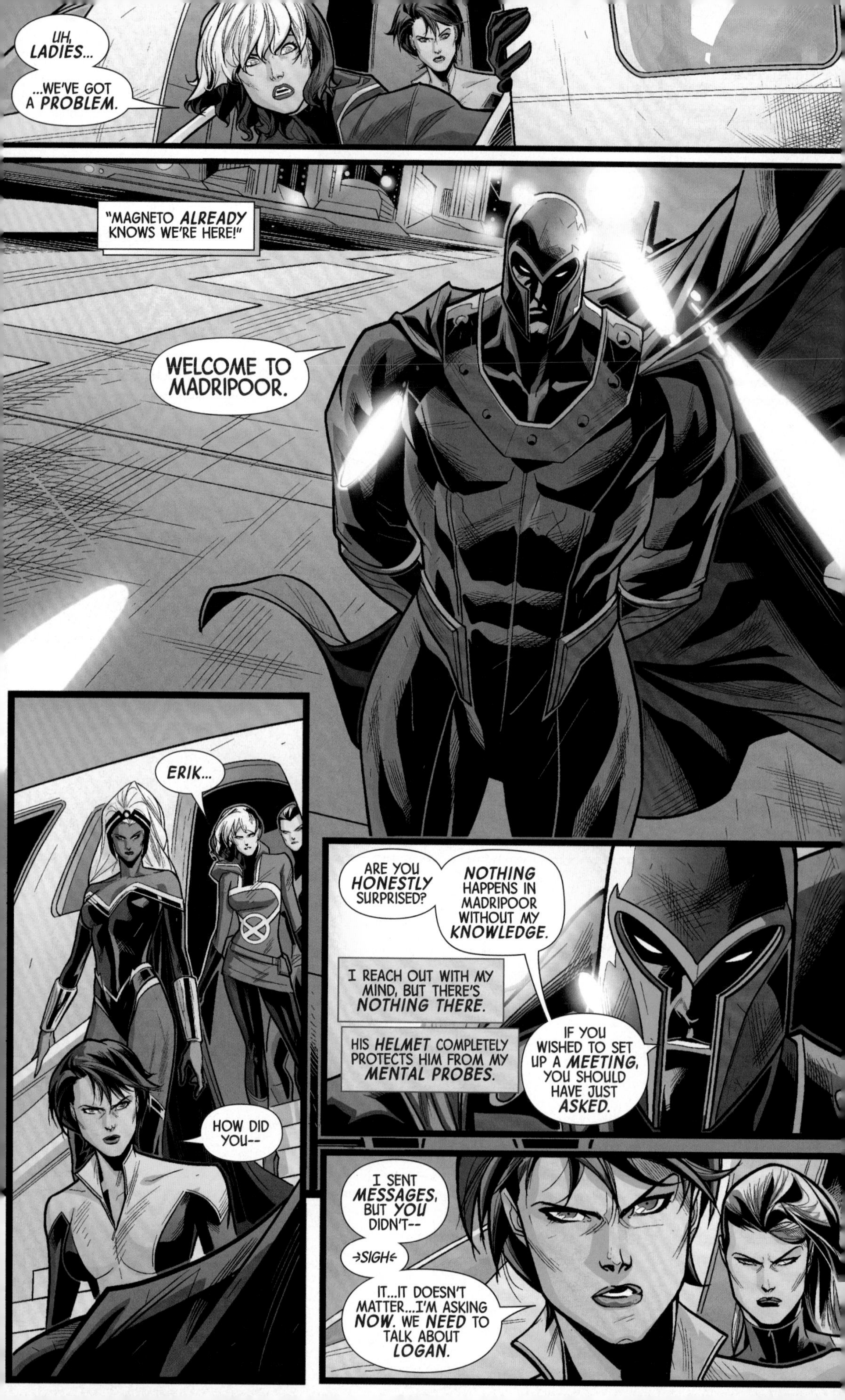

UH, LADIES...
...WE'VE GOT A PROBLEM.
"MAGNETO ALREADY KNOWS WE'RE HERE!"
WELCOME TO MADRIPOOR.
ERIK...
HOW DID YOU--
ARE YOU HONESTLY SURPRISED?
NOTHING HAPPENS IN MADRIPOOR WITHOUT MY KNOWLEDGE.
I REACH OUT WITH MY MIND, BUT THERE'S NOTHING THERE.
HIS HELMET COMPLETELY PROTECTS HIM FROM MY MENTAL PROBES.
IF YOU WISHED TO SET UP A MEETING, YOU SHOULD HAVE JUST ASKED.
I SENT MESSAGES, BUT YOU DIDN'T--
⇒SIGH⇐
IT...IT DOESN'T MATTER...I'M ASKING NOW. WE NEED TO TALK ABOUT LOGAN.

AND WE WILL...BUT NOT HERE.

TONIGHT. 10 PM. THE KING'S IMPRESARIO RESTAURANT.

YOU'LL LIKE THE LAKSA.

HOW DO WE KNOW WE CAN TRUST YOU?

PSYLOCKE IS HERE. I WON'T BRING MY HELMET TO DINNER.

YOU WON'T?

I HAVE NOTHING TO HIDE...

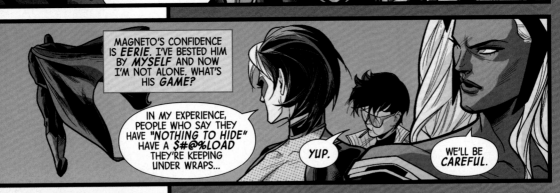

MAGNETO'S CONFIDENCE IS EERIE. I'VE BESTED HIM BY MYSELF AND NOW I'M NOT ALONE. WHAT'S HIS GAME?

IN MY EXPERIENCE, PEOPLE WHO SAY THEY HAVE "NOTHING TO HIDE" HAVE A $#@%LOAD THEY'RE KEEPING UNDER WRAPS...

YUP.

WE'LL BE CAREFUL.

NOT CAREFUL ENOUGH, ORORO...

MY LADY, THE X-MEN HAVE ARRIVED. SIX IN TOTAL.

GOOD. AFTER NEARLY DRAINING OUR GUEST DRY, SAPPHIRE IS STILL QUITE HUNGRY...

...SHE'S INSATIABLE NOWADAYS.

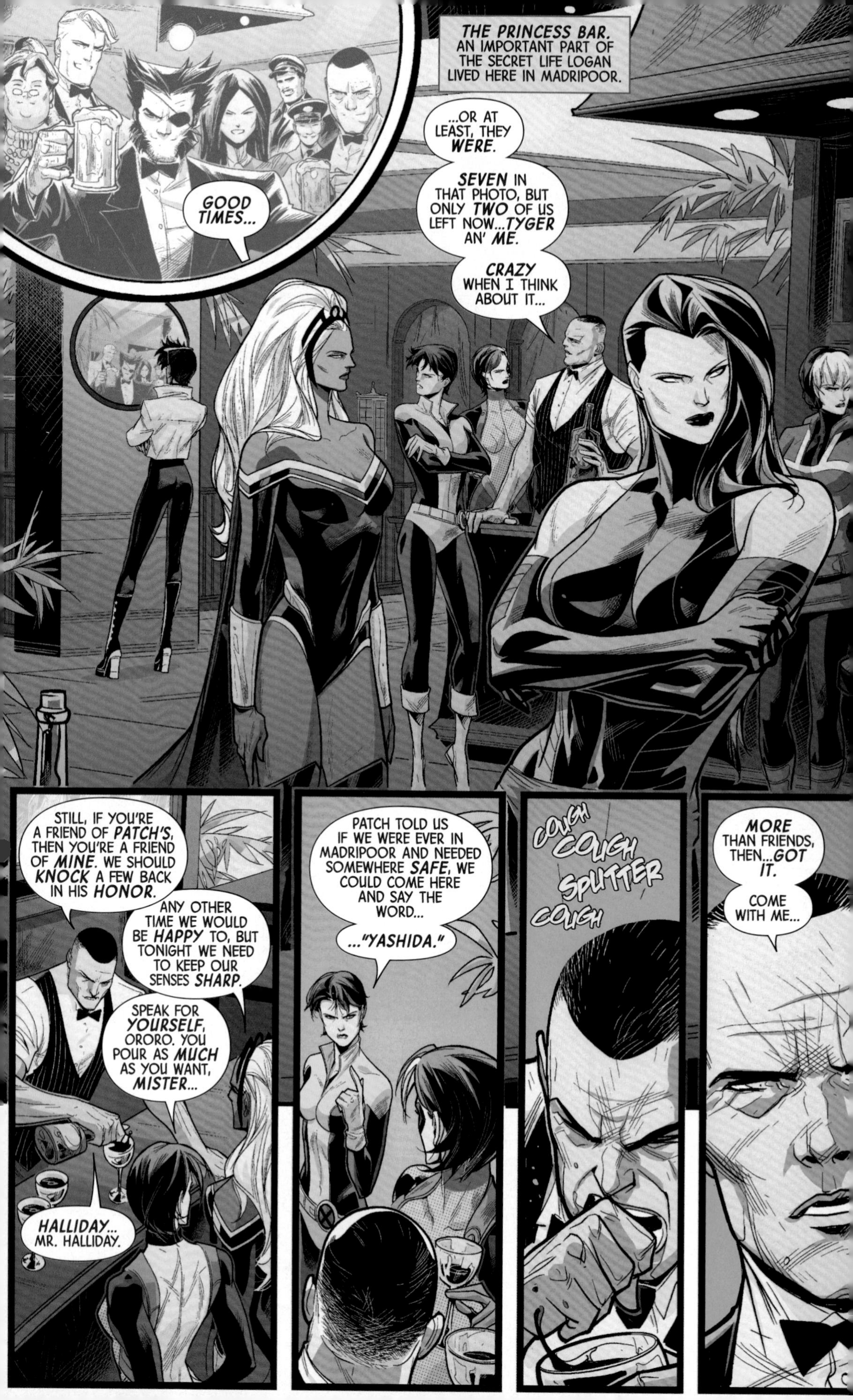

THE PRINCESS BAR. AN IMPORTANT PART OF THE SECRET LIFE LOGAN LIVED HERE IN MADRIPOOR.
GOOD TIMES...
...OR AT LEAST, THEY WERE.
SEVEN IN THAT PHOTO, BUT ONLY TWO OF US LEFT NOW...TYGER AN' ME.
CRAZY WHEN I THINK ABOUT IT...
STILL, IF YOU'RE A FRIEND OF PATCH'S, THEN YOU'RE A FRIEND OF MINE. WE SHOULD KNOCK A FEW BACK IN HIS HONOR.
ANY OTHER TIME WE WOULD BE HAPPY TO, BUT TONIGHT WE NEED TO KEEP OUR SENSES SHARP.
SPEAK FOR YOURSELF, ORORO. YOU POUR AS MUCH AS YOU WANT, MISTER...
HALLIDAY... MR. HALLIDAY.
PATCH TOLD US IF WE WERE EVER IN MADRIPOOR AND NEEDED SOMEWHERE SAFE, WE COULD COME HERE AND SAY THE WORD...
..."YASHIDA."
COUGH
COUGH
SPUTTER
COUGH
MORE THAN FRIENDS, THEN...GOT IT.
COME WITH ME...

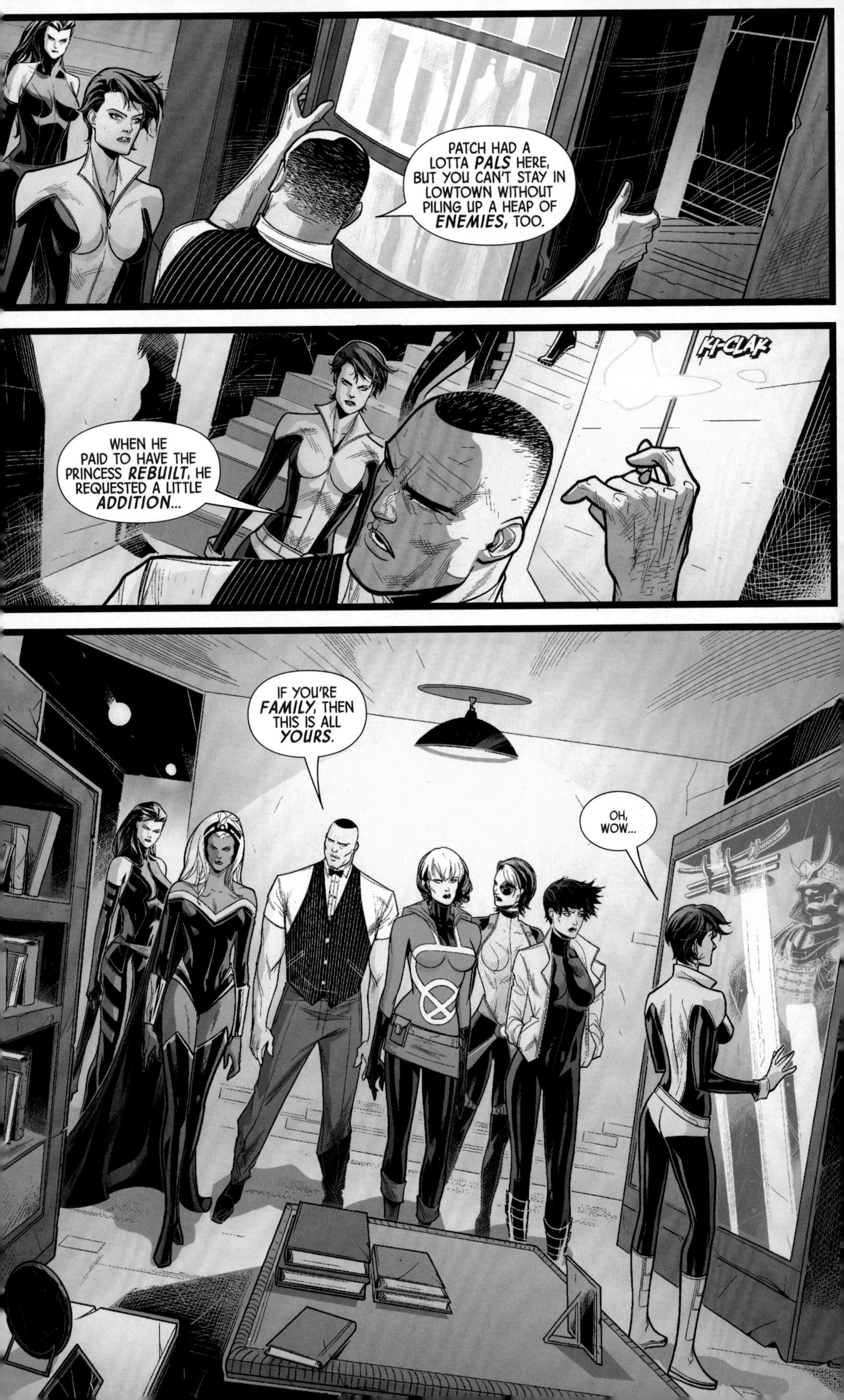
PATCH HAD A LOTTA PALS HERE, BUT YOU CAN'T STAY IN LOWTOWN WITHOUT PILING UP A HEAP OF ENEMIES, TOO.
WHEN HE PAID TO HAVE THE PRINCESS REBUILT, HE REQUESTED A LITTLE ADDITION...
KI-CLAK
IF YOU'RE FAMILY, THEN THIS IS ALL YOURS.
OH, WOW...

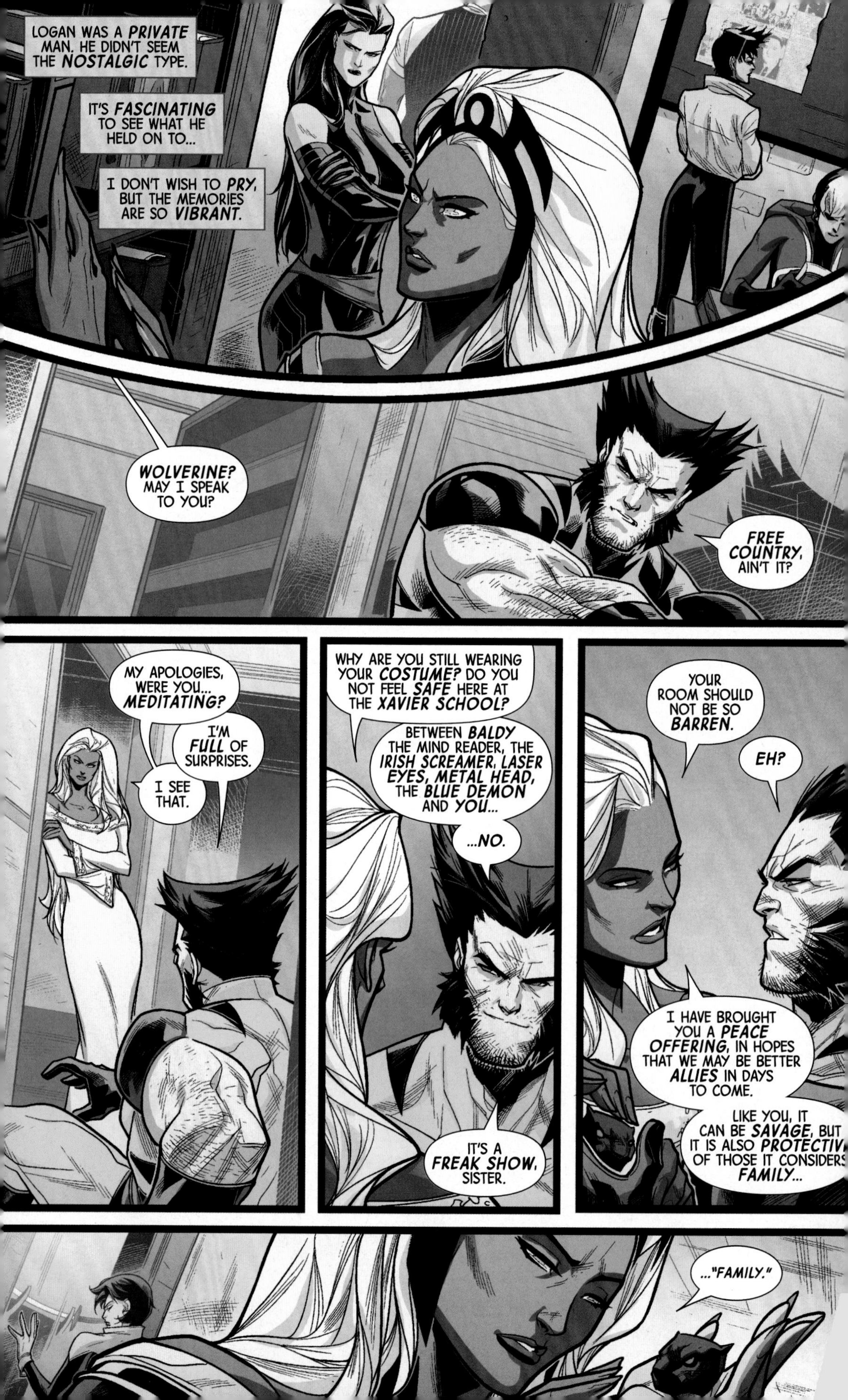

LOGAN WAS A PRIVATE MAN. HE DIDN'T SEEM THE NOSTALGIC TYPE.
IT'S FASCINATING TO SEE WHAT HE HELD ON TO...
I DON'T WISH TO PRY, BUT THE MEMORIES ARE SO VIBRANT.
WOLVERINE? MAY I SPEAK TO YOU?
FREE COUNTRY, AIN'T IT?
MY APOLOGIES, WERE YOU... MEDITATING?
I'M FULL OF SURPRISES.
I SEE THAT.
WHY ARE YOU STILL WEARING YOUR COSTUME? DO YOU NOT FEEL SAFE HERE AT THE XAVIER SCHOOL?
BETWEEN BALDY THE MIND READER, THE IRISH SCREAMER, LASER EYES, METAL HEAD, THE BLUE DEMON AND YOU...
...NO.
IT'S A FREAK SHOW, SISTER.
YOUR ROOM SHOULD NOT BE SO BARREN.
EH?
I HAVE BROUGHT YOU A PEACE OFFERING, IN HOPES THAT WE MAY BE BETTER ALLIES IN DAYS TO COME.
LIKE YOU, IT CAN BE SAVAGE, BUT IT IS ALSO PROTECTIV OF THOSE IT CONSIDERS FAMILY...
..."FAMILY."

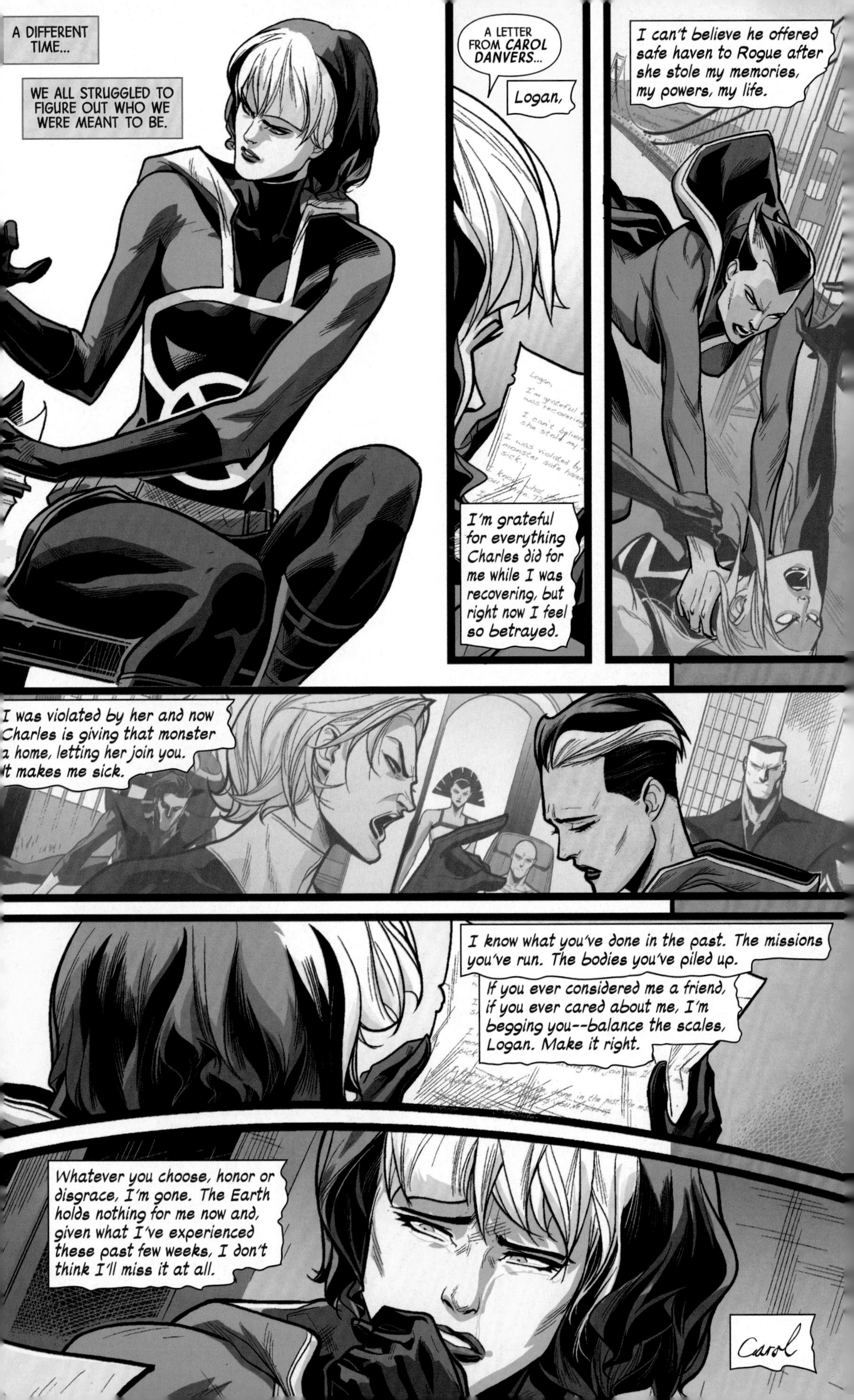
A DIFFERENT TIME...
WE ALL STRUGGLED TO FIGURE OUT WHO WE WERE MEANT TO BE.
A LETTER FROM CAROL DANVERS...
Logan,
I'm grateful for everything Charles did for me while I was recovering, but right now I feel so betrayed.
I can't believe he offered safe haven to Rogue after she stole my memories, my powers, my life.
I was violated by her and now Charles is giving that monster a home, letting her join you. It makes me sick.
I know what you've done in the past. The missions you've run. The bodies you've piled up.
If you ever considered me a friend, if you ever cared about me, I'm begging you--balance the scales, Logan. Make it right.
Whatever you choose, honor or disgrace, I'm gone. The Earth holds nothing for me now and, given what I've experienced these past few weeks, I don't think I'll miss it at all.
Carol

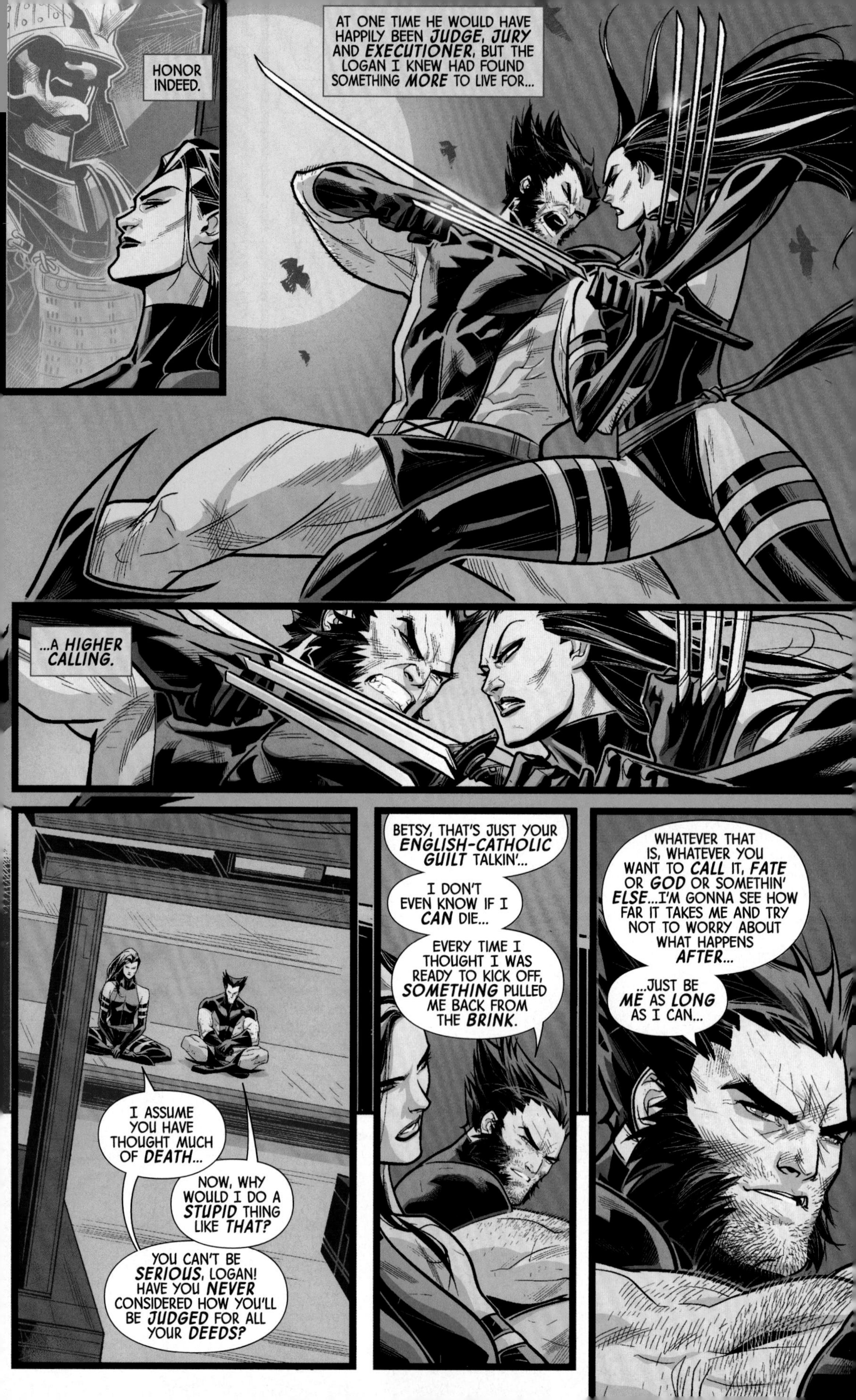
HONOR INDEED.
AT ONE TIME HE WOULD HAVE HAPPILY BEEN JUDGE, JURY AND EXECUTIONER, BUT THE LOGAN I KNEW HAD FOUND SOMETHING MORE TO LIVE FOR...
...A HIGHER CALLING.
I ASSUME YOU HAVE THOUGHT MUCH OF DEATH...
NOW, WHY WOULD I DO A STUPID THING LIKE THAT?
YOU CAN'T BE SERIOUS, LOGAN! HAVE YOU NEVER CONSIDERED HOW YOU'LL BE JUDGED FOR ALL YOUR DEEDS?
BETSY, THAT'S JUST YOUR ENGLISH-CATHOLIC GUILT TALKIN'...
I DON'T EVEN KNOW IF I CAN DIE...
EVERY TIME I THOUGHT I WAS READY TO KICK OFF, SOMETHING PULLED ME BACK FROM THE BRINK.
WHATEVER THAT IS, WHATEVER YOU WANT TO CALL IT, FATE OR GOD OR SOMETHIN' ELSE...I'M GONNA SEE HOW FAR IT TAKES ME AND TRY NOT TO WORRY ABOUT WHAT HAPPENS AFTER...
...JUST BE ME AS LONG AS I CAN...

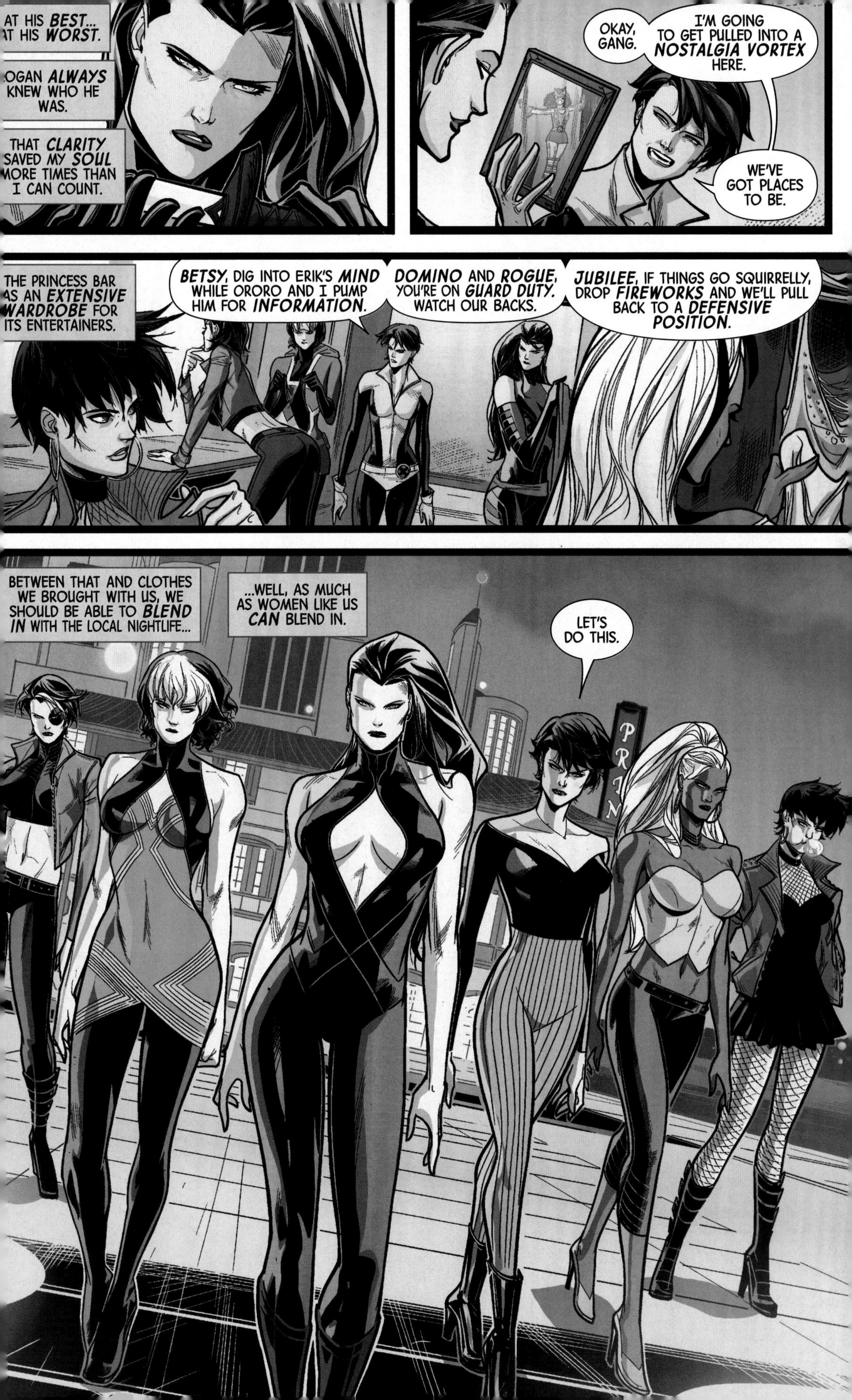

AT HIS BEST... AT HIS WORST.
OGAN ALWAYS KNEW WHO HE WAS.
THAT CLARITY SAVED MY SOUL MORE TIMES THAN I CAN COUNT.
OKAY, GANG.
I'M GOING TO GET PULLED INTO A NOSTALGIA VORTEX HERE.
WE'VE GOT PLACES TO BE.
THE PRINCESS BAR AS AN EXTENSIVE WARDROBE FOR ITS ENTERTAINERS.
BETSY, DIG INTO ERIK'S MIND WHILE ORORO AND I PUMP HIM FOR INFORMATION.
DOMINO AND ROGUE, YOU'RE ON GUARD DUTY. WATCH OUR BACKS.
JUBILEE, IF THINGS GO SQUIRRELLY, DROP FIREWORKS AND WE'LL PULL BACK TO A DEFENSIVE POSITION.
BETWEEN THAT AND CLOTHES WE BROUGHT WITH US, WE SHOULD BE ABLE TO BLEND IN WITH THE LOCAL NIGHTLIFE...
...WELL, AS MUCH AS WOMEN LIKE US CAN BLEND IN.
LET'S DO THIS.
PRIN

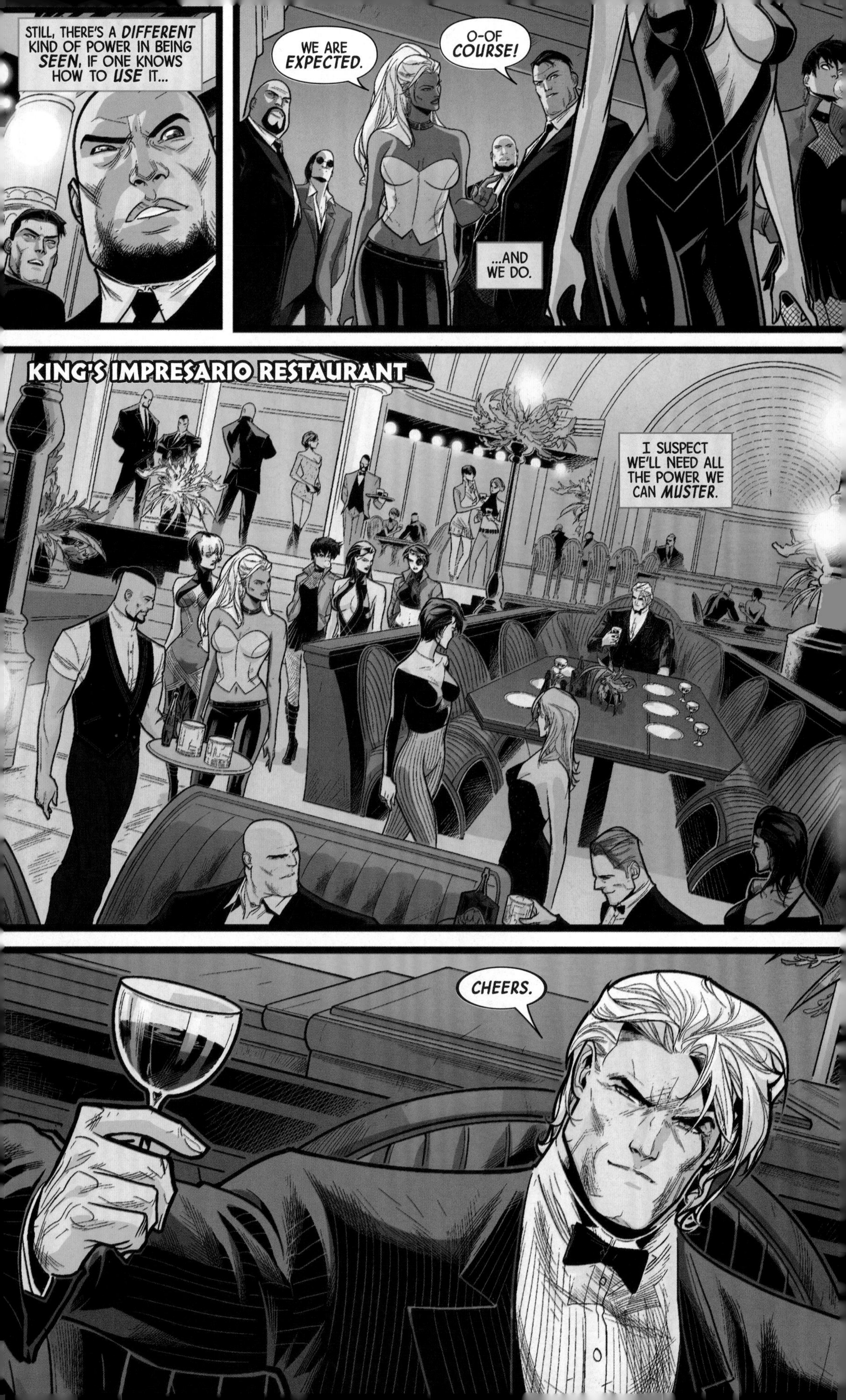

STILL, THERE'S A DIFFERENT KIND OF POWER IN BEING SEEN, IF ONE KNOWS HOW TO USE IT...
WE ARE EXPECTED.
O-OF COURSE!
...AND WE DO.
KING'S IMPRESARIO RESTAURANT
I SUSPECT WE'LL NEED ALL THE POWER WE CAN MUSTER.
CHEERS.

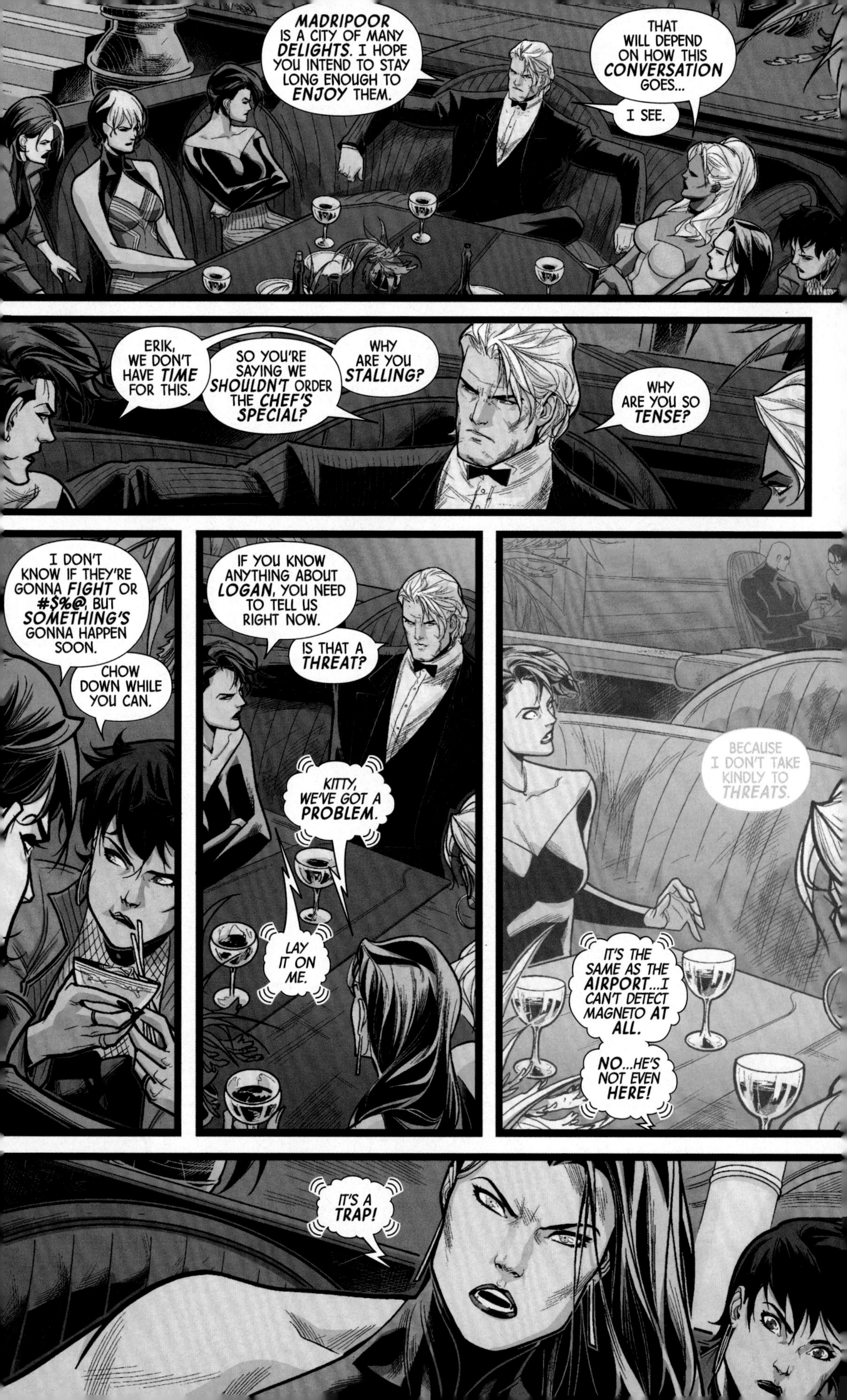
MADRIPOOR IS A CITY OF MANY DELIGHTS. I HOPE YOU INTEND TO STAY LONG ENOUGH TO ENJOY THEM.
THAT WILL DEPEND ON HOW THIS CONVERSATION GOES...
I SEE.
ERIK, WE DON'T HAVE TIME FOR THIS.
SO YOU'RE SAYING WE SHOULDN'T ORDER THE CHEF'S SPECIAL?
WHY ARE YOU STALLING?
WHY ARE YOU SO TENSE?
I DON'T KNOW IF THEY'RE GONNA FIGHT OR #$%@, BUT SOMETHING'S GONNA HAPPEN SOON.
CHOW DOWN WHILE YOU CAN.
IF YOU KNOW ANYTHING ABOUT LOGAN, YOU NEED TO TELL US RIGHT NOW.
IS THAT A THREAT?
KITTY, WE'VE GOT A PROBLEM.
LAY IT ON ME.
BECAUSE I DON'T TAKE KINDLY TO THREATS.
IT'S THE SAME AS THE AIRPORT...I CAN'T DETECT MAGNETO AT ALL.
NO...HE'S NOT EVEN HERE!
IT'S A TRAP!

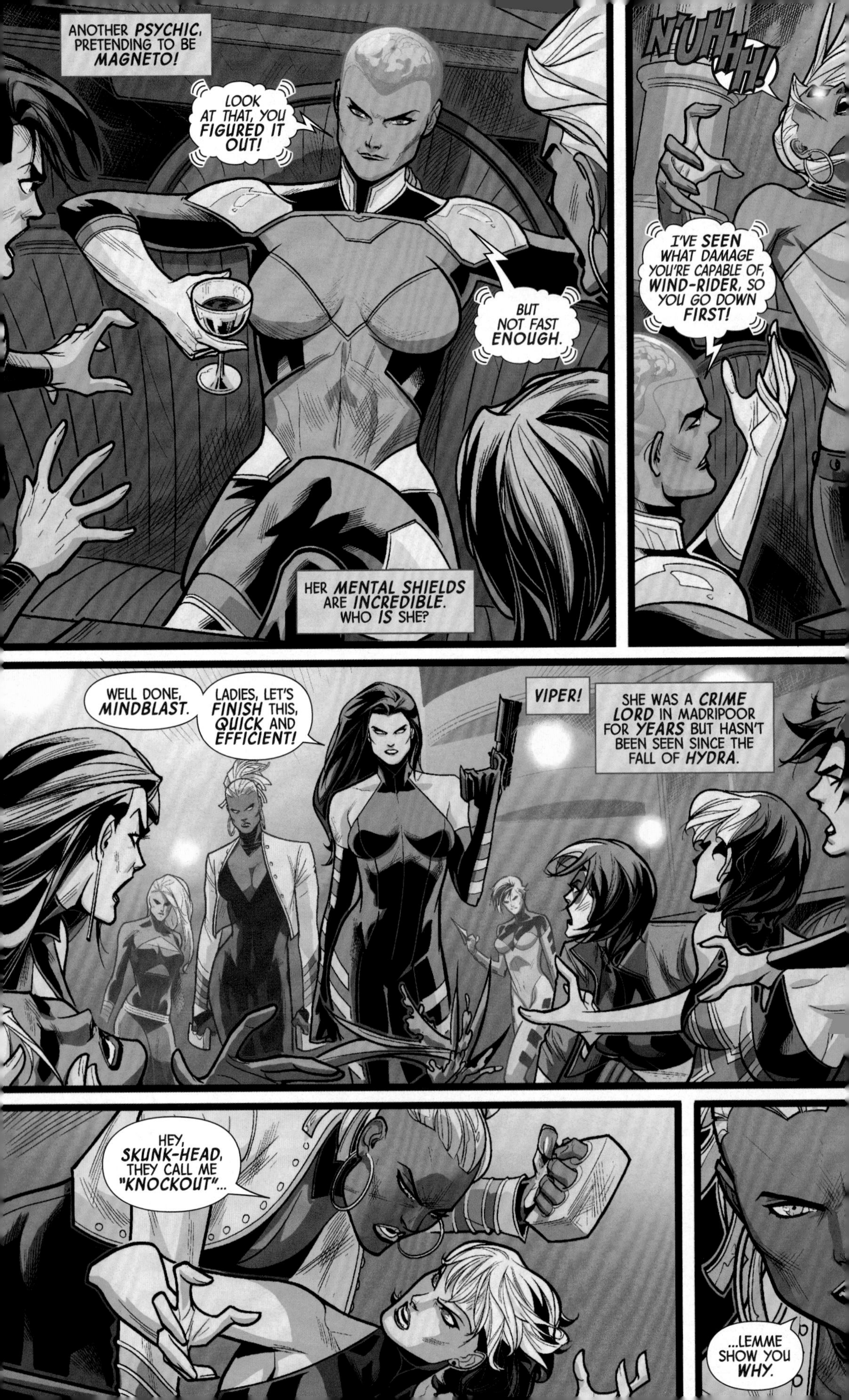
ANOTHER PSYCHIC, PRETENDING TO BE MAGNETO!
LOOK AT THAT, YOU FIGURED IT OUT!
BUT NOT FAST ENOUGH.
HER MENTAL SHIELDS ARE INCREDIBLE. WHO IS SHE?
N'UHHH!
I'VE SEEN WHAT DAMAGE YOU'RE CAPABLE OF, WIND-RIDER, SO YOU GO DOWN FIRST!
WELL DONE, MINDBLAST.
LADIES, LET'S FINISH THIS, QUICK AND EFFICIENT!
VIPER!
SHE WAS A CRIME LORD IN MADRIPOOR FOR YEARS BUT HASN'T BEEN SEEN SINCE THE FALL OF HYDRA.
HEY, SKUNK-HEAD, THEY CALL ME "KNOCKOUT"...
...LEMME SHOW YOU WHY.

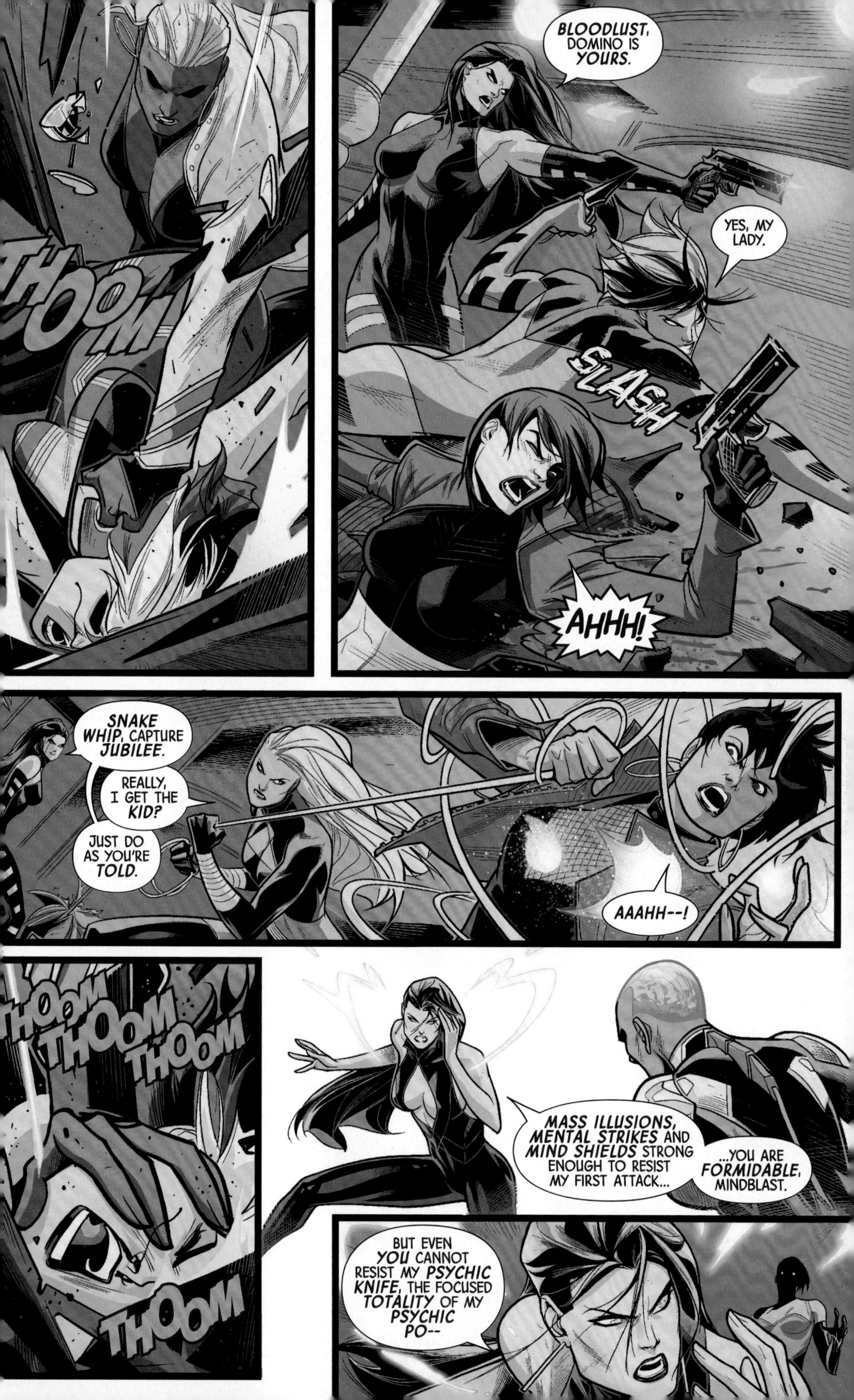
THOOM
BLOODLUST, DOMINO IS YOURS.
YES, MY LADY.
SLASH
AHHH!
SNAKE WHIP, CAPTURE JUBILEE.
REALLY, I GET THE KID?
JUST DO AS YOU'RE TOLD.
AAAHH--!
THOOM THOOM THOOM
THOOM
MASS ILLUSIONS, MENTAL STRIKES AND MIND SHIELDS STRONG ENOUGH TO RESIST MY FIRST ATTACK...
...YOU ARE FORMIDABLE, MINDBLAST.
BUT EVEN YOU CANNOT RESIST MY PSYCHIC KNIFE, THE FOCUSED TOTALITY OF MY PSYCHIC PO--

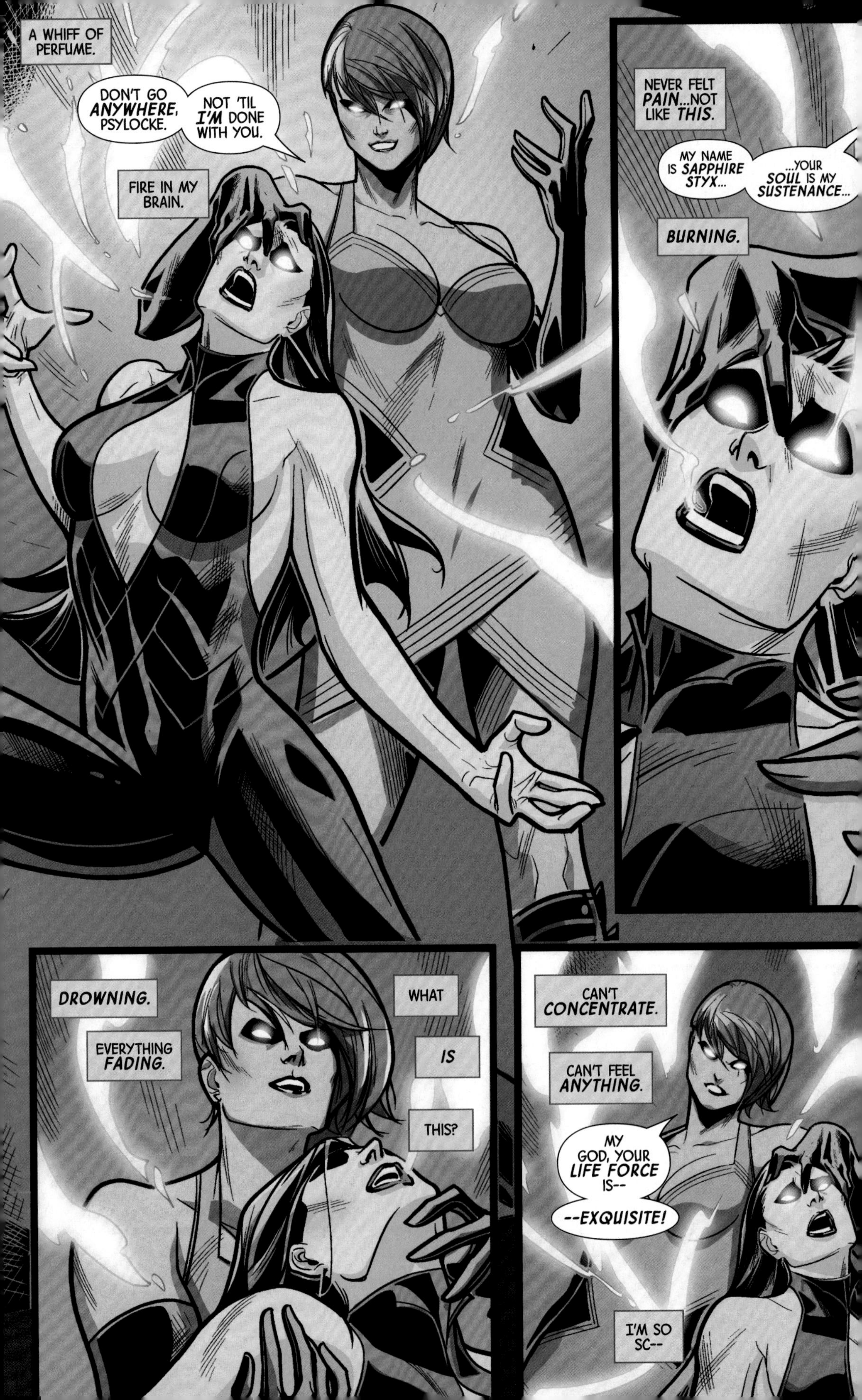

A WHIFF OF PERFUME.
DON'T GO ANYWHERE, PSYLOCKE.
NOT 'TIL I'M DONE WITH YOU.
FIRE IN MY BRAIN.
NEVER FELT PAIN...NOT LIKE THIS.
MY NAME IS SAPPHIRE STYX...
...YOUR SOUL IS MY SUSTENANCE...
BURNING.
DROWNING.
EVERYTHING FADING.
WHAT
IS
THIS?
CAN'T CONCENTRATE.
CAN'T FEEL ANYTHING.
MY GOD, YOUR LIFE FORCE IS--
--EXQUISITE!
I'M SO SC--

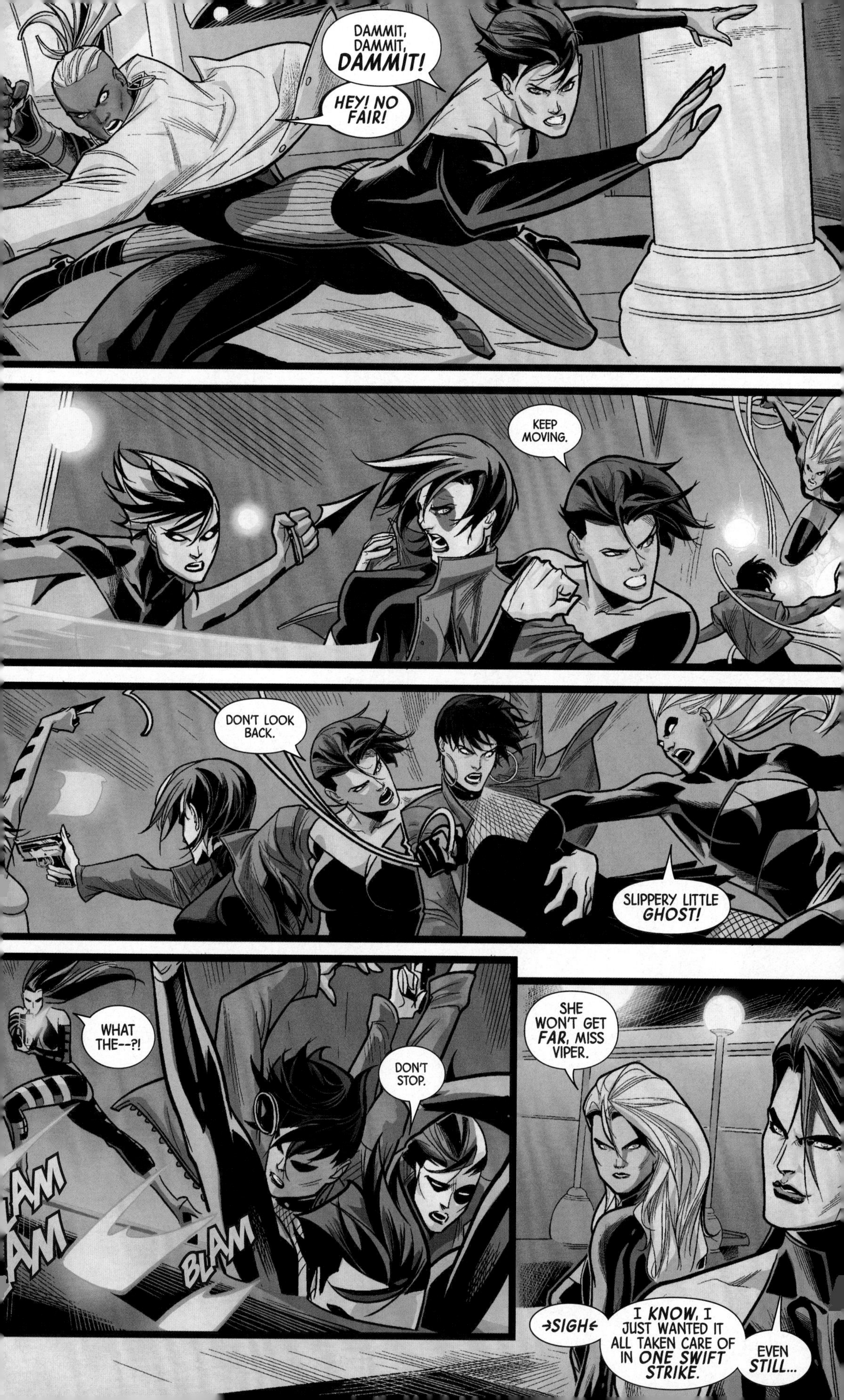
DAMMIT, DAMMIT, DAMMIT!
HEY! NO FAIR!
KEEP MOVING.
DON'T LOOK BACK.
SLIPPERY LITTLE GHOST!
WHAT THE--?!
DON'T STOP.
LAM
AM
BLAM
SHE WON'T GET FAR, MISS VIPER.
→SIGH←
I KNOW, I JUST WANTED IT ALL TAKEN CARE OF IN ONE SWIFT STRIKE.
EVEN STILL...

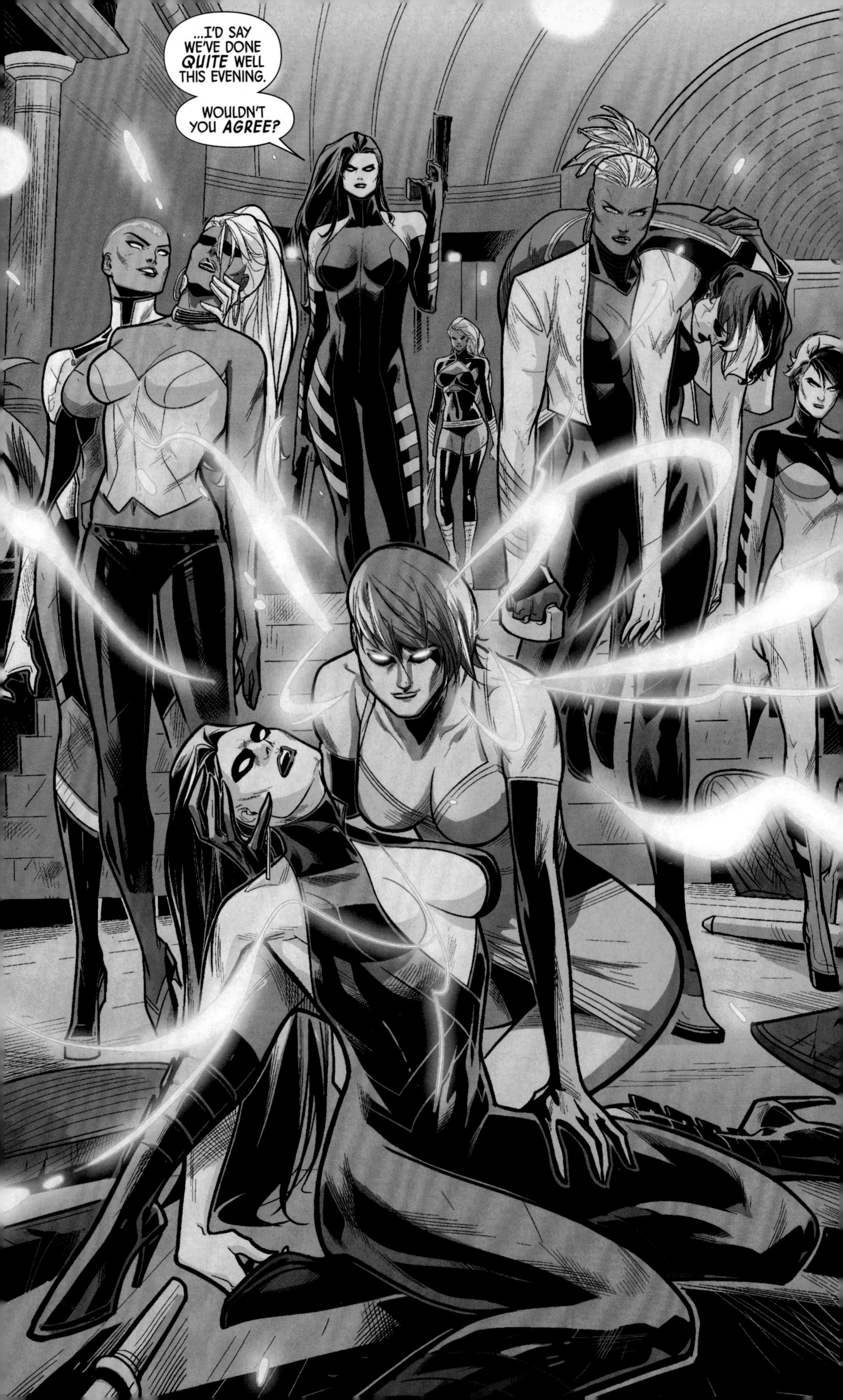
...I'D SAY WE'VE DONE QUITE WELL THIS EVENING.
WOULDN'T YOU AGREE?

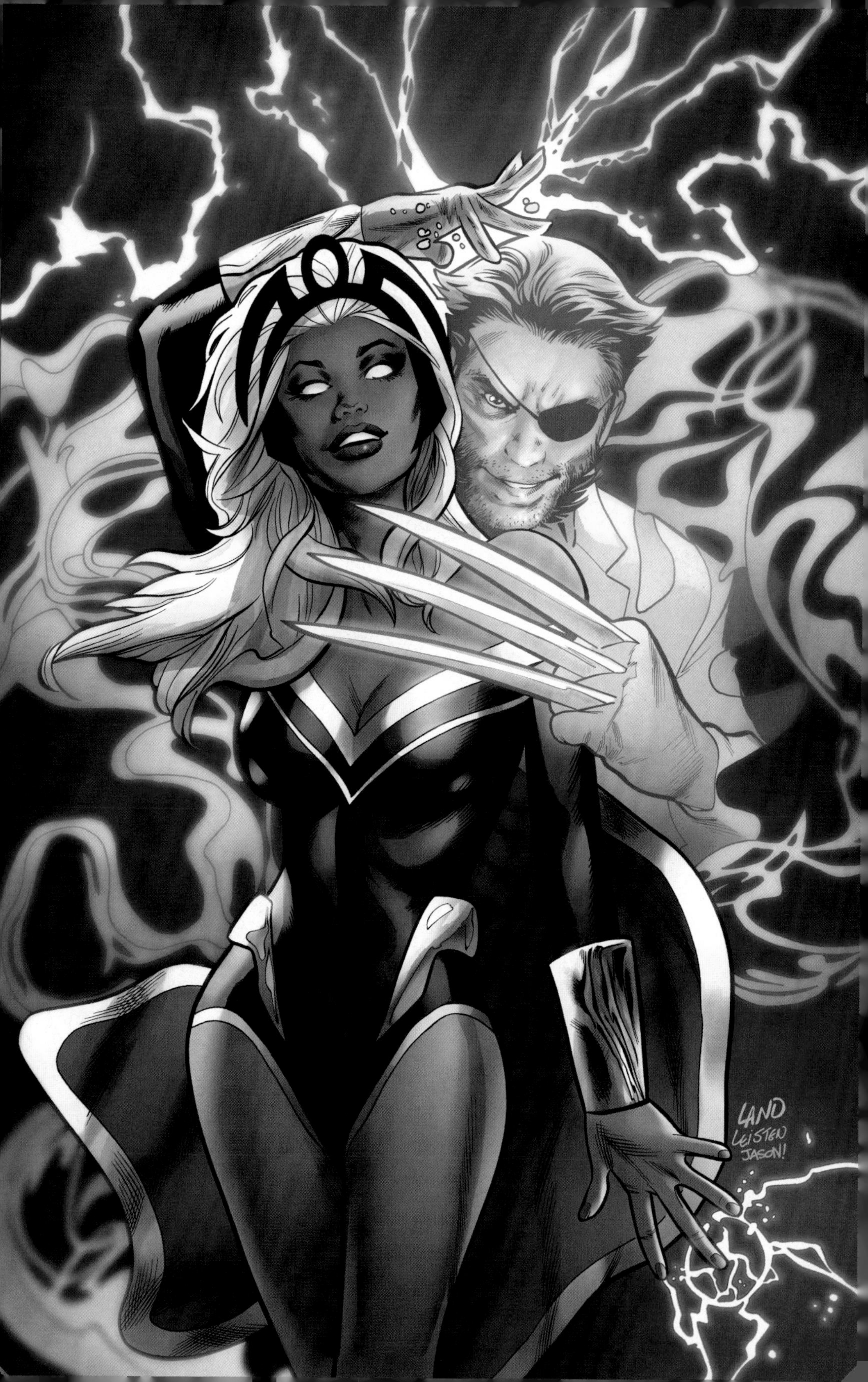
LAND
LEISTEN
JASON!

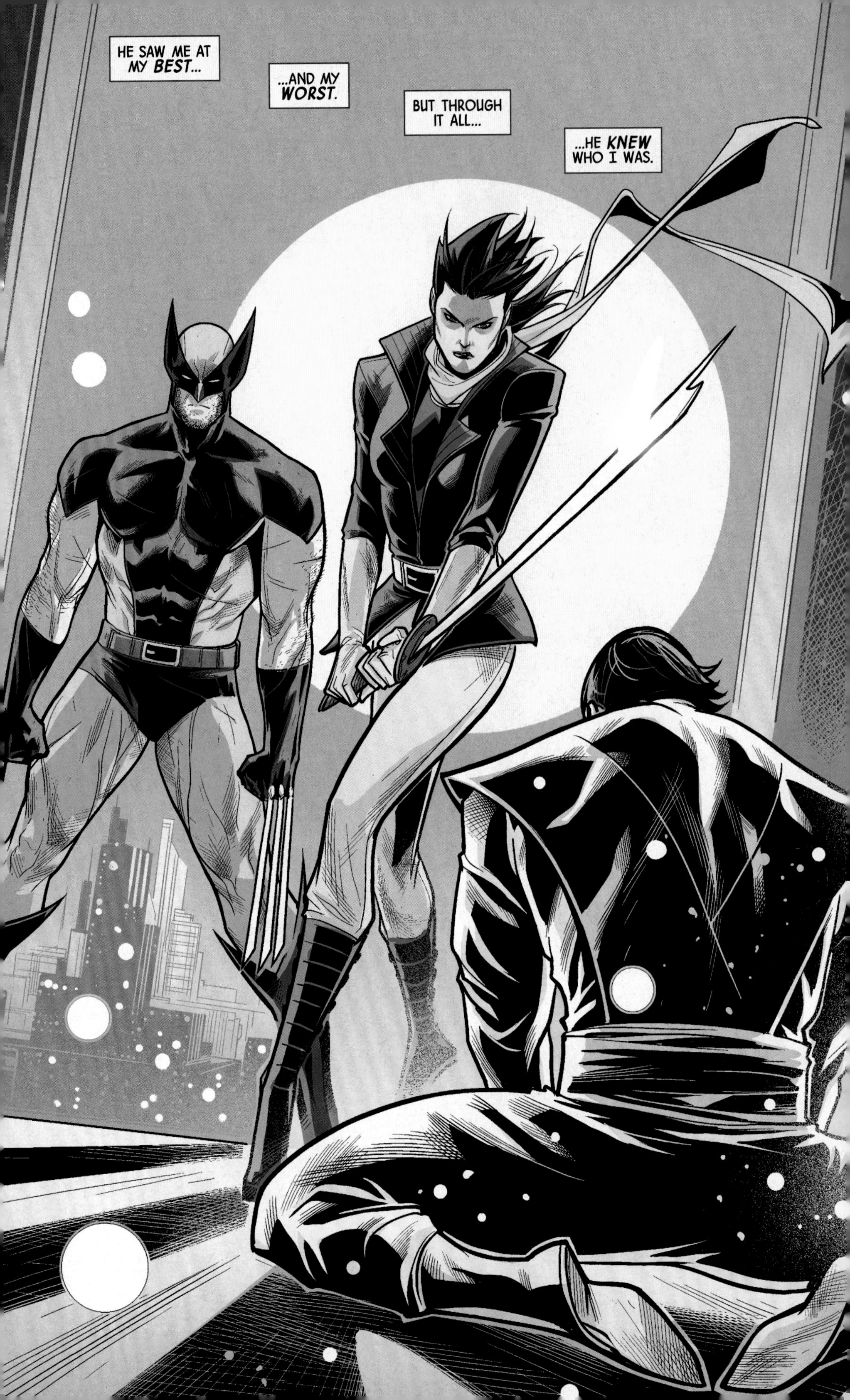
HE SAW ME AT MY BEST...
...AND MY WORST.
BUT THROUGH IT ALL...
...HE KNEW WHO I WAS.

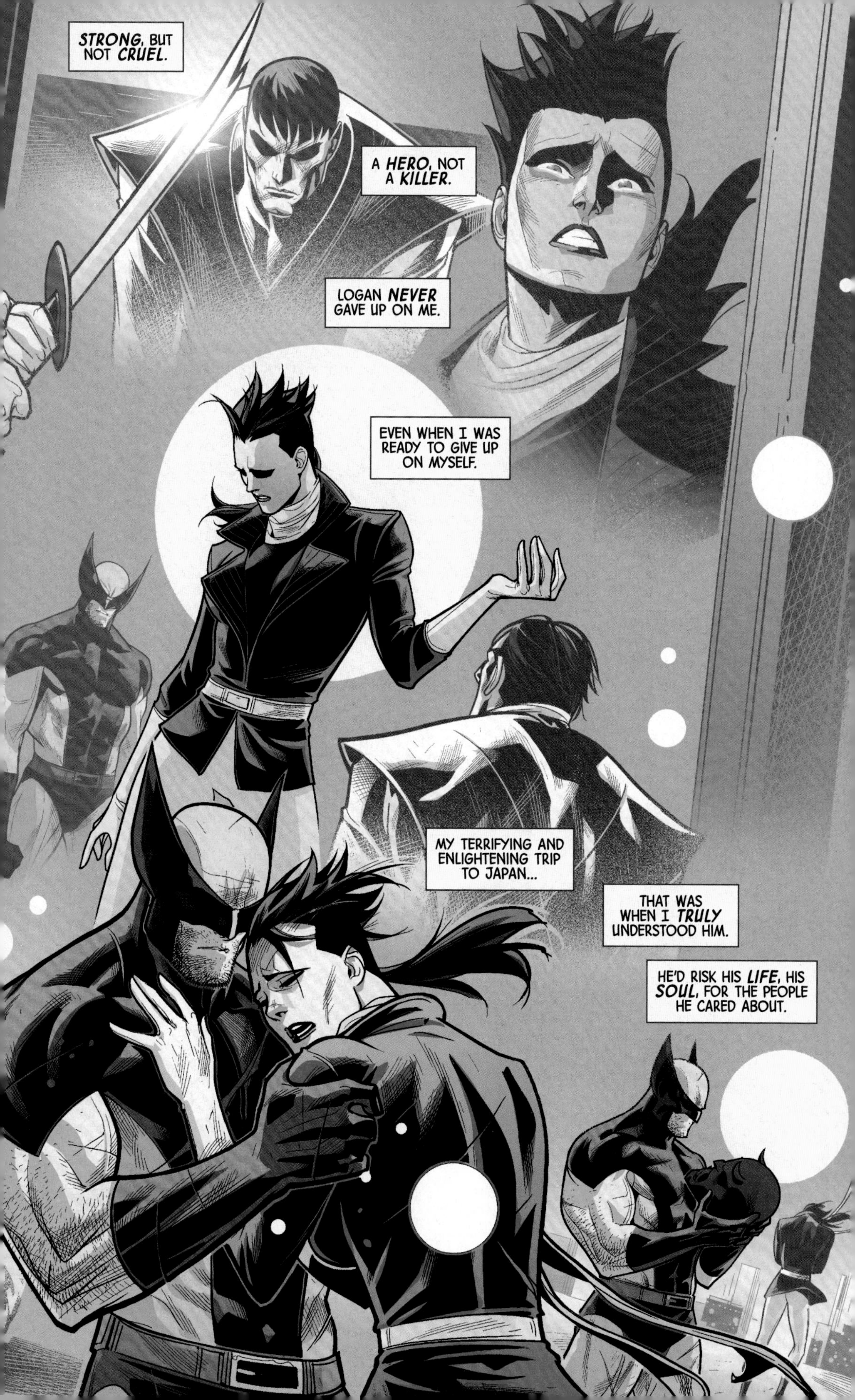
STRONG, BUT NOT CRUEL.
A HERO, NOT A KILLER.
LOGAN NEVER GAVE UP ON ME.
EVEN WHEN I WAS READY TO GIVE UP ON MYSELF.
MY TERRIFYING AND ENLIGHTENING TRIP TO JAPAN...
THAT WAS WHEN I TRULY UNDERSTOOD HIM.
HE'D RISK HIS LIFE, HIS SOUL, FOR THE PEOPLE HE CARED ABOUT.

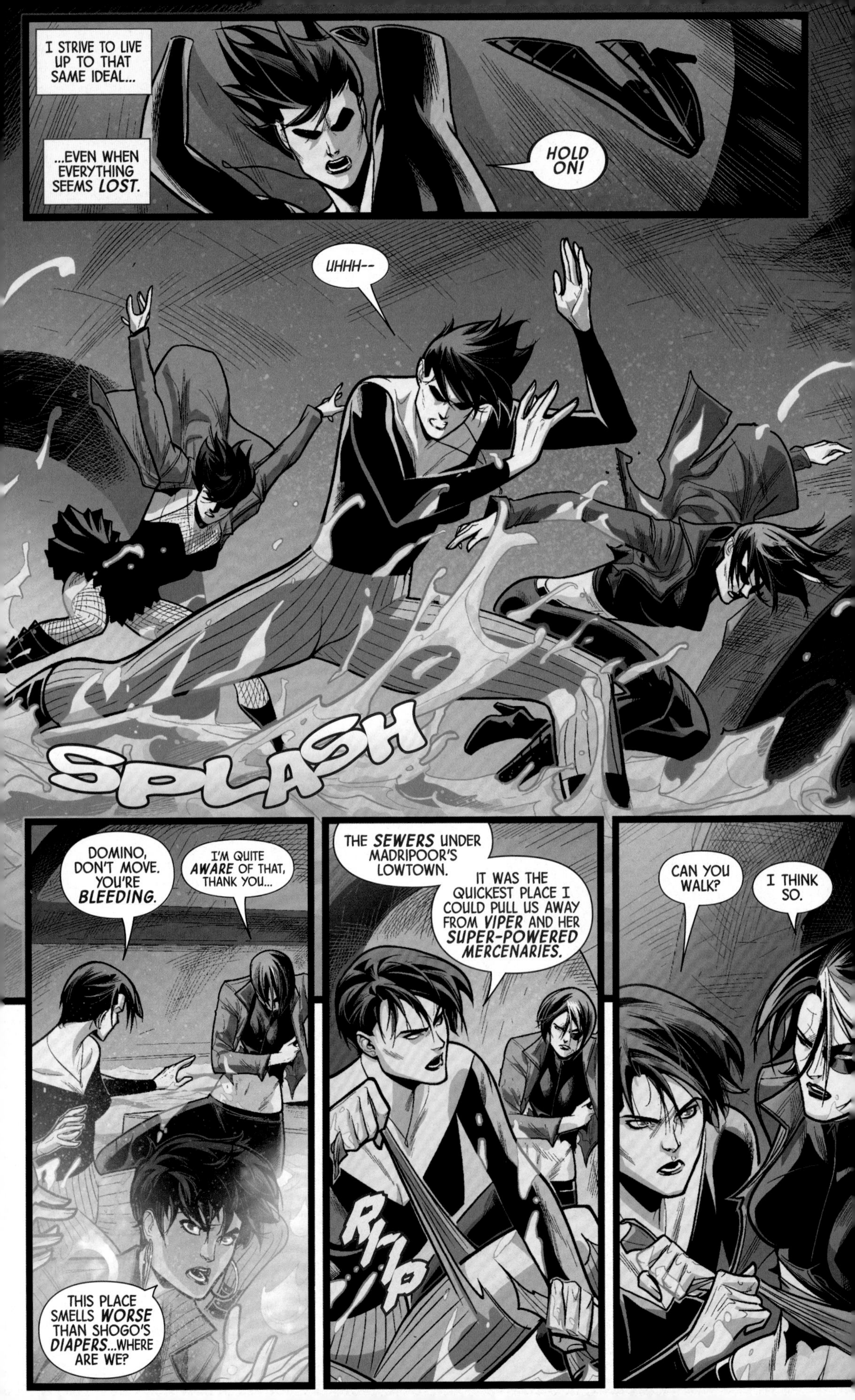
I STRIVE TO LIVE UP TO THAT SAME IDEAL...
...EVEN WHEN EVERYTHING SEEMS LOST.
HOLD ON!
UHHH--
SPLASH
DOMINO, DON'T MOVE. YOU'RE BLEEDING.
I'M QUITE AWARE OF THAT, THANK YOU...
THIS PLACE SMELLS WORSE THAN SHOGO'S DIAPERS...WHERE ARE WE?
THE SEWERS UNDER MADRIPOOR'S LOWTOWN.
IT WAS THE QUICKEST PLACE I COULD PULL US AWAY FROM VIPER AND HER SUPER-POWERED MERCENARIES.
RIIP
CAN YOU WALK?
I THINK SO.

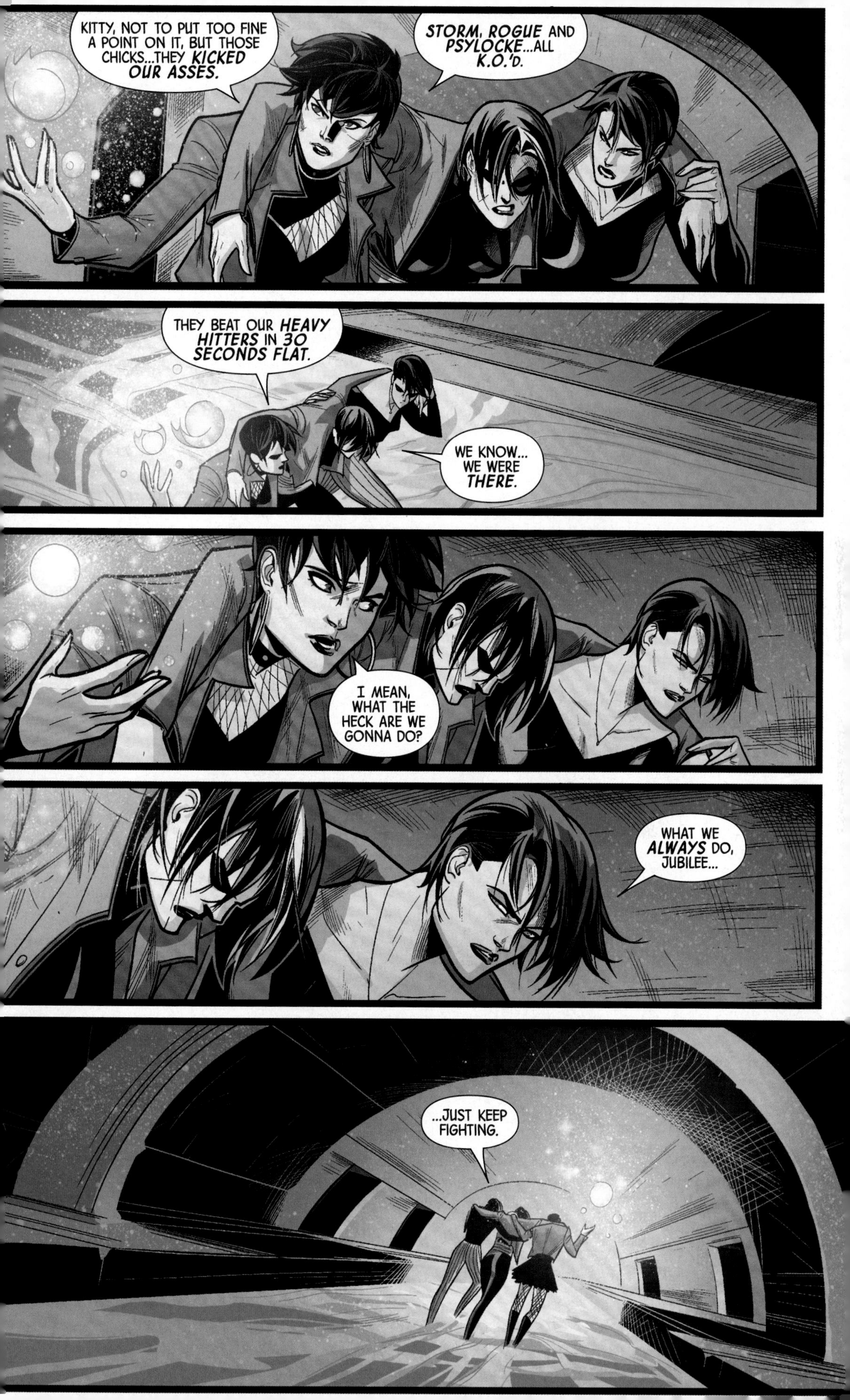
KITTY, NOT TO PUT TOO FINE A POINT ON IT, BUT THOSE CHICKS...THEY KICKED OUR ASSES.
STORM, ROGUE AND PSYLOCKE...ALL K.O.'D.
THEY BEAT OUR HEAVY HITTERS IN 30 SECONDS FLAT.
WE KNOW... WE WERE THERE.
I MEAN, WHAT THE HECK ARE WE GONNA DO?
WHAT WE ALWAYS DO, JUBILEE...
...JUST KEEP FIGHTING.

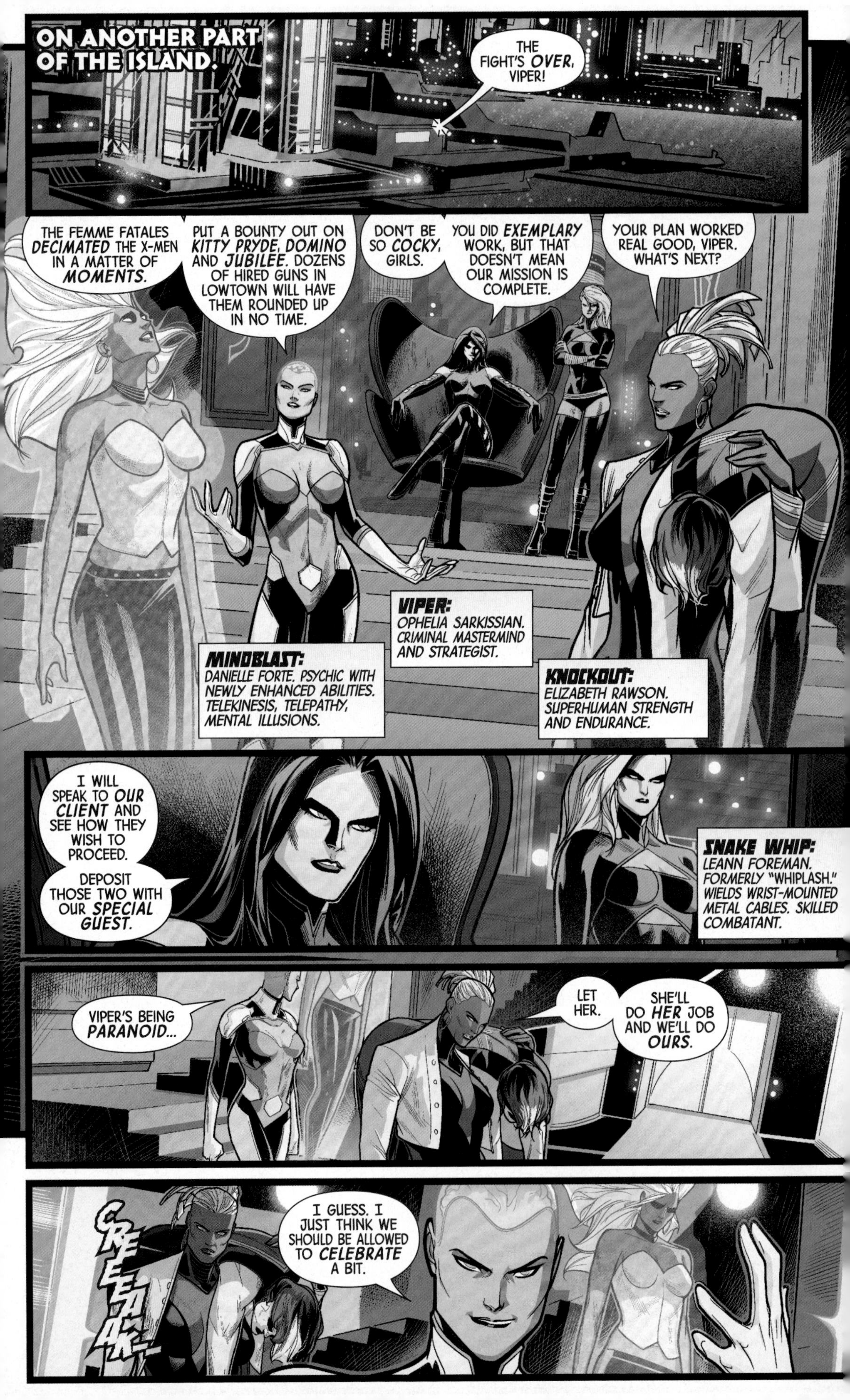

ON ANOTHER PART OF THE ISLAND.
THE FIGHT'S OVER, VIPER!
THE FEMME FATALES DECIMATED THE X-MEN IN A MATTER OF MOMENTS.
PUT A BOUNTY OUT ON KITTY PRYDE, DOMINO AND JUBILEE. DOZENS OF HIRED GUNS IN LOWTOWN WILL HAVE THEM ROUNDED UP IN NO TIME.
DON'T BE SO COCKY, GIRLS.
YOU DID EXEMPLARY WORK, BUT THAT DOESN'T MEAN OUR MISSION IS COMPLETE.
YOUR PLAN WORKED REAL GOOD, VIPER. WHAT'S NEXT?
VIPER: OPHELIA SARKISSIAN. CRIMINAL MASTERMIND AND STRATEGIST.
MINDBLAST: DANIELLE FORTE. PSYCHIC WITH NEWLY ENHANCED ABILITIES. TELEKINESIS, TELEPATHY, MENTAL ILLUSIONS.
KNOCKOUT: ELIZABETH RAWSON. SUPERHUMAN STRENGTH AND ENDURANCE.
I WILL SPEAK TO OUR CLIENT AND SEE HOW THEY WISH TO PROCEED.
DEPOSIT THOSE TWO WITH OUR SPECIAL GUEST.
SNAKE WHIP: LEANN FOREMAN. FORMERLY "WHIPLASH." WIELDS WRIST-MOUNTED METAL CABLES. SKILLED COMBATANT.
VIPER'S BEING PARANOID...
LET HER.
SHE'LL DO HER JOB AND WE'LL DO OURS.
CREEEAAK—
I GUESS. I JUST THINK WE SHOULD BE ALLOWED TO CELEBRATE A BIT.

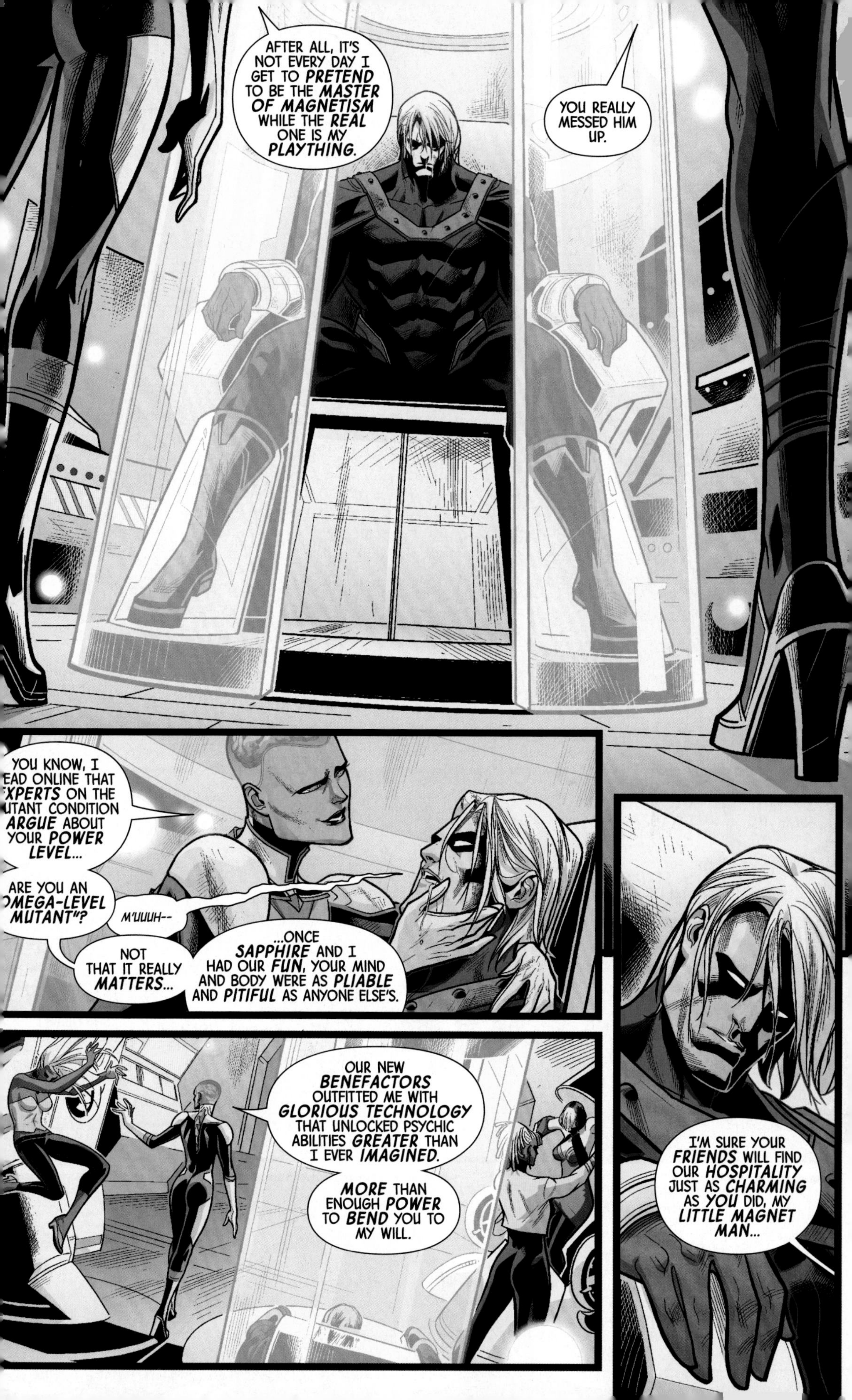
AFTER ALL, IT'S NOT EVERY DAY I GET TO PRETEND TO BE THE MASTER OF MAGNETISM WHILE THE REAL ONE IS MY PLAYTHING.
YOU REALLY MESSED HIM UP.
YOU KNOW, I EAD ONLINE THAT XPERTS ON THE UTANT CONDITION ARGUE ABOUT YOUR POWER LEVEL...
ARE YOU AN OMEGA-LEVEL MUTANT"?
M'UUUH--
NOT THAT IT REALLY MATTERS...
...ONCE SAPPHIRE AND I HAD OUR FUN, YOUR MIND AND BODY WERE AS PLIABLE AND PITIFUL AS ANYONE ELSE'S.
OUR NEW BENEFACTORS OUTFITTED ME WITH GLORIOUS TECHNOLOGY THAT UNLOCKED PSYCHIC ABILITIES GREATER THAN I EVER IMAGINED.
MORE THAN ENOUGH POWER TO BEND YOU TO MY WILL.
I'M SURE YOUR FRIENDS WILL FIND OUR HOSPITALITY JUST AS CHARMING AS YOU DID, MY LITTLE MAGNET MAN...

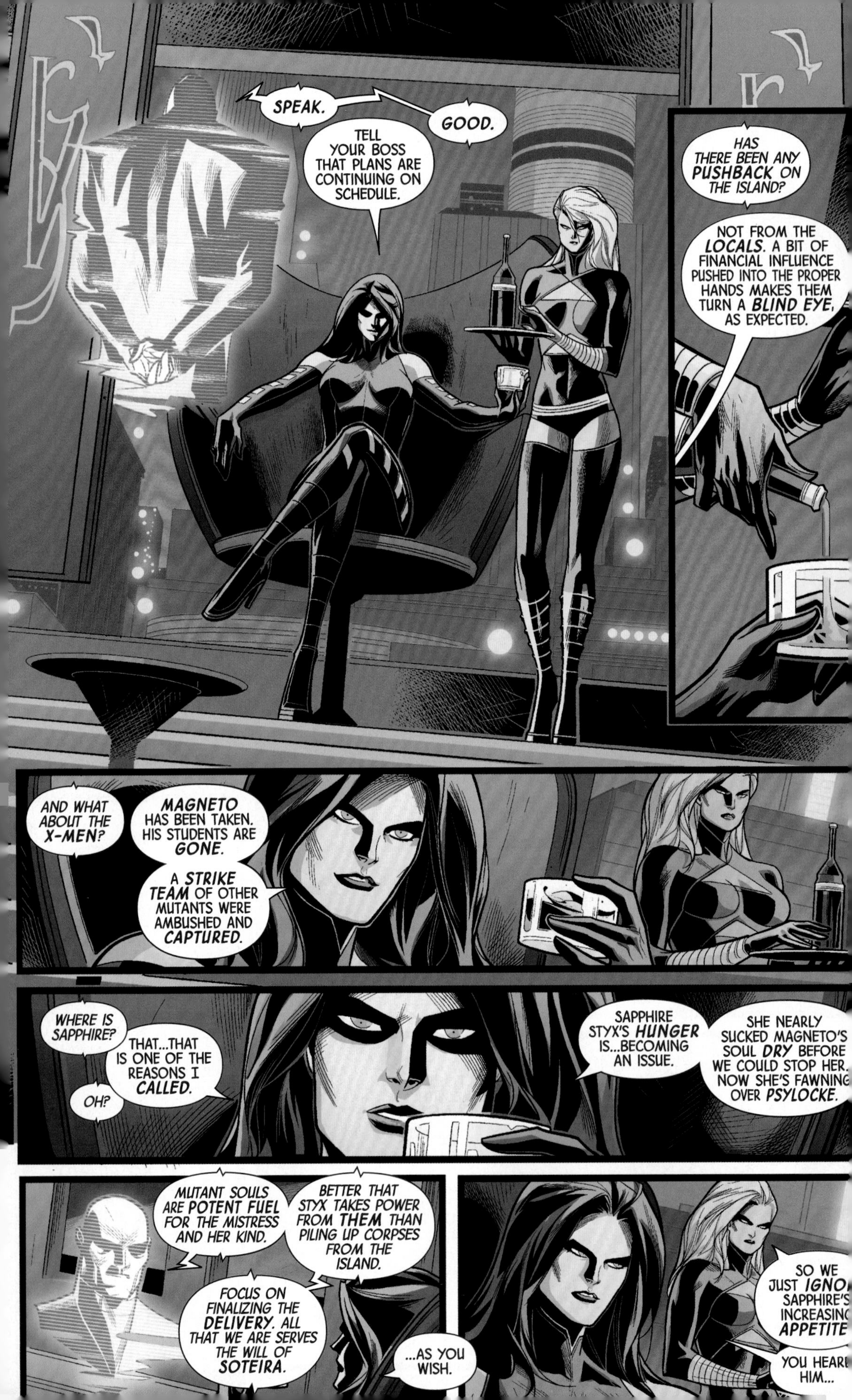
SPEAK.
GOOD.
TELL YOUR BOSS THAT PLANS ARE CONTINUING ON SCHEDULE.
HAS THERE BEEN ANY PUSHBACK ON THE ISLAND?
NOT FROM THE LOCALS. A BIT OF FINANCIAL INFLUENCE PUSHED INTO THE PROPER HANDS MAKES THEM TURN A BLIND EYE, AS EXPECTED.
AND WHAT ABOUT THE X-MEN?
MAGNETO HAS BEEN TAKEN. HIS STUDENTS ARE GONE.
A STRIKE TEAM OF OTHER MUTANTS WERE AMBUSHED AND CAPTURED.
WHERE IS SAPPHIRE?
THAT...THAT IS ONE OF THE REASONS I CALLED.
OH?
SAPPHIRE STYX'S HUNGER IS...BECOMING AN ISSUE.
SHE NEARLY SUCKED MAGNETO'S SOUL DRY BEFORE WE COULD STOP HER. NOW SHE'S FAWNING OVER PSYLOCKE.
MUTANT SOULS ARE POTENT FUEL FOR THE MISTRESS AND HER KIND.
BETTER THAT STYX TAKES POWER FROM THEM THAN PILING UP CORPSES FROM THE ISLAND.
FOCUS ON FINALIZING THE DELIVERY. ALL THAT WE ARE SERVES THE WILL OF SOTEIRA.
...AS YOU WISH.

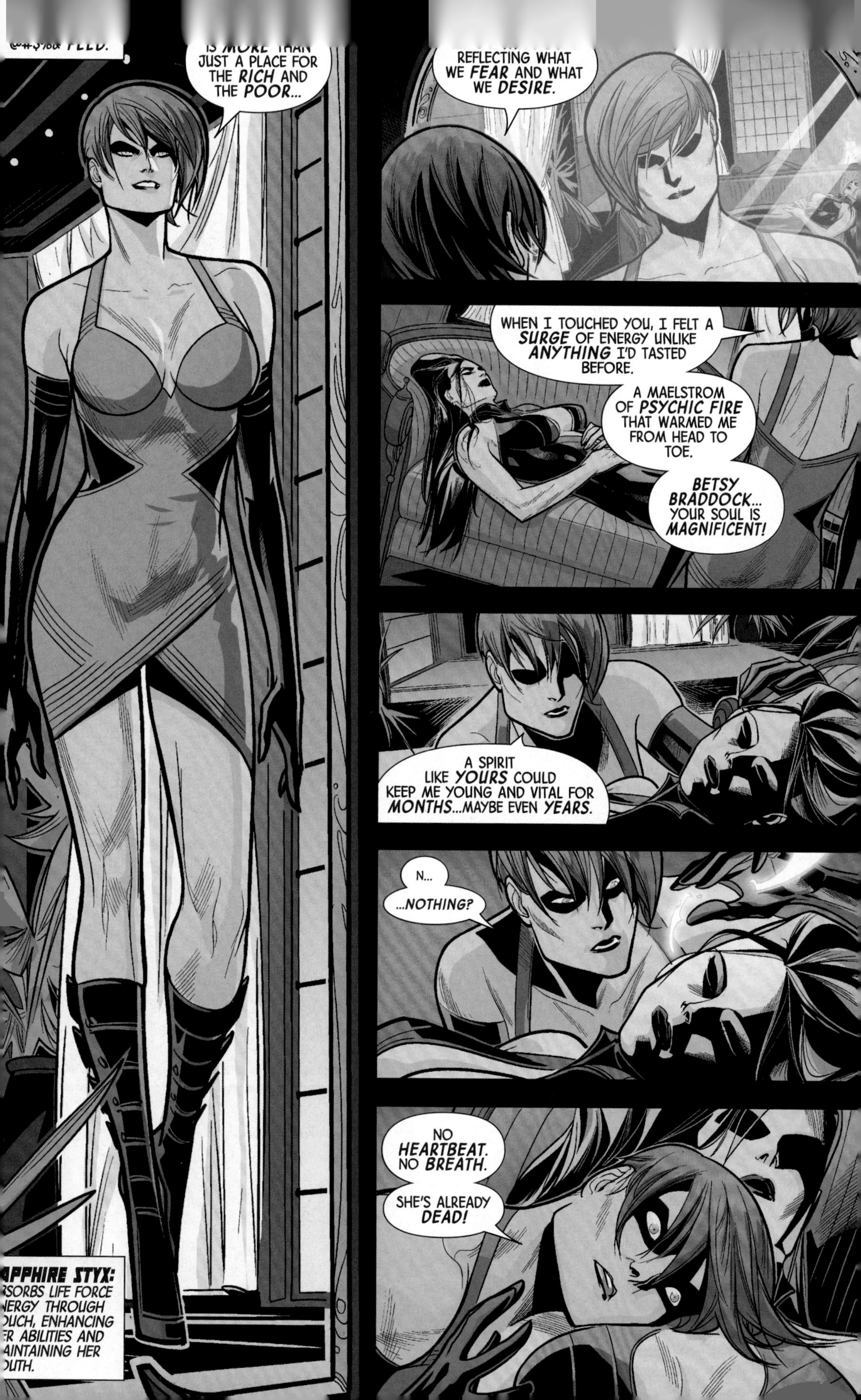
IS MORE THAN JUST A PLACE FOR THE RICH AND THE POOR...
REFLECTING WHAT WE FEAR AND WHAT WE DESIRE.
WHEN I TOUCHED YOU, I FELT A SURGE OF ENERGY UNLIKE ANYTHING I'D TASTED BEFORE.
A MAELSTROM OF PSYCHIC FIRE THAT WARMED ME FROM HEAD TO TOE.
BETSY BRADDOCK... YOUR SOUL IS MAGNIFICENT!
A SPIRIT LIKE YOURS COULD KEEP ME YOUNG AND VITAL FOR MONTHS...MAYBE EVEN YEARS.
N...
...NOTHING?
NO HEARTBEAT. NO BREATH.
SHE'S ALREADY DEAD!
APPHIRE STYX: BSORBS LIFE FORCE NERGY THROUGH OUCH, ENHANCING ER ABILITIES AND AINTAINING HER OUTH.

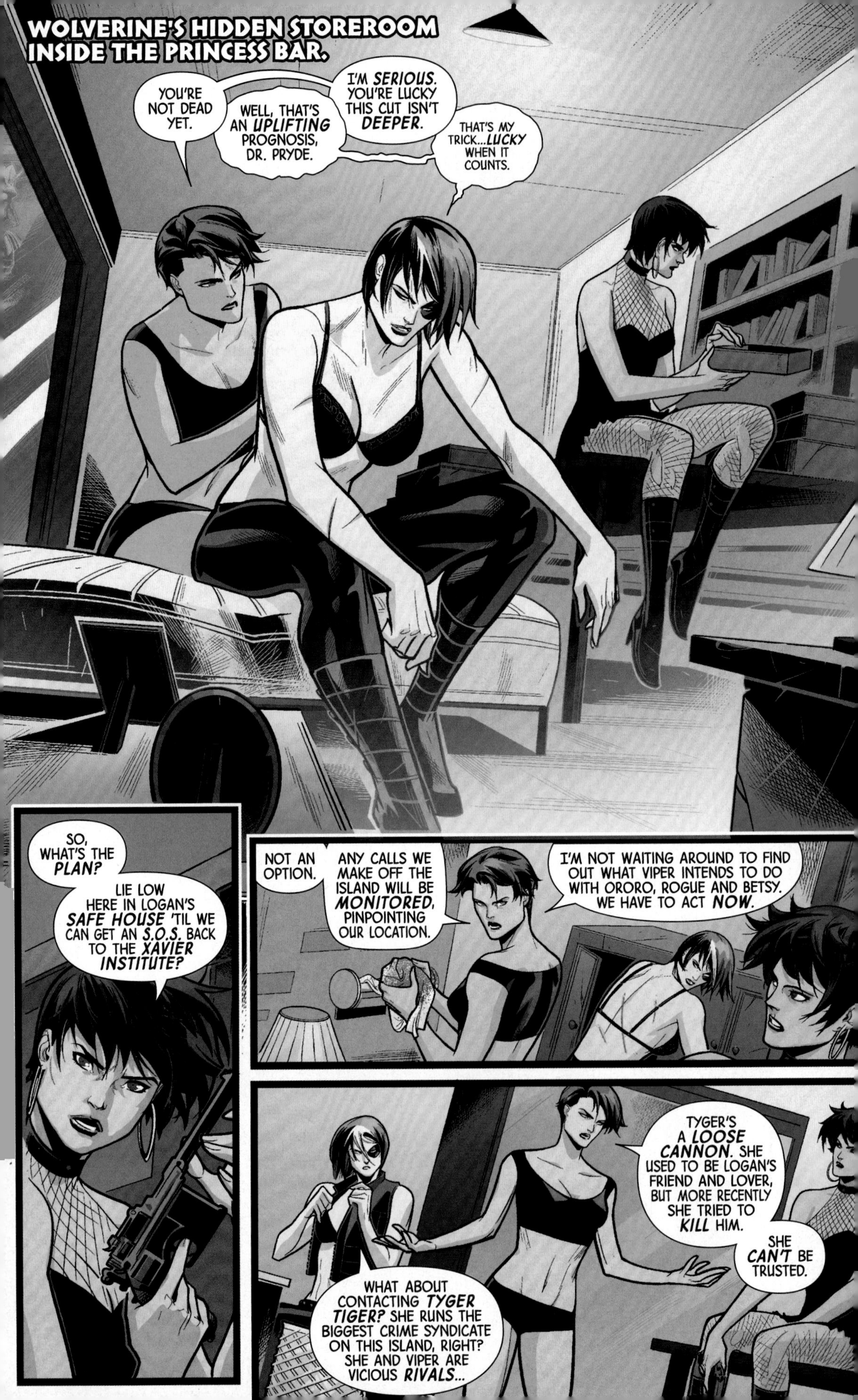
WOLVERINE'S HIDDEN STOREROOM INSIDE THE PRINCESS BAR.
YOU'RE NOT DEAD YET.
WELL, THAT'S AN UPLIFTING PROGNOSIS, DR. PRYDE.
I'M SERIOUS. YOU'RE LUCKY THIS CUT ISN'T DEEPER.
THAT'S MY TRICK...LUCKY WHEN IT COUNTS.
SO, WHAT'S THE PLAN?
LIE LOW HERE IN LOGAN'S SAFE HOUSE 'TIL WE CAN GET AN S.O.S. BACK TO THE XAVIER INSTITUTE?
NOT AN OPTION.
ANY CALLS WE MAKE OFF THE ISLAND WILL BE MONITORED, PINPOINTING OUR LOCATION.
I'M NOT WAITING AROUND TO FIND OUT WHAT VIPER INTENDS TO DO WITH ORORO, ROGUE AND BETSY. WE HAVE TO ACT NOW.
WHAT ABOUT CONTACTING TYGER TIGER? SHE RUNS THE BIGGEST CRIME SYNDICATE ON THIS ISLAND, RIGHT? SHE AND VIPER ARE VICIOUS RIVALS...
TYGER'S A LOOSE CANNON. SHE USED TO BE LOGAN'S FRIEND AND LOVER, BUT MORE RECENTLY SHE TRIED TO KILL HIM.
SHE CAN'T BE TRUSTED.

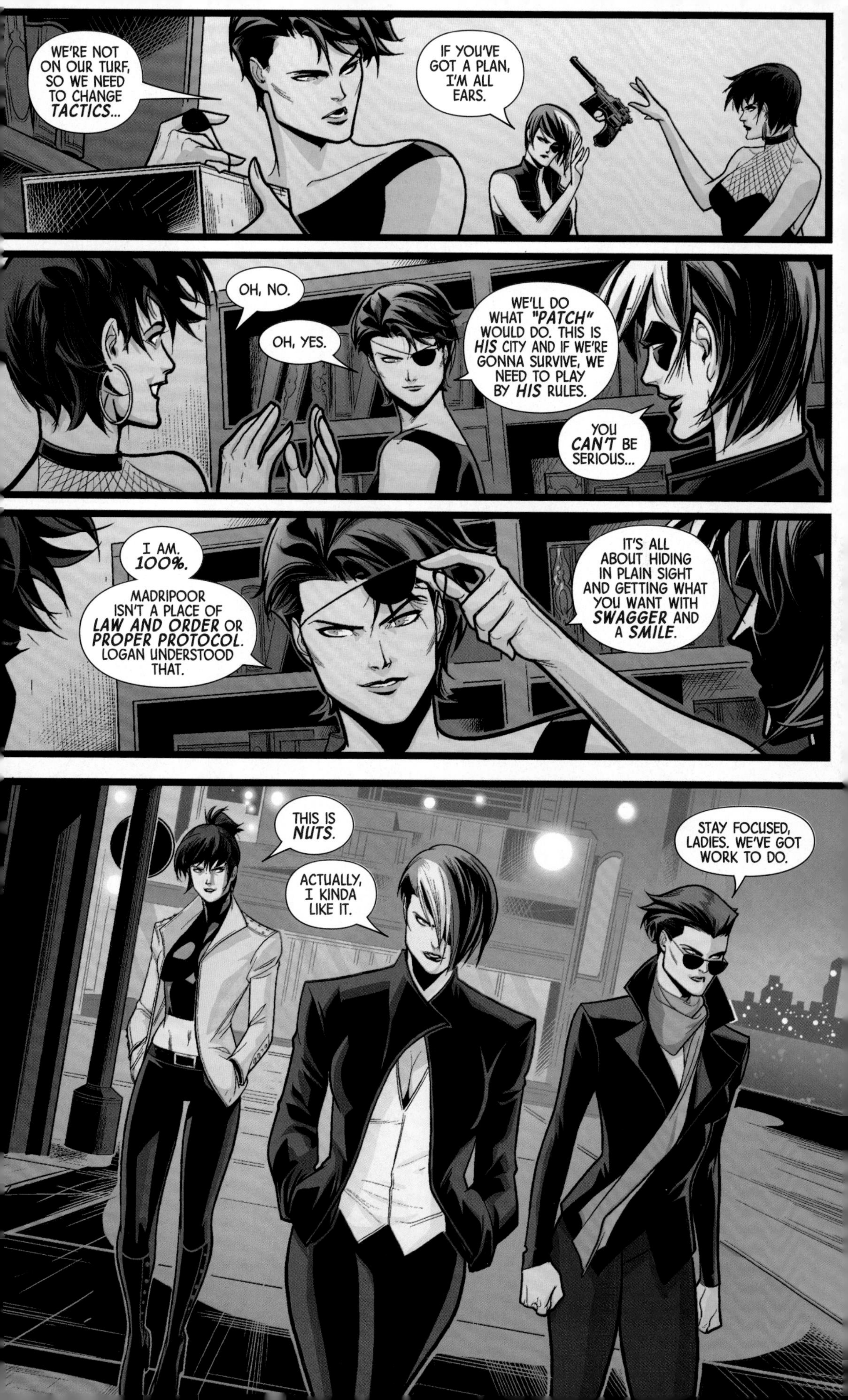
WE'RE NOT ON OUR TURF, SO WE NEED TO CHANGE *TACTICS*...
IF YOU'VE GOT A PLAN, I'M ALL EARS.
OH, NO.
OH, YES.
WE'LL DO WHAT **"PATCH"** WOULD DO. THIS IS **HIS** CITY AND IF WE'RE GONNA SURVIVE, WE NEED TO PLAY BY **HIS** RULES.
YOU **CAN'T** BE SERIOUS...
I AM. **100%.**
MADRIPOOR ISN'T A PLACE OF **LAW AND ORDER** OR **PROPER PROTOCOL**. LOGAN UNDERSTOOD THAT.
IT'S ALL ABOUT HIDING IN PLAIN SIGHT AND GETTING WHAT YOU WANT WITH **SWAGGER** AND A **SMILE**.
THIS IS **NUTS**.
ACTUALLY, I KINDA LIKE IT.
STAY FOCUSED, LADIES. WE'VE GOT WORK TO DO.

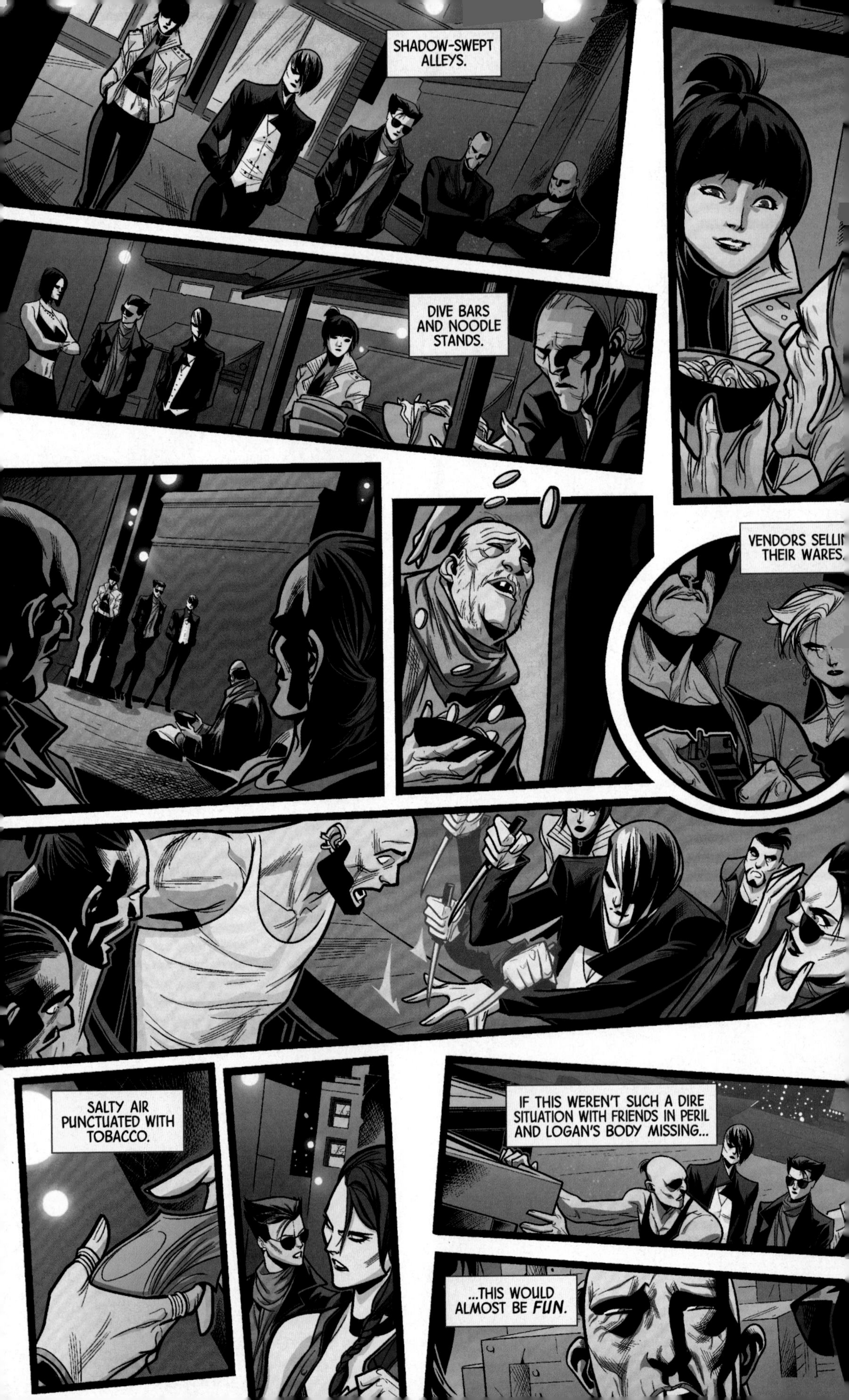
SHADOW-SWEPT ALLEYS.
DIVE BARS AND NOODLE STANDS.
VENDORS SELLI
THEIR WARES.
SALTY AIR PUNCTUATED WITH TOBACCO.
IF THIS WEREN'T SUCH A DIRE SITUATION WITH FRIENDS IN PERIL AND LOGAN'S BODY MISSING...
...THIS WOULD ALMOST BE *FUN*.

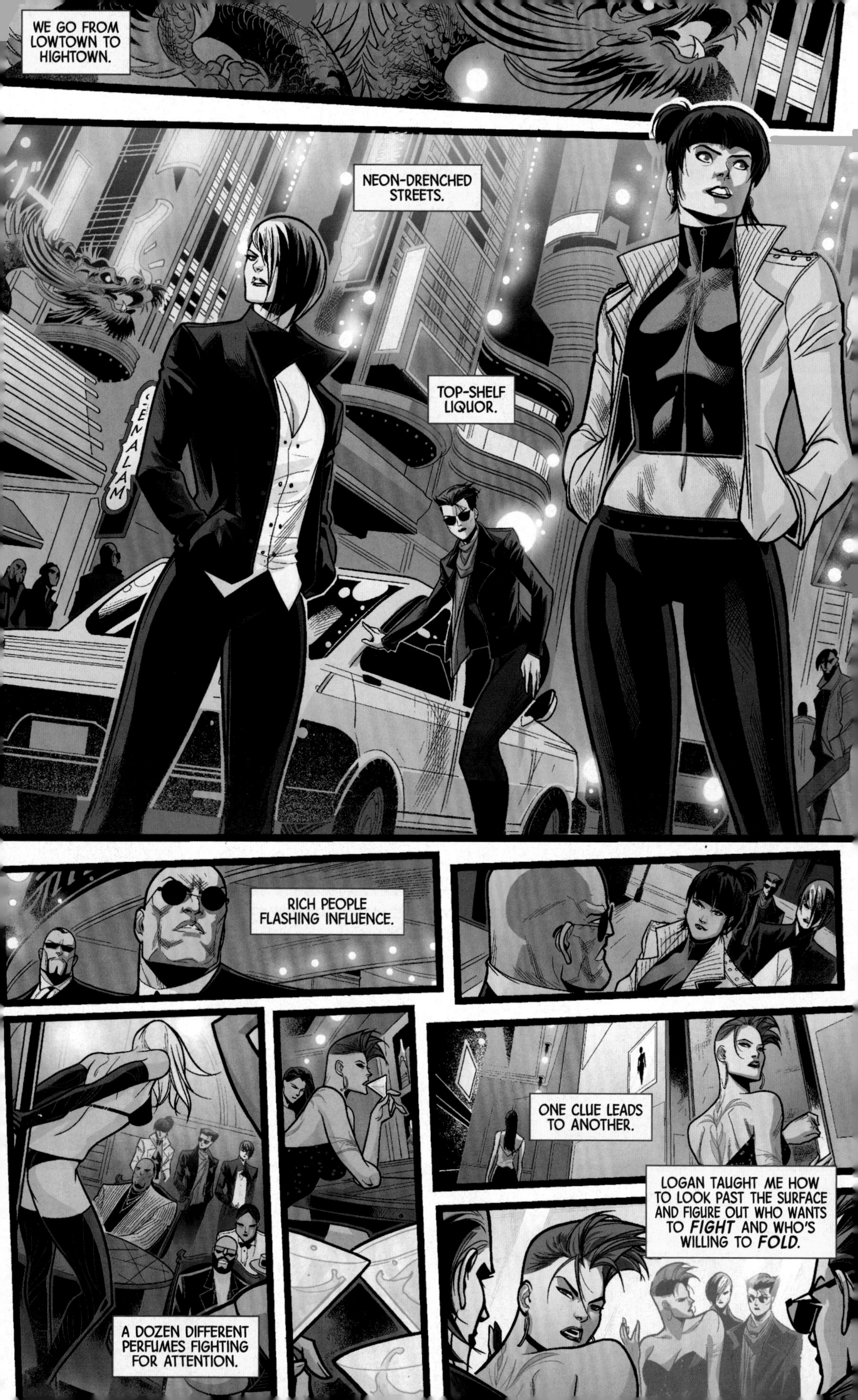
WE GO FROM LOWTOWN TO HIGHTOWN.
NEON-DRENCHED STREETS.
TOP-SHELF LIQUOR.
MALANE
RICH PEOPLE FLASHING INFLUENCE.
A DOZEN DIFFERENT PERFUMES FIGHTING FOR ATTENTION.
ONE CLUE LEADS TO ANOTHER.
LOGAN TAUGHT ME HOW TO LOOK PAST THE SURFACE AND FIGURE OUT WHO WANTS TO *FIGHT* AND WHO'S WILLING TO *FOLD*.

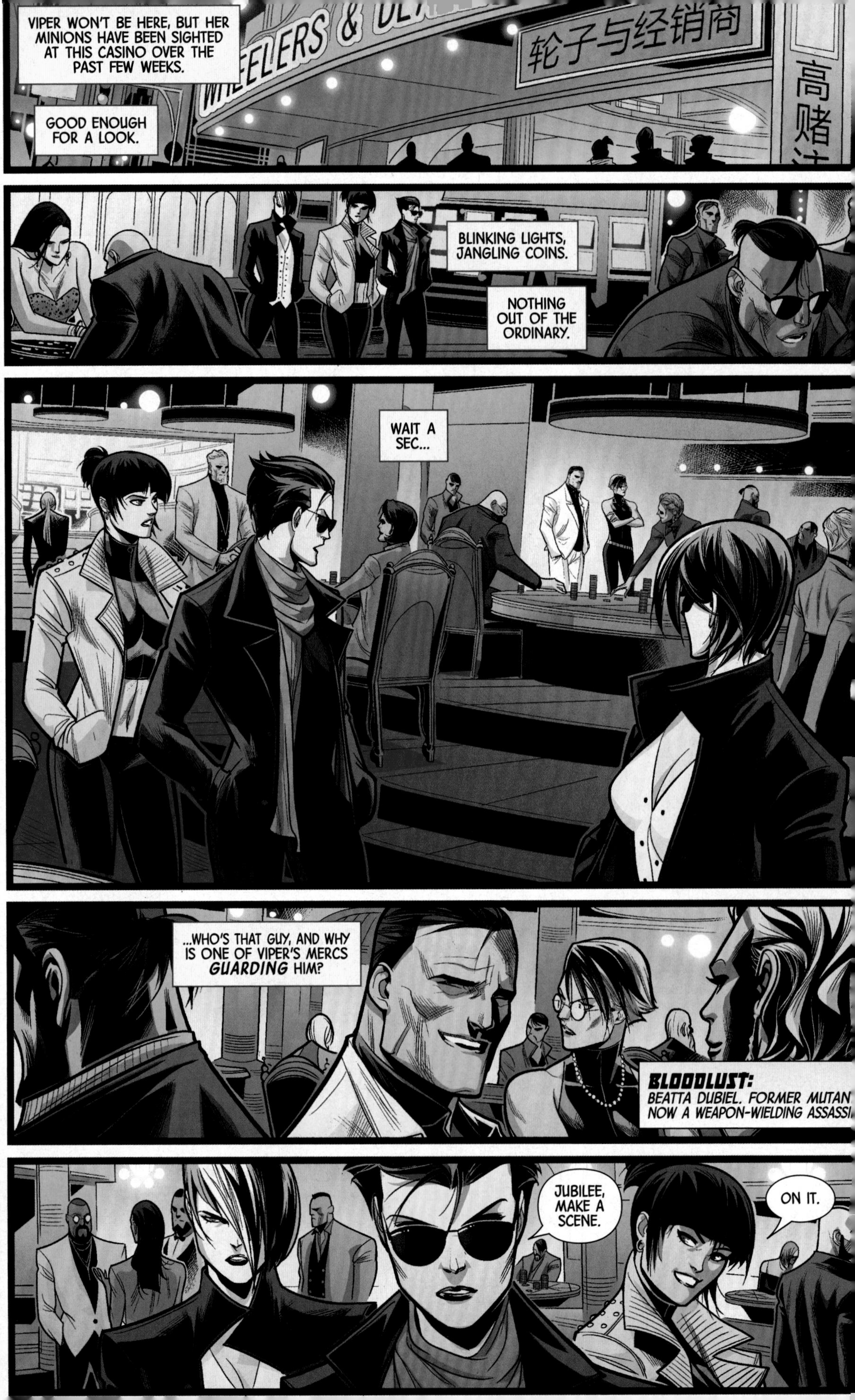
VIPER WON'T BE HERE, BUT HER MINIONS HAVE BEEN SIGHTED AT THIS CASINO OVER THE PAST FEW WEEKS.
GOOD ENOUGH FOR A LOOK.
WHEELERS &
轮子与经销商
高赌
BLINKING LIGHTS, JANGLING COINS.
NOTHING OUT OF THE ORDINARY.
WAIT A SEC...
...WHO'S THAT GUY, AND WHY IS ONE OF VIPER'S MERCS *GUARDING* HIM?
BLOODLUST:
BEATTA DUBIEL. FORMER MUTAN
NOW A WEAPON-WIELDING ASSASSI
JUBILEE, MAKE A SCENE.
ON IT.

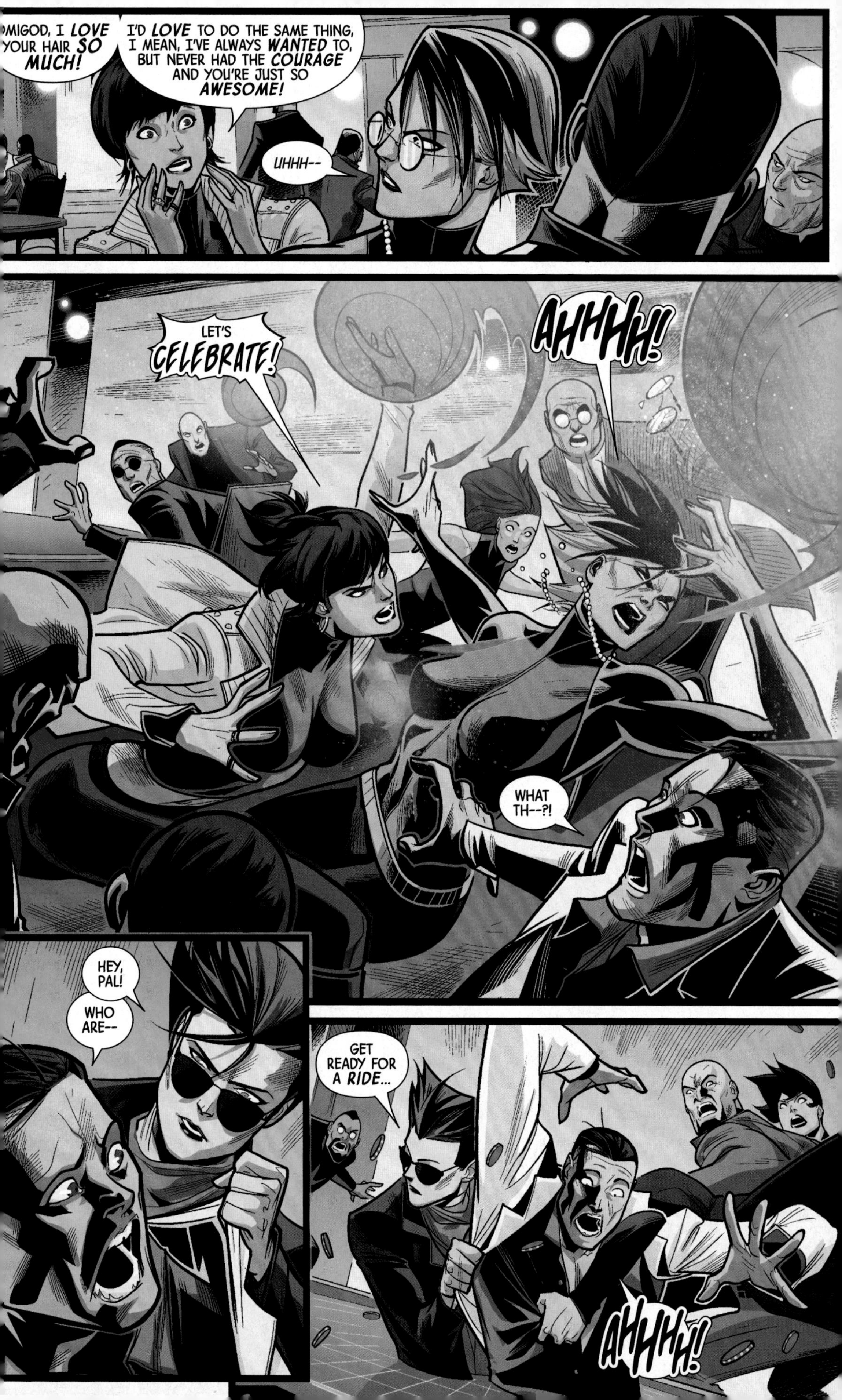

OMIGOD, I LOVE YOUR HAIR SO MUCH!
I'D LOVE TO DO THE SAME THING, I MEAN, I'VE ALWAYS WANTED TO, BUT NEVER HAD THE COURAGE AND YOU'RE JUST SO AWESOME!
UHHH--
LET'S CELEBRATE!
AHHHH!
WHAT TH--?!
HEY, PAL!
WHO ARE--
GET READY FOR A RIDE...
AHHHH!

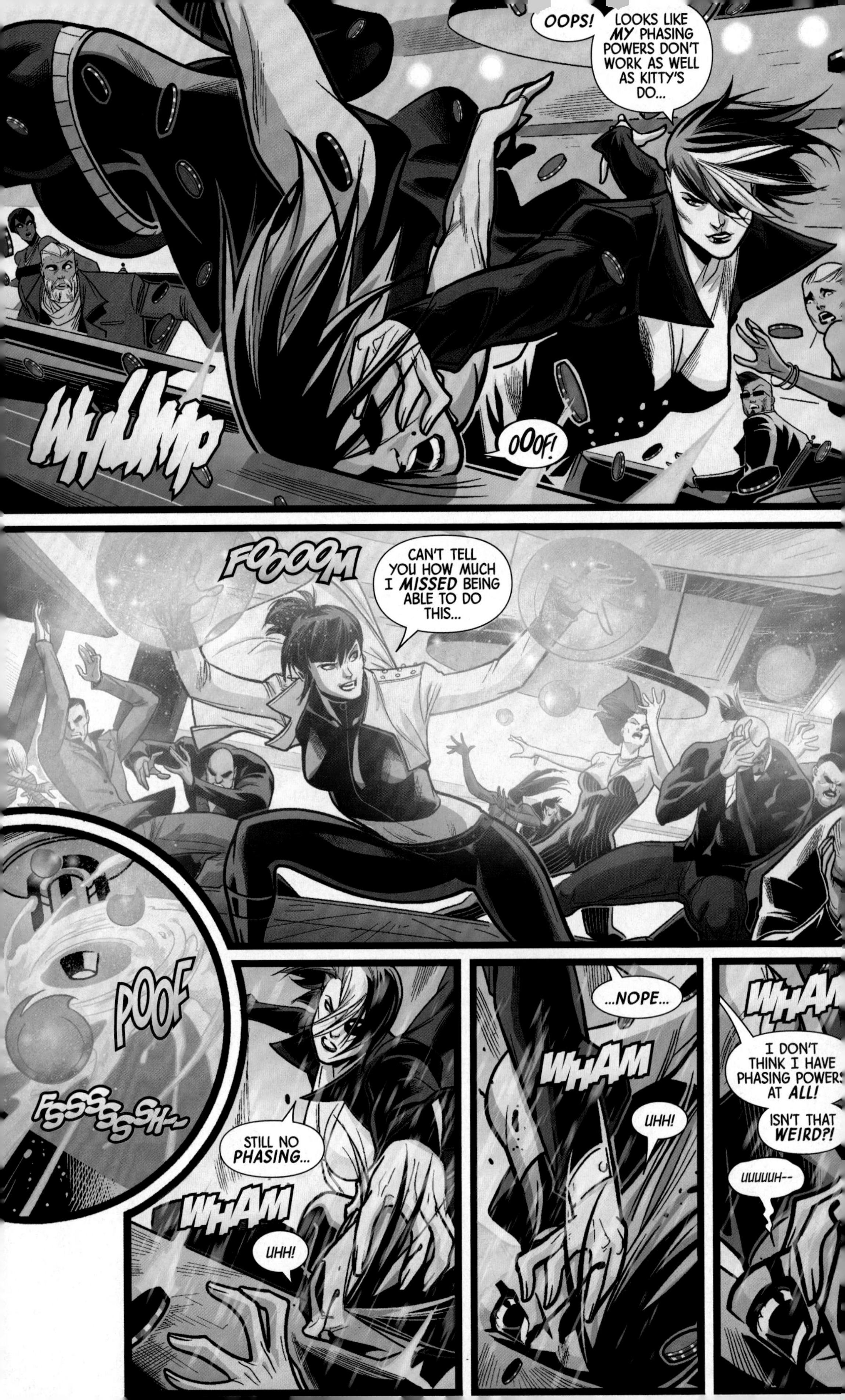
OOPS!
LOOKS LIKE MY PHASING POWERS DON'T WORK AS WELL AS KITTY'S DO...
WHUMP
OOOF!
FOOOOM
CAN'T TELL YOU HOW MUCH I MISSED BEING ABLE TO DO THIS...
POOF
FSSSSSSH--
STILL NO PHASING...
WHAM
UHH!
...NOPE...
WHAM
UHH!
WHAM
I DON'T THINK I HAVE PHASING POWERS AT ALL!
ISN'T THAT WEIRD?!
UUUUUH--

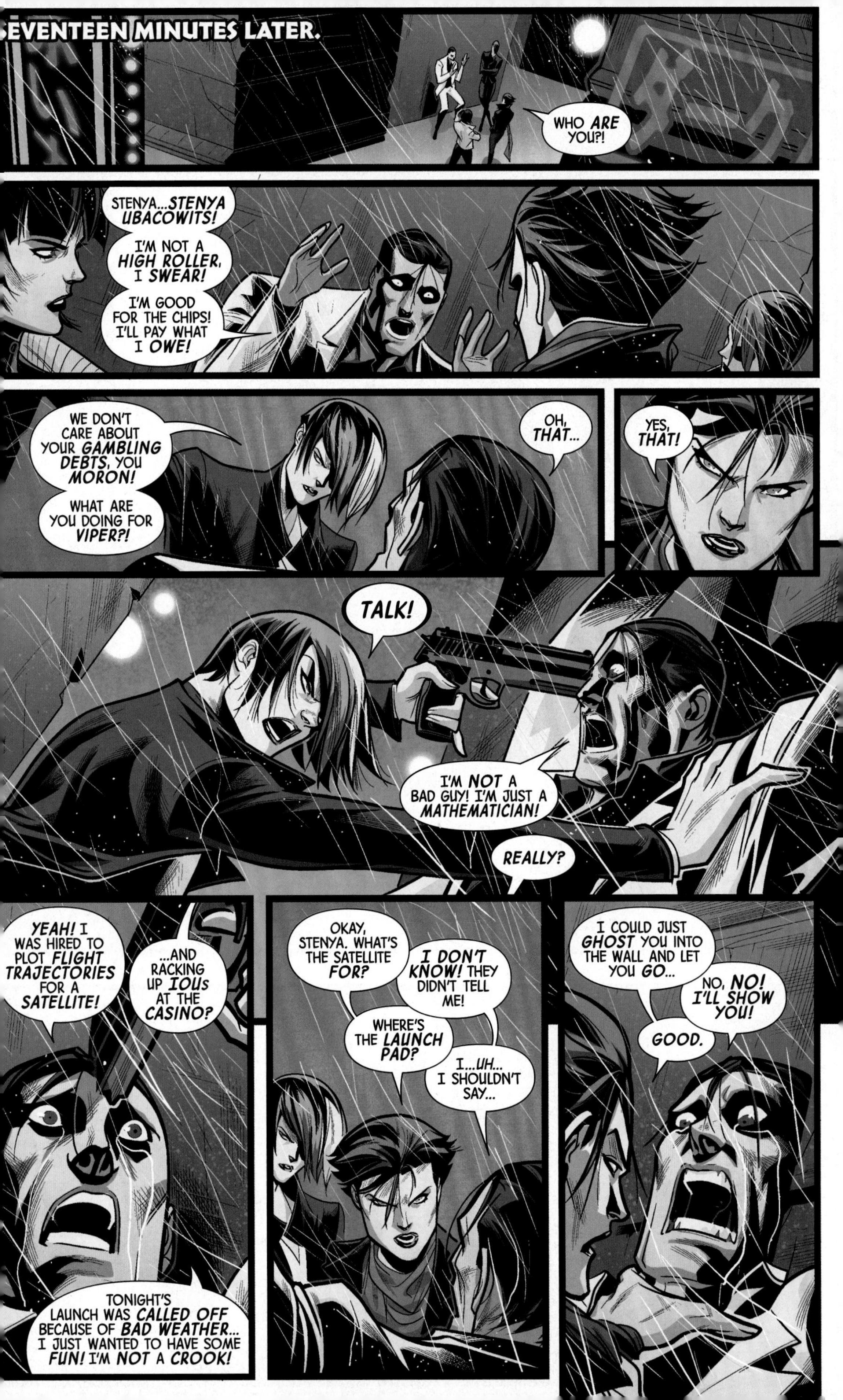
EVENTEEN MINUTES LATER.
WHO ARE YOU?!
STENYA...STENYA UBACOWITS!
I'M NOT A HIGH ROLLER, I SWEAR!
I'M GOOD FOR THE CHIPS! I'LL PAY WHAT I OWE!
WE DON'T CARE ABOUT YOUR GAMBLING DEBTS, YOU MORON!
WHAT ARE YOU DOING FOR VIPER?!
OH, THAT...
YES, THAT!
TALK!
I'M NOT A BAD GUY! I'M JUST A MATHEMATICIAN!
REALLY?
YEAH! I WAS HIRED TO PLOT FLIGHT TRAJECTORIES FOR A SATELLITE!
...AND RACKING UP IOUs AT THE CASINO?
TONIGHT'S LAUNCH WAS CALLED OFF BECAUSE OF BAD WEATHER... I JUST WANTED TO HAVE SOME FUN! I'M NOT A CROOK!
OKAY, STENYA. WHAT'S THE SATELLITE FOR?
I DON'T KNOW! THEY DIDN'T TELL ME!
WHERE'S THE LAUNCH PAD?
I...UH... I SHOULDN'T SAY...
I COULD JUST GHOST YOU INTO THE WALL AND LET YOU GO...
NO, NO! I'LL SHOW YOU!
GOOD.

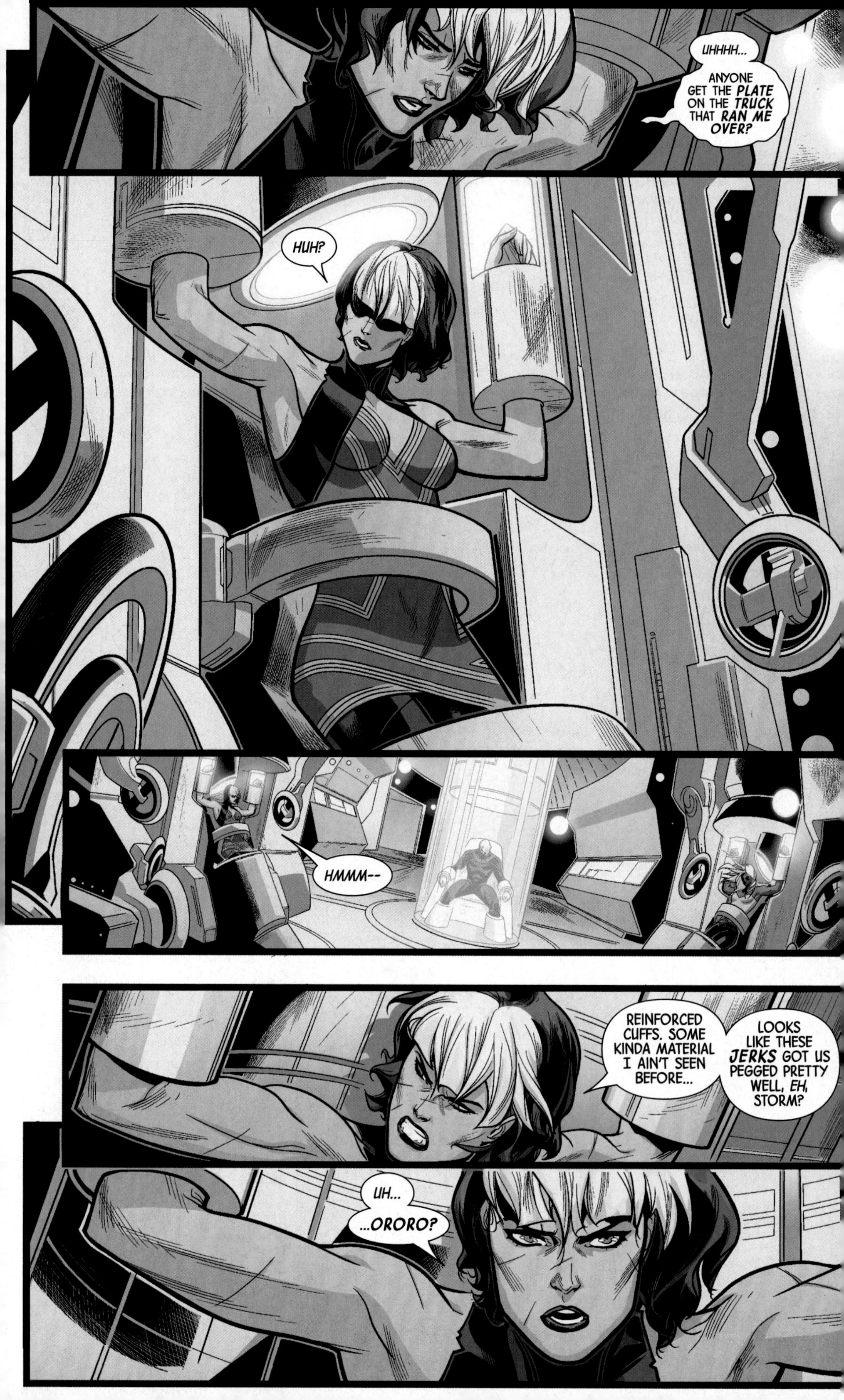
UHHHH...
ANYONE GET THE PLATE ON THE TRUCK THAT RAN ME OVER?
HUH?
HMMM--
REINFORCED CUFFS. SOME KINDA MATERIAL I AIN'T SEEN BEFORE...
LOOKS LIKE THESE JERKS GOT US PEGGED PRETTY WELL, EH, STORM?
UH...
...ORORO?

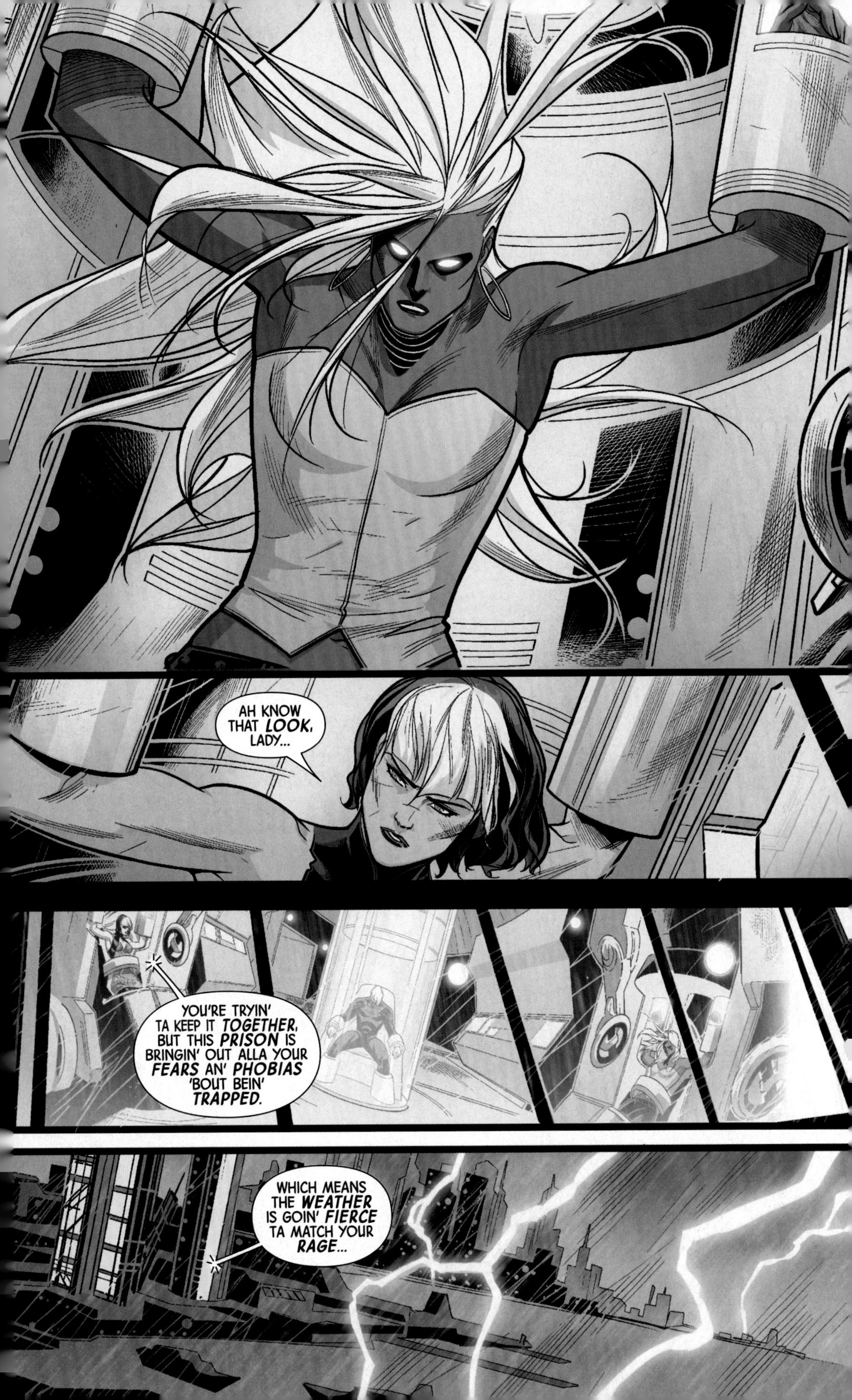
AH KNOW THAT LOOK, LADY...
YOU'RE TRYIN' TA KEEP IT TOGETHER, BUT THIS PRISON IS BRINGIN' OUT ALLA YOUR FEARS AN' PHOBIAS 'BOUT BEIN' TRAPPED.
WHICH MEANS THE WEATHER IS GOIN' FIERCE TA MATCH YOUR RAGE...

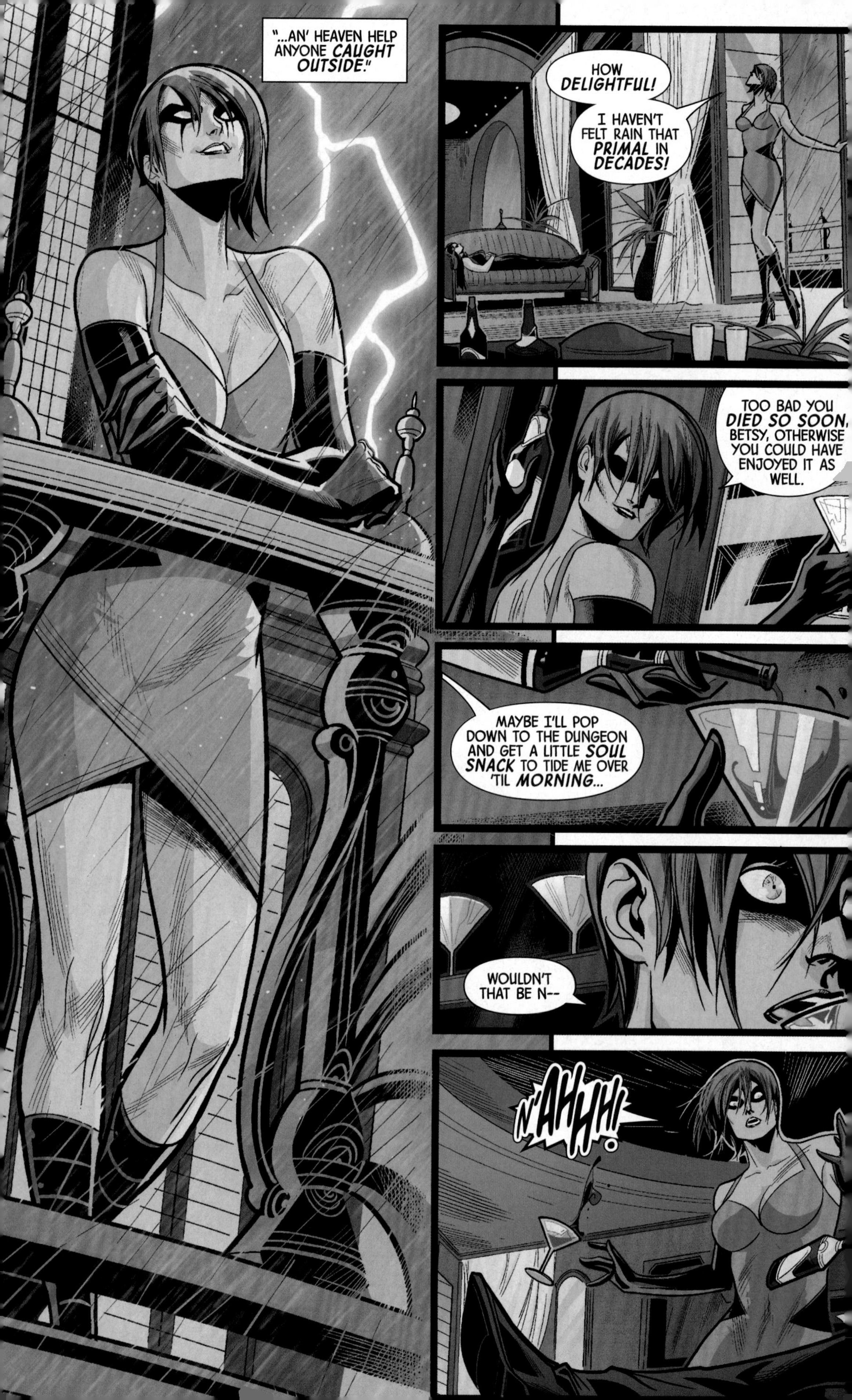
"...AN' HEAVEN HELP ANYONE CAUGHT OUTSIDE."
HOW DELIGHTFUL!
I HAVEN'T FELT RAIN THAT PRIMAL IN DECADES!
TOO BAD YOU DIED SO SOON, BETSY, OTHERWISE YOU COULD HAVE ENJOYED IT AS WELL.
MAYBE I'LL POP DOWN TO THE DUNGEON AND GET A LITTLE SOUL SNACK TO TIDE ME OVER 'TIL MORNING...
WOULDN'T THAT BE N--
N'AHHH!

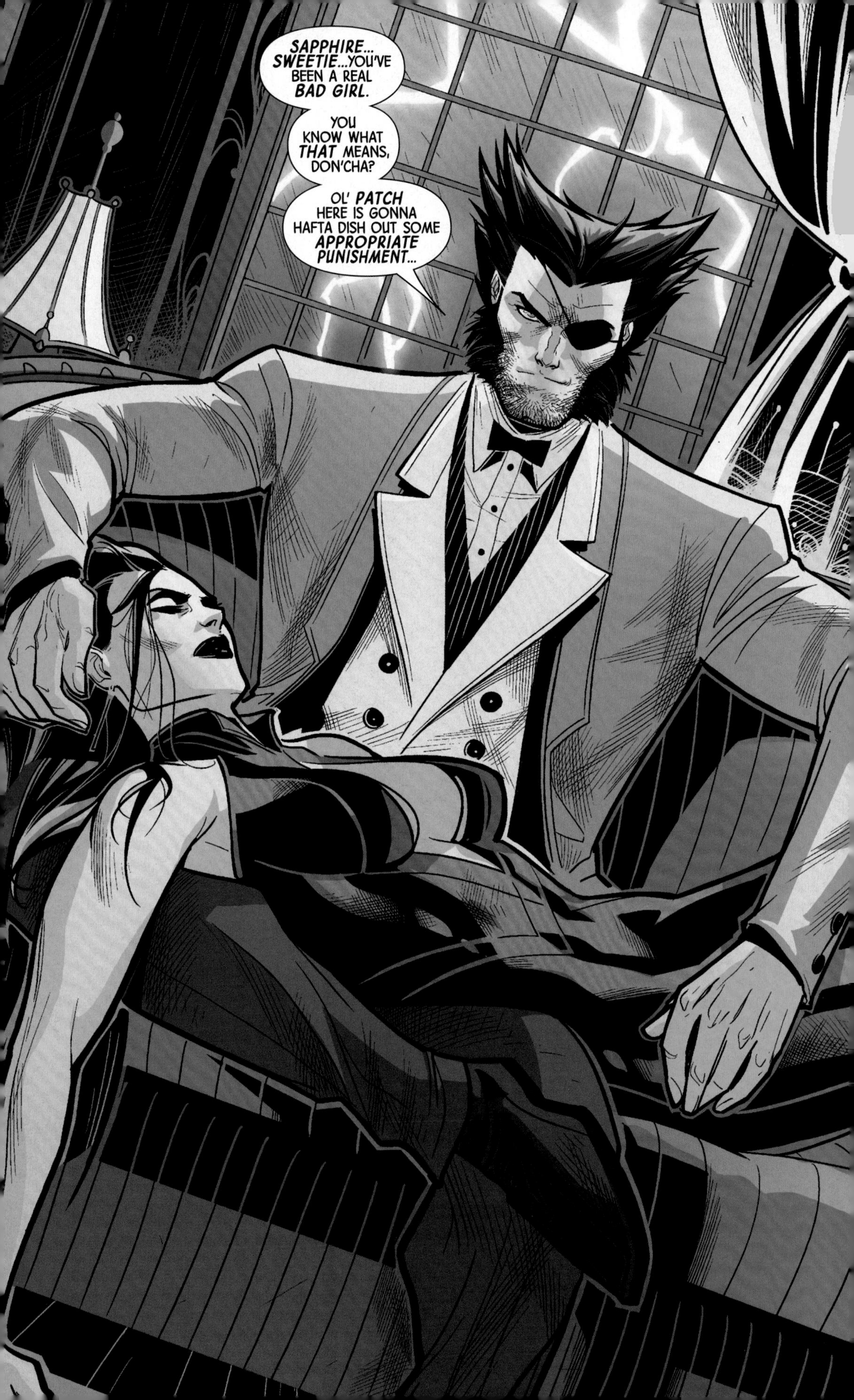
SAPPHIRE... SWEETIE...YOU'VE BEEN A REAL BAD GIRL.
YOU KNOW WHAT THAT MEANS, DON'CHA?
OL' PATCH HERE IS GONNA HAFTA DISH OUT SOME APPROPRIATE PUNISHMENT...

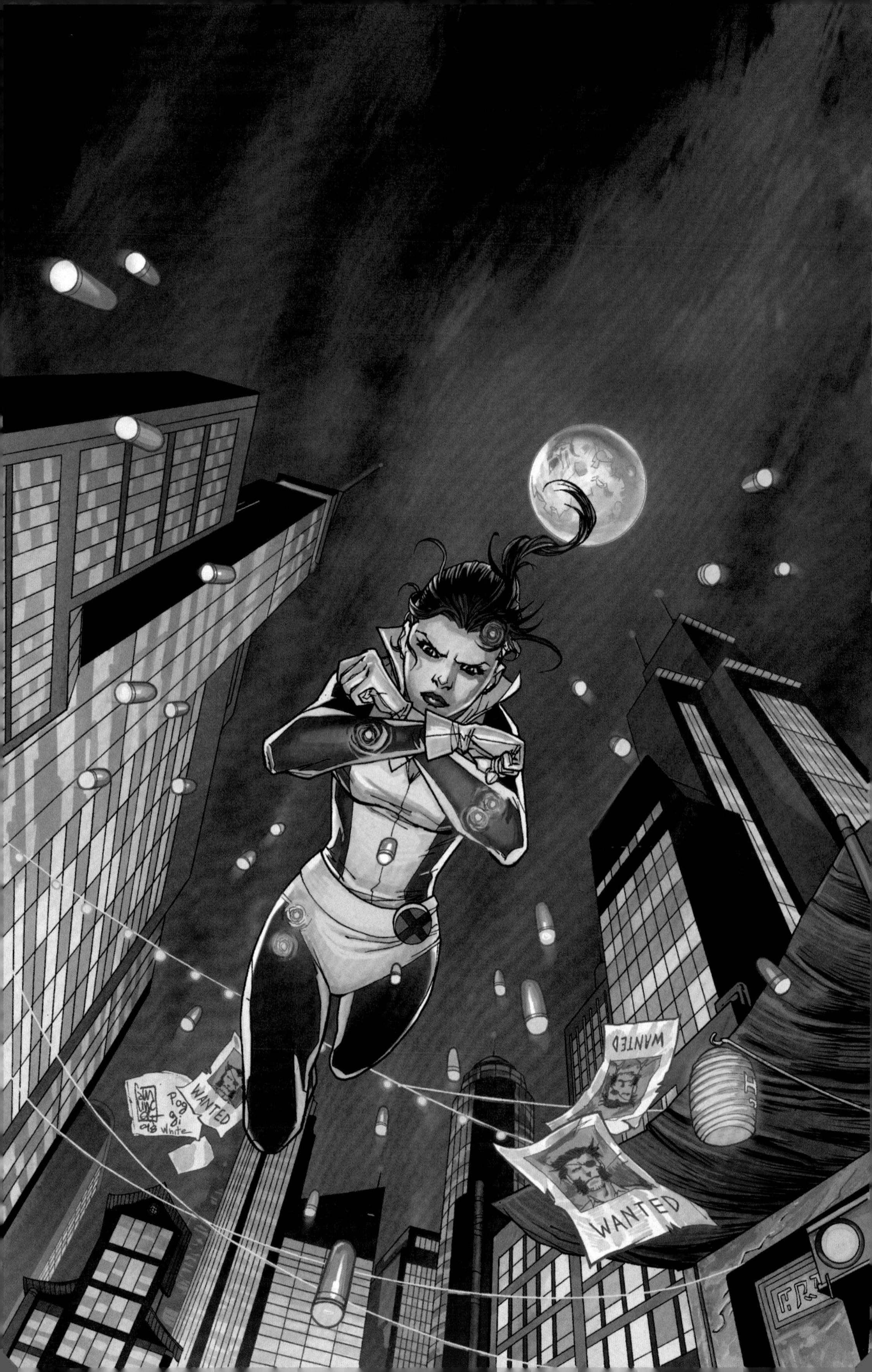
WANTED
WANTED
WANTED

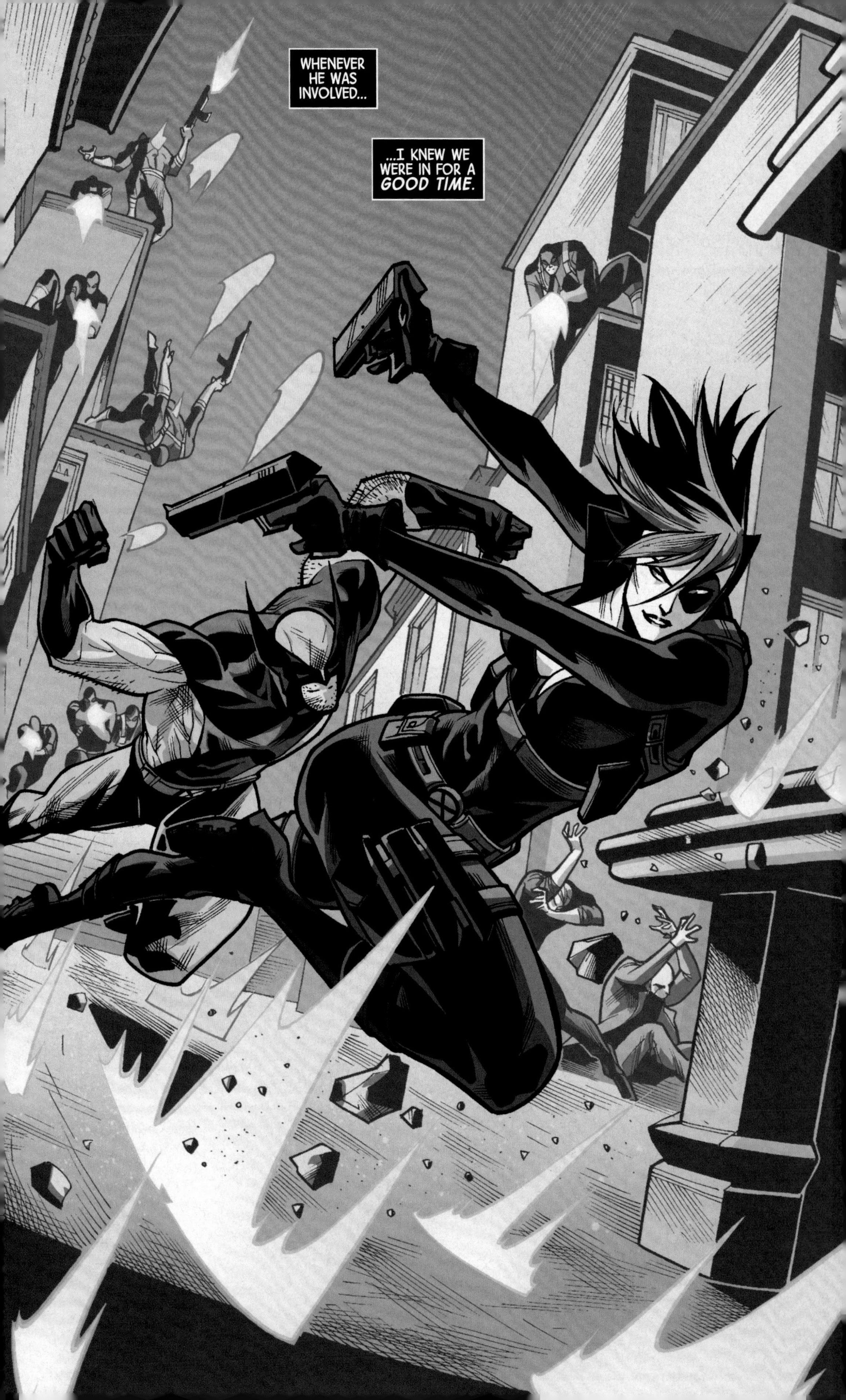
WHENEVER HE WAS INVOLVED...
...I KNEW WE WERE IN FOR A *GOOD TIME*.

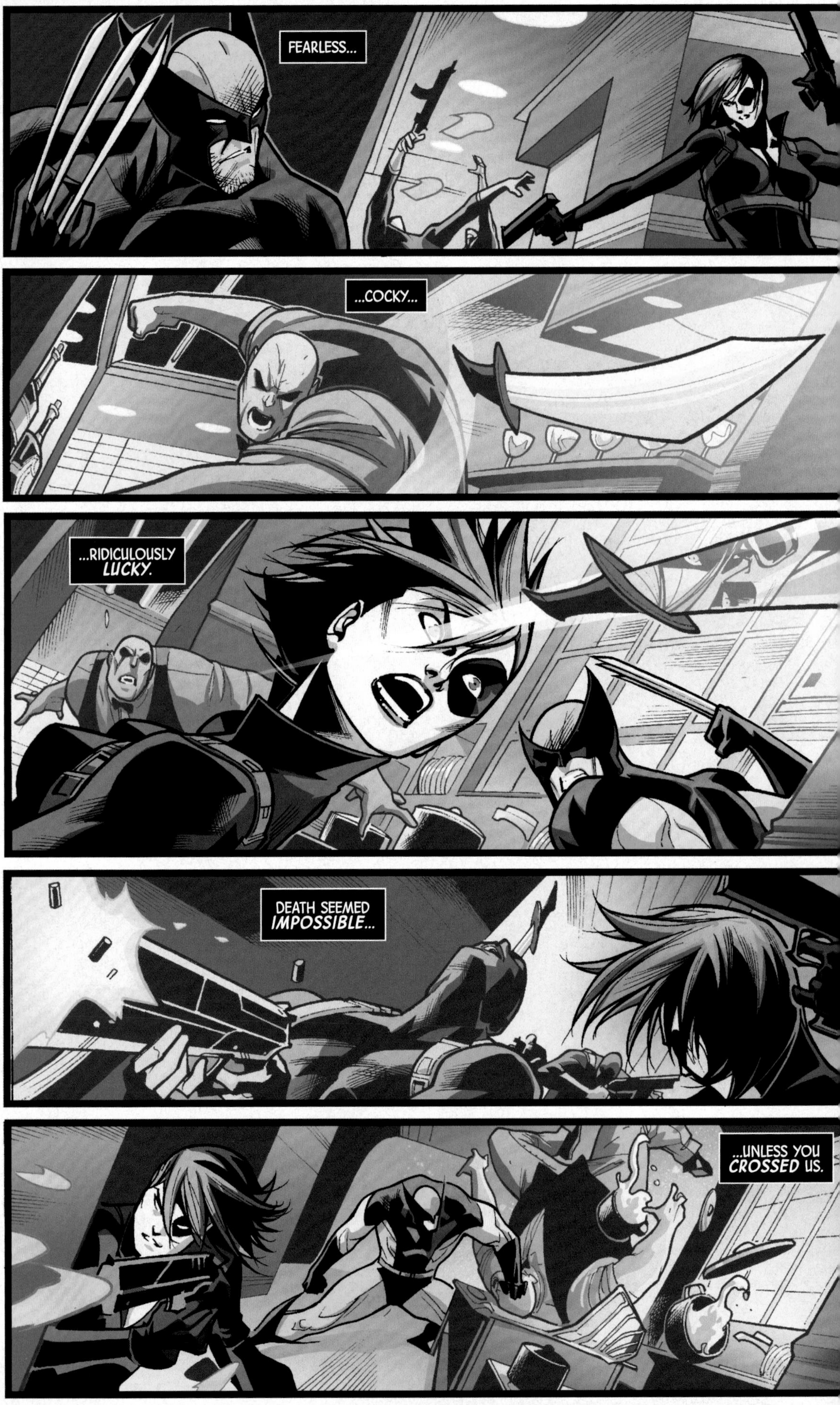
FEARLESS...
...COCKY...
...RIDICULOUSLY LUCKY.
DEATH SEEMED IMPOSSIBLE...
...UNLESS YOU CROSSED US.

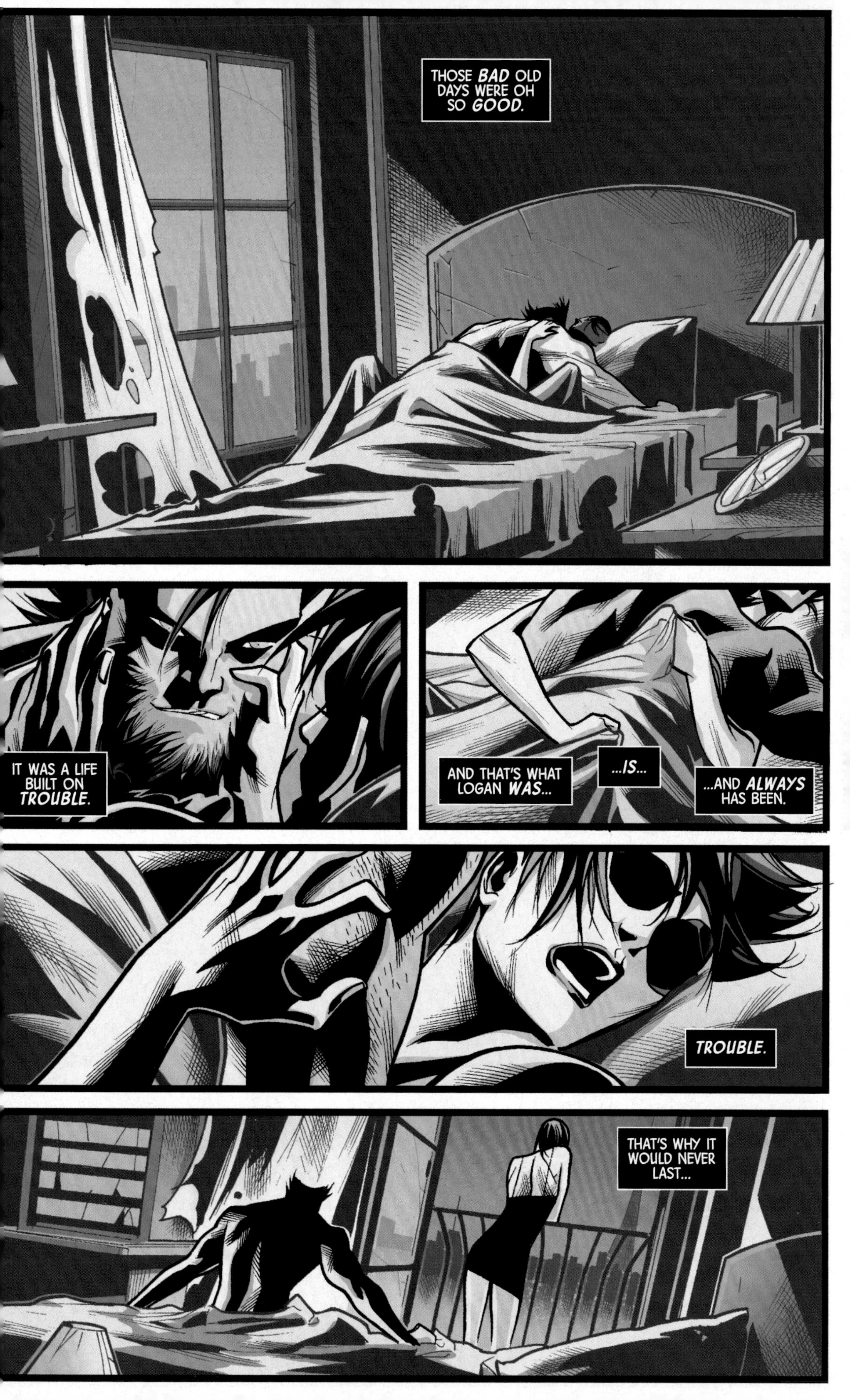
THOSE BAD OLD DAYS WERE OH SO GOOD.
IT WAS A LIFE BUILT ON TROUBLE.
AND THAT'S WHAT LOGAN WAS...
...IS...
...AND ALWAYS HAS BEEN.
TROUBLE.
THAT'S WHY IT WOULD NEVER LAST...

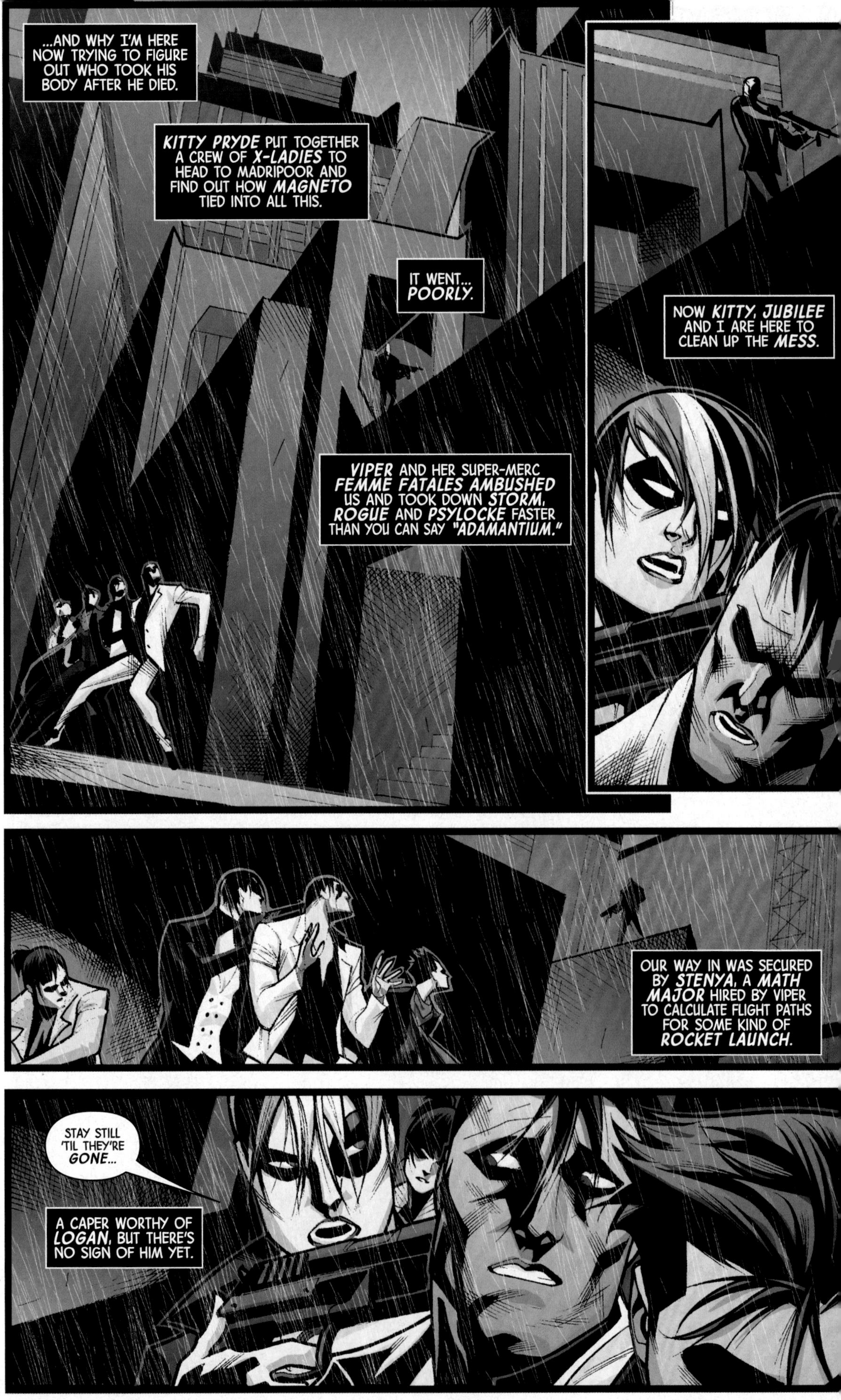

...AND WHY I'M HERE NOW TRYING TO FIGURE OUT WHO TOOK HIS BODY AFTER HE DIED.
KITTY PRYDE PUT TOGETHER A CREW OF X-LADIES TO HEAD TO MADRIPOOR AND FIND OUT HOW MAGNETO TIED INTO ALL THIS.
IT WENT... POORLY.
VIPER AND HER SUPER-MERC FEMME FATALES AMBUSHED US AND TOOK DOWN STORM, ROGUE AND PSYLOCKE FASTER THAN YOU CAN SAY "ADAMANTIUM."
NOW KITTY, JUBILEE AND I ARE HERE TO CLEAN UP THE MESS.
OUR WAY IN WAS SECURED BY STENYA, A MATH MAJOR HIRED BY VIPER TO CALCULATE FLIGHT PATHS FOR SOME KIND OF ROCKET LAUNCH.
STAY STILL 'TIL THEY'RE GONE...
A CAPER WORTHY OF LOGAN, BUT THERE'S NO SIGN OF HIM YET.

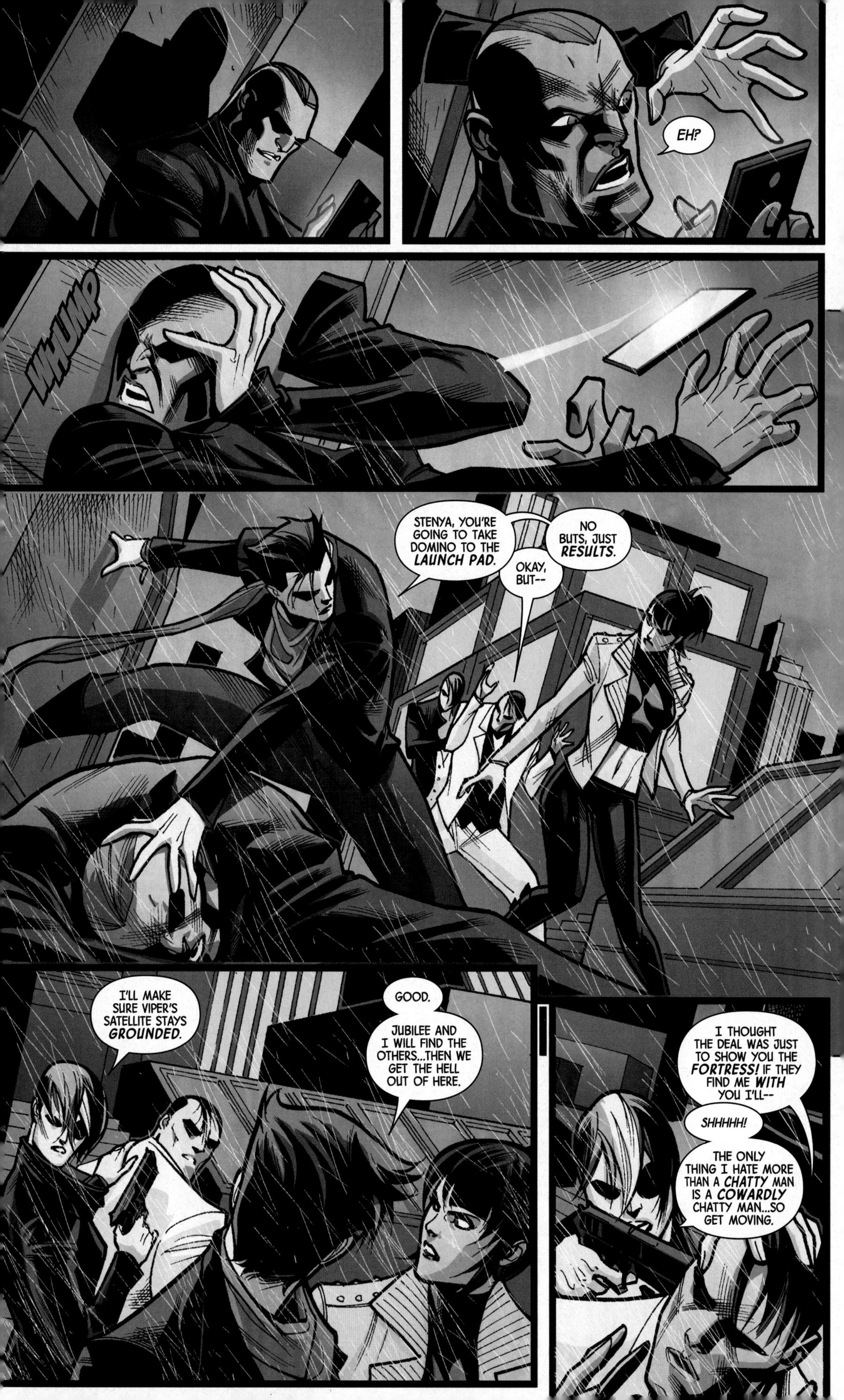
EH?
WHUMP
STENYA, YOU'RE GOING TO TAKE DOMINO TO THE LAUNCH PAD.
OKAY, BUT--
NO BUTS, JUST RESULTS.
I'LL MAKE SURE VIPER'S SATELLITE STAYS GROUNDED.
GOOD.
JUBILEE AND I WILL FIND THE OTHERS...THEN WE GET THE HELL OUT OF HERE.
I THOUGHT THE DEAL WAS JUST TO SHOW YOU THE FORTRESS! IF THEY FIND ME WITH YOU I'LL--
SHHHHH!
THE ONLY THING I HATE MORE THAN A CHATTY MAN IS A COWARDLY CHATTY MAN...SO GET MOVING.

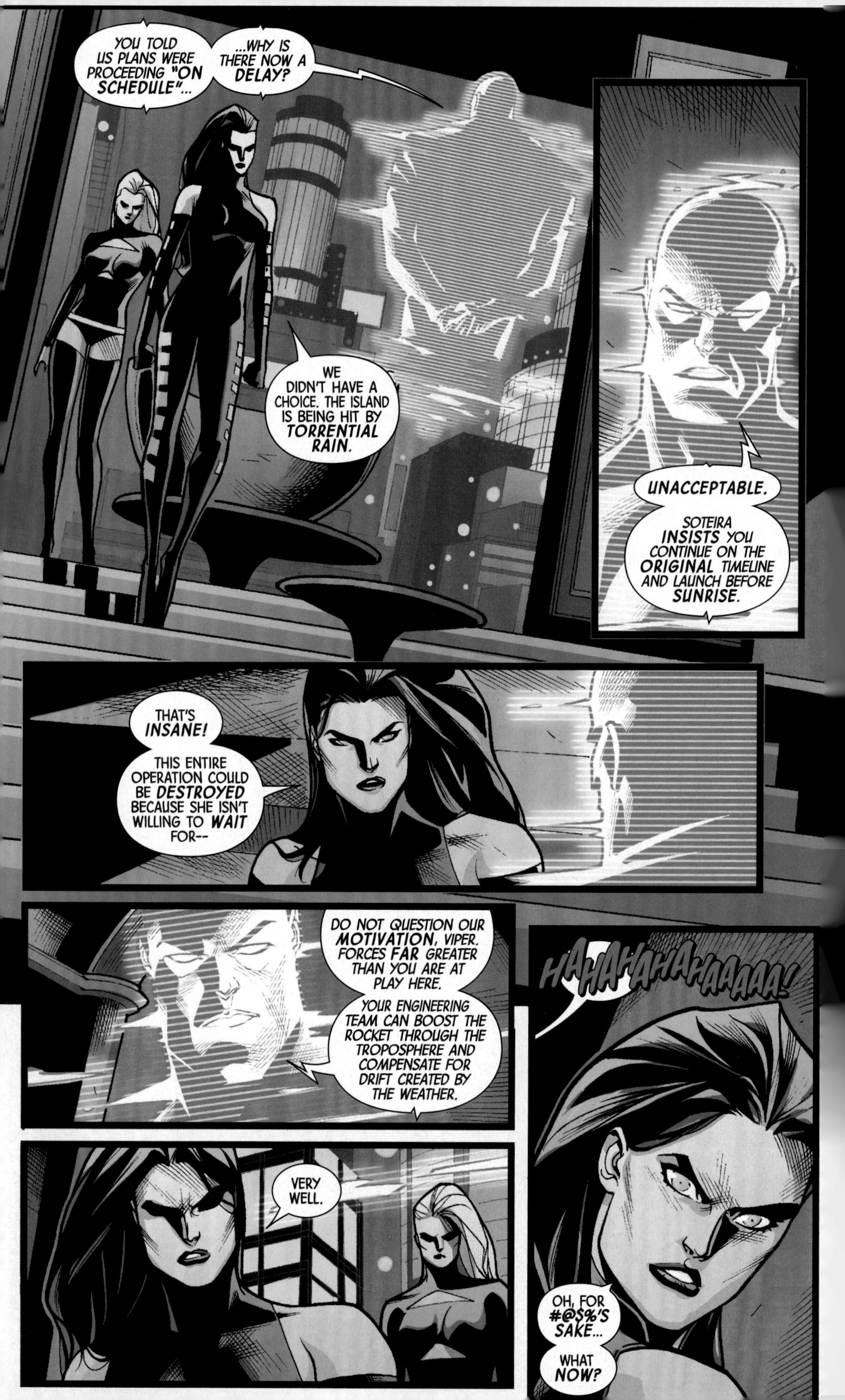
YOU TOLD US PLANS WERE PROCEEDING "ON SCHEDULE"...
...WHY IS THERE NOW A DELAY?
WE DIDN'T HAVE A CHOICE. THE ISLAND IS BEING HIT BY TORRENTIAL RAIN.
UNACCEPTABLE.
SOTEIRA INSISTS YOU CONTINUE ON THE ORIGINAL TIMELINE AND LAUNCH BEFORE SUNRISE.
THAT'S INSANE!
THIS ENTIRE OPERATION COULD BE DESTROYED BECAUSE SHE ISN'T WILLING TO WAIT FOR--
DO NOT QUESTION OUR MOTIVATION, VIPER. FORCES FAR GREATER THAN YOU ARE AT PLAY HERE.
YOUR ENGINEERING TEAM CAN BOOST THE ROCKET THROUGH THE TROPOSPHERE AND COMPENSATE FOR DRIFT CREATED BY THE WEATHER.
VERY WELL.
HAHAHAHAHAHAAAAAA!
OH, FOR #@$%'S SAKE...
WHAT NOW?

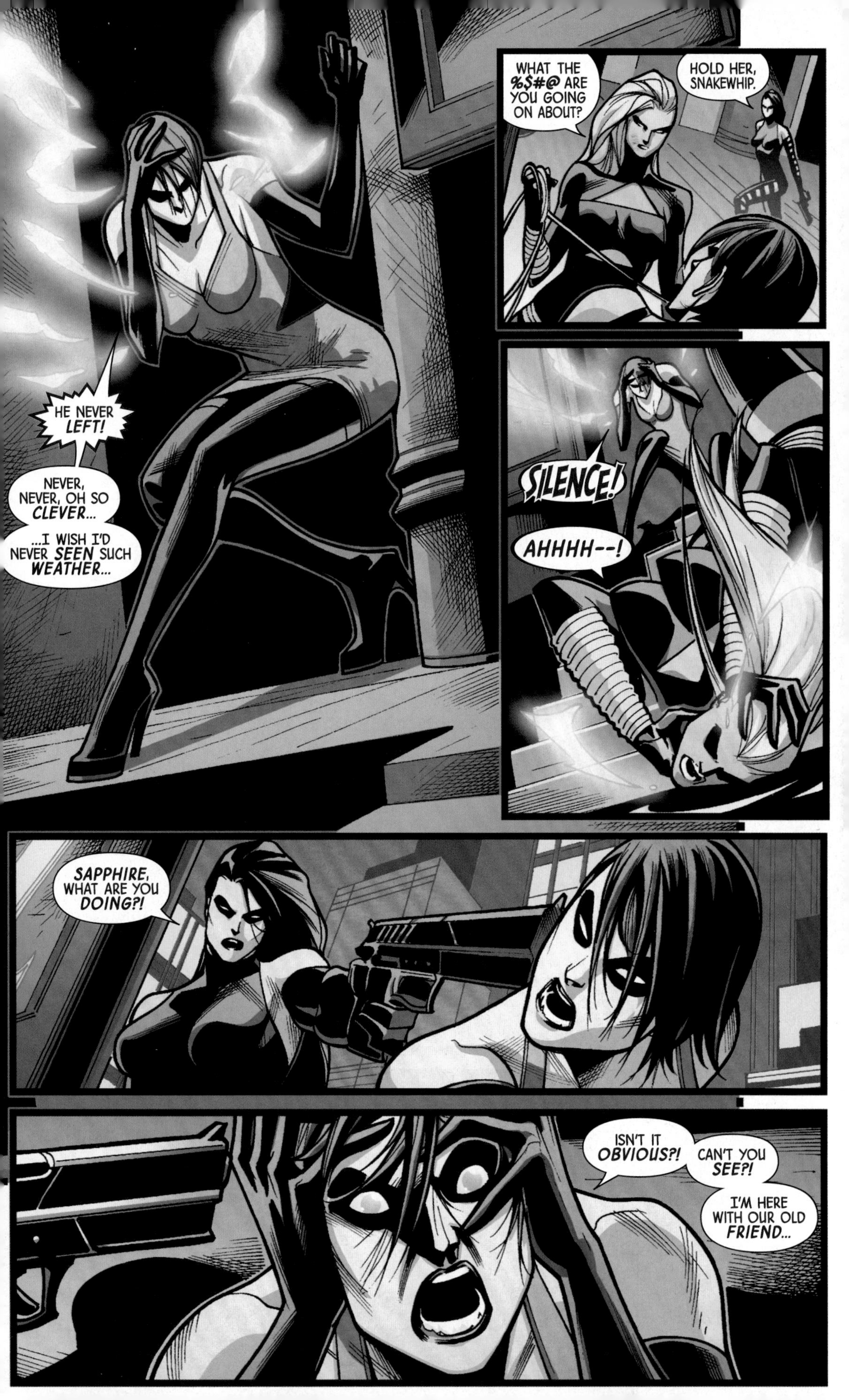
HE NEVER LEFT!
NEVER, NEVER, OH SO CLEVER...
...I WISH I'D NEVER SEEN SUCH WEATHER...
WHAT THE %$#@ ARE YOU GOING ON ABOUT?
HOLD HER, SNAKEWHIP.
SILENCE!
AHHHH--!
SAPPHIRE, WHAT ARE YOU DOING?!
ISN'T IT OBVIOUS?!
CAN'T YOU SEE?!
I'M HERE WITH OUR OLD FRIEND...

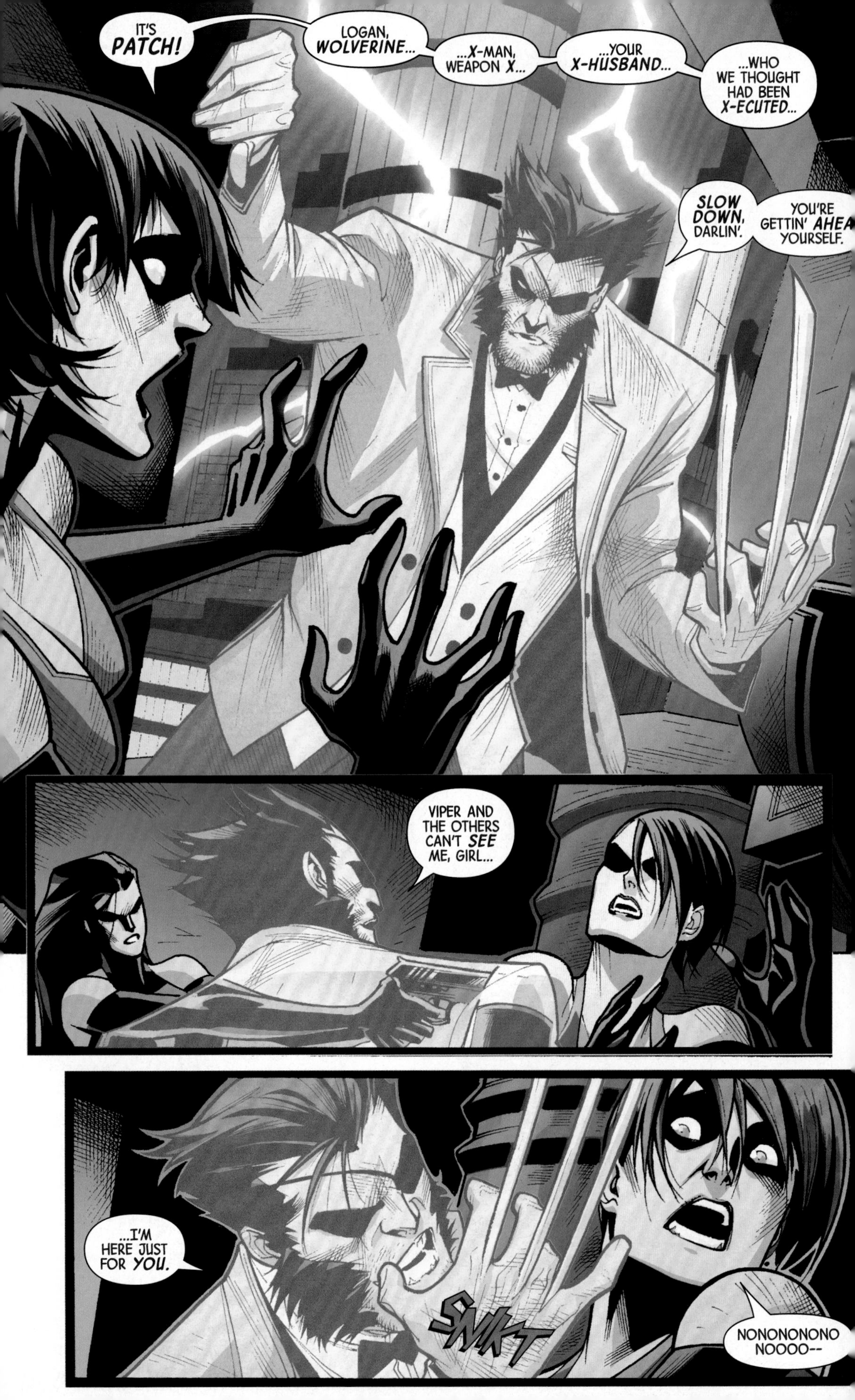
IT'S PATCH!
LOGAN, WOLVERINE...
...X-MAN, WEAPON X...
...YOUR X-HUSBAND...
...WHO WE THOUGHT HAD BEEN X-ECUTED...
SLOW DOWN, DARLIN'.
YOU'RE GETTIN' AHEA YOURSELF.
VIPER AND THE OTHERS CAN'T SEE ME, GIRL...
...I'M HERE JUST FOR YOU.
SNIKT
NONONONONO NOOOO--

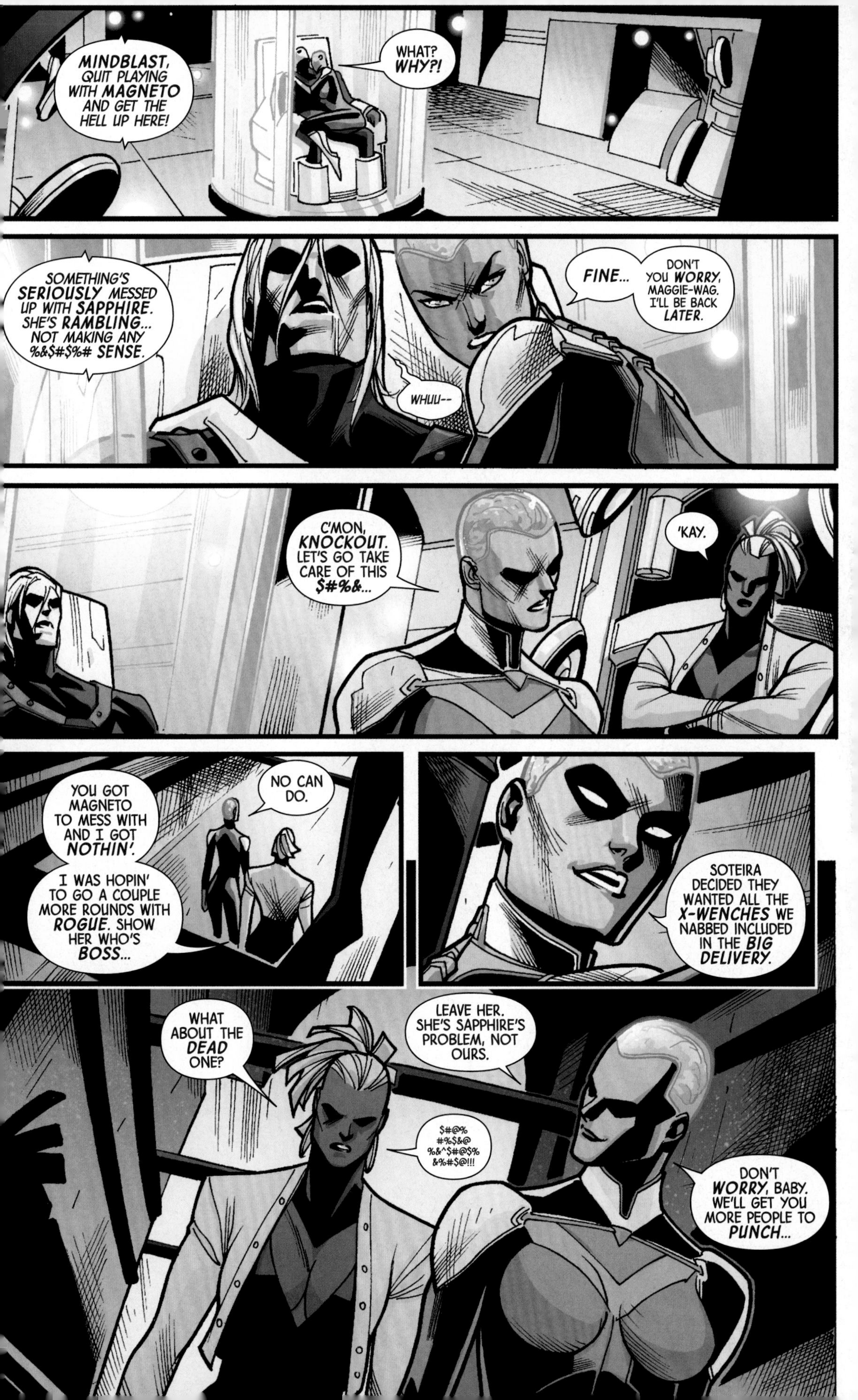
MINDBLAST, QUIT PLAYING WITH MAGNETO AND GET THE HELL UP HERE!
WHAT? WHY?!
SOMETHING'S SERIOUSLY MESSED UP WITH SAPPHIRE. SHE'S RAMBLING... NOT MAKING ANY %&$#$%# SENSE.
WHUU--
FINE...
DON'T YOU WORRY, MAGGIE-WAG. I'LL BE BACK LATER.
C'MON, KNOCKOUT. LET'S GO TAKE CARE OF THIS $#%&...
'KAY.
YOU GOT MAGNETO TO MESS WITH AND I GOT NOTHIN'.
I WAS HOPIN' TO GO A COUPLE MORE ROUNDS WITH ROGUE. SHOW HER WHO'S BOSS...
NO CAN DO.
SOTEIRA DECIDED THEY WANTED ALL THE X-WENCHES WE NABBED INCLUDED IN THE BIG DELIVERY.
WHAT ABOUT THE DEAD ONE?
LEAVE HER. SHE'S SAPPHIRE'S PROBLEM, NOT OURS.
$#@% #%$&@ %&^$#@$% &%#$@!!!
DON'T WORRY, BABY. WE'LL GET YOU MORE PEOPLE TO PUNCH...

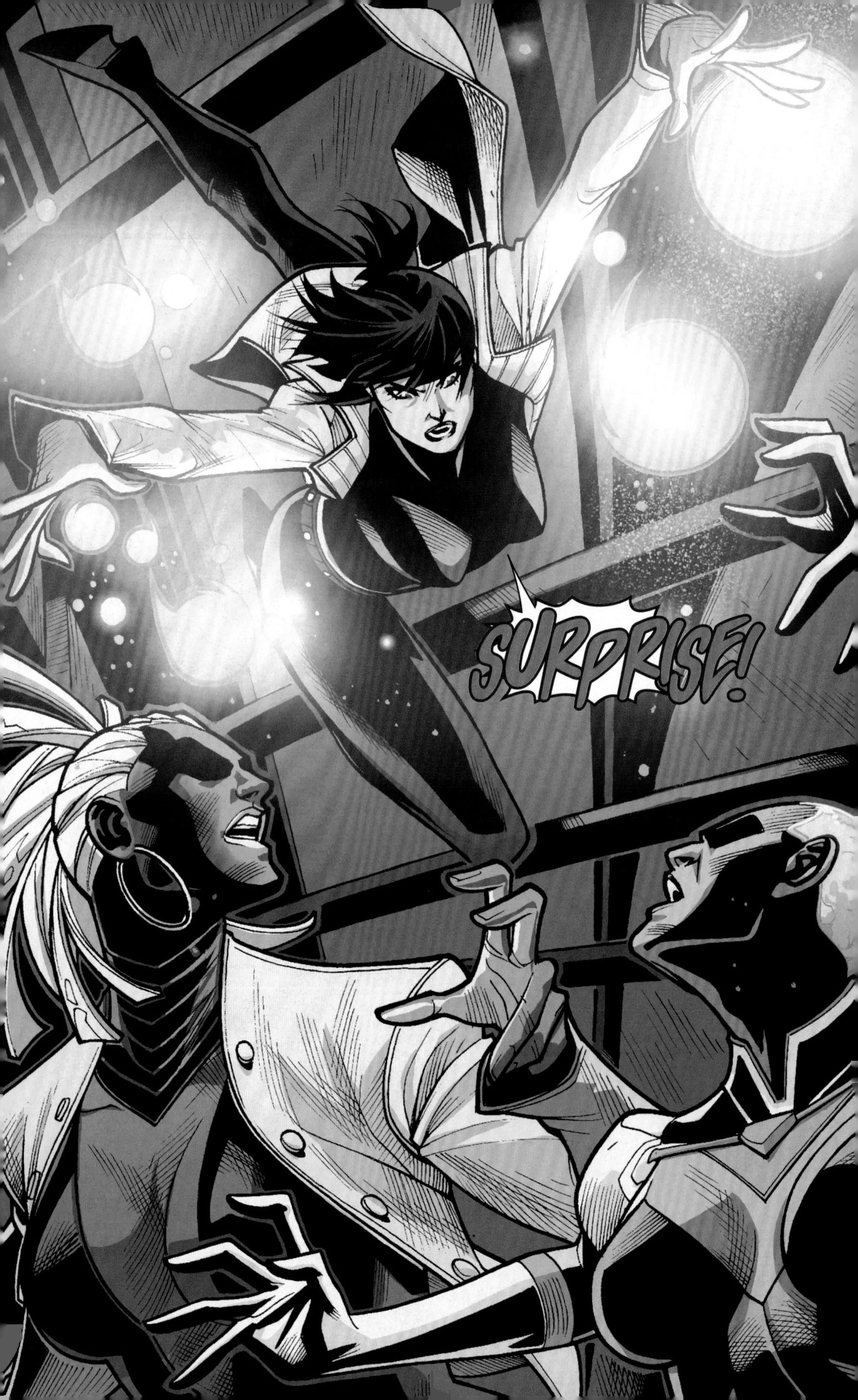
SURPRISE!

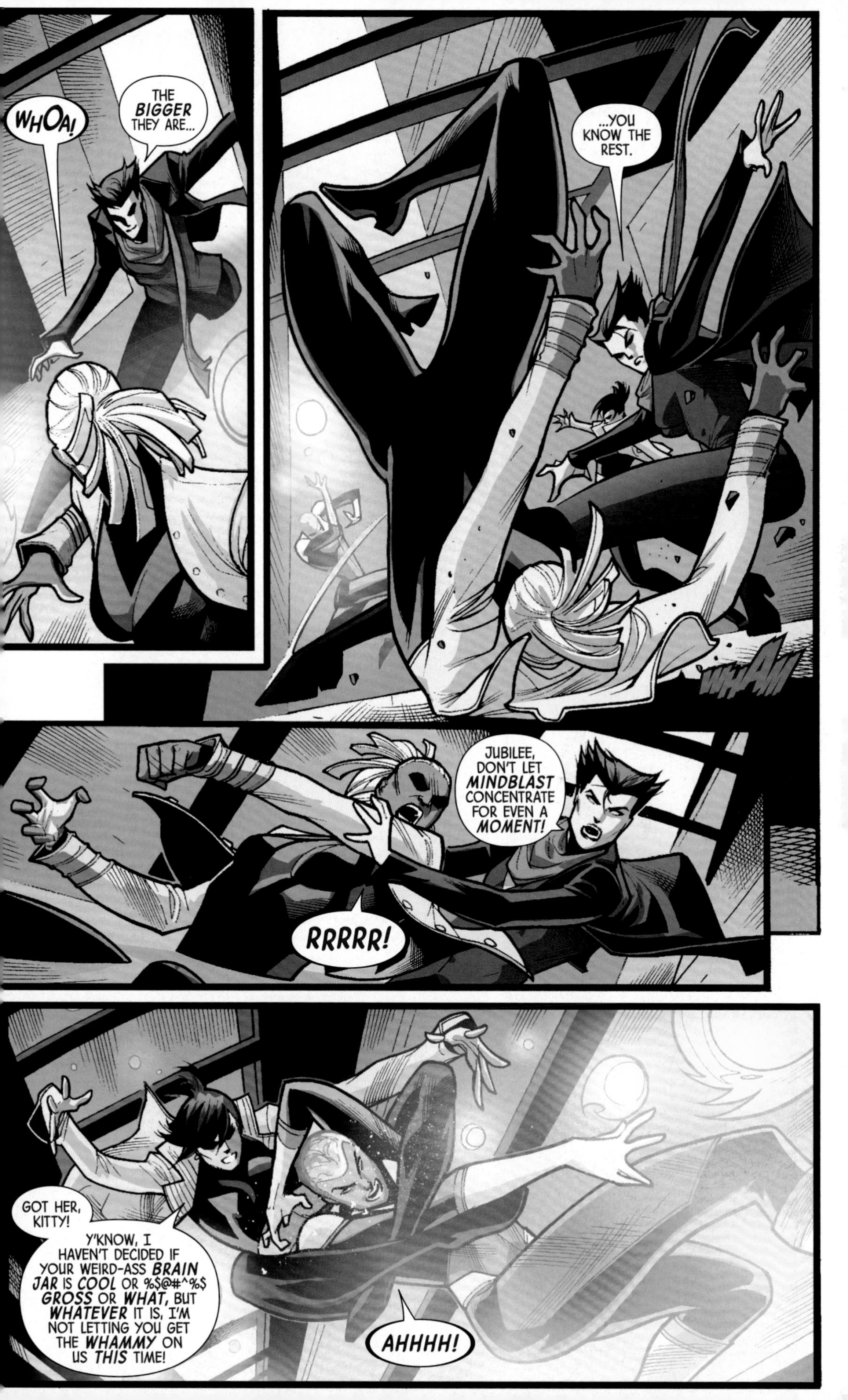
WHOA!
THE BIGGER THEY ARE...
...YOU KNOW THE REST.
WHAM
JUBILEE, DON'T LET MINDBLAST CONCENTRATE FOR EVEN A MOMENT!
RRRRR!
GOT HER, KITTY!
Y'KNOW, I HAVEN'T DECIDED IF YOUR WEIRD-ASS BRAIN JAR IS COOL OR %$@#^%$ GROSS OR WHAT, BUT WHATEVER IT IS, I'M NOT LETTING YOU GET THE WHAMMY ON US THIS TIME!
AHHHH!

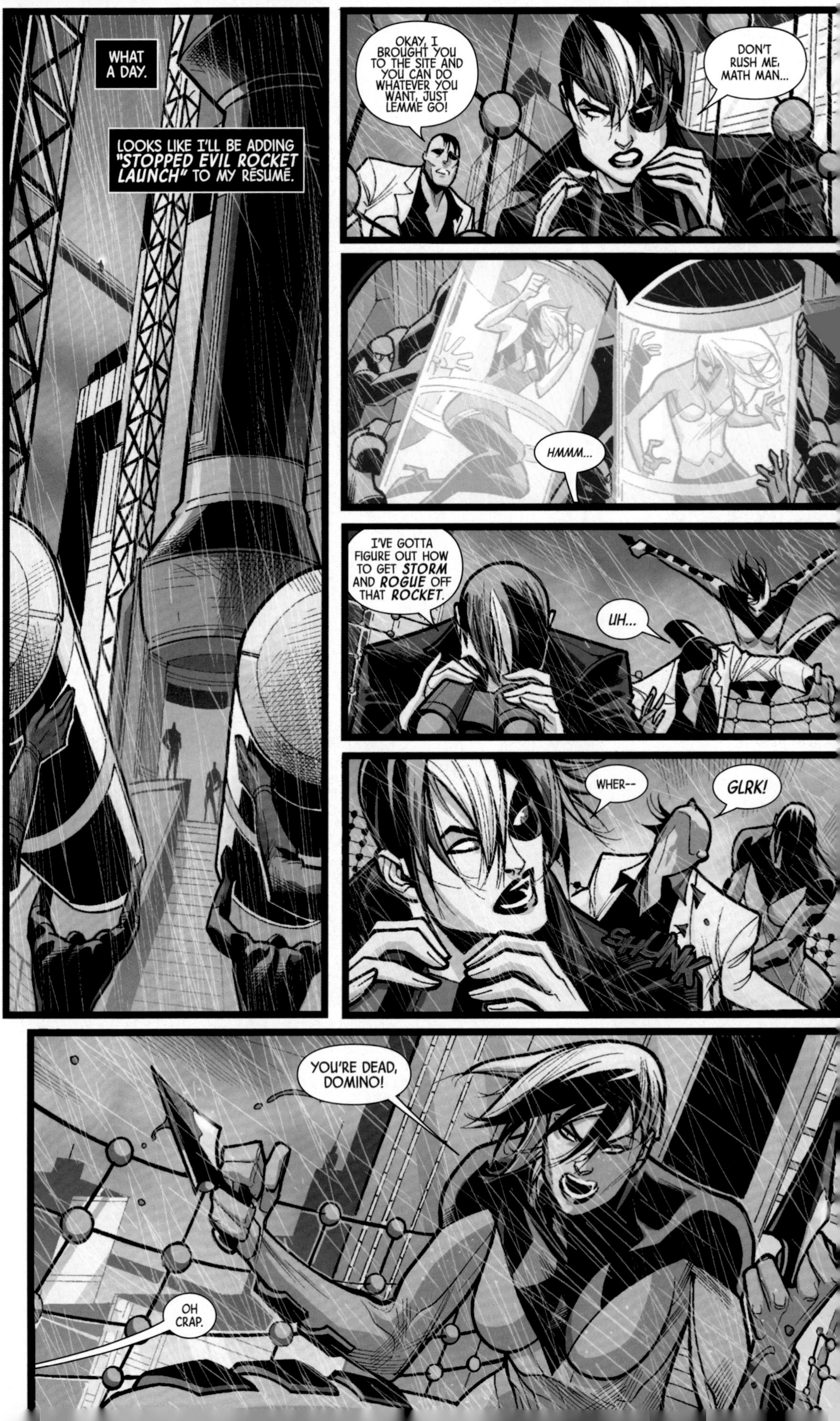
WHAT A DAY.
LOOKS LIKE I'LL BE ADDING "STOPPED EVIL ROCKET LAUNCH" TO MY RESUMÉ.
OKAY, I BROUGHT YOU TO THE SITE AND YOU CAN DO WHATEVER YOU WANT, JUST LEMME GO!
DON'T RUSH ME, MATH MAN...
HMMM...
I'VE GOTTA FIGURE OUT HOW TO GET STORM AND ROGUE OFF THAT ROCKET.
UH...
WHER--
GLRK!
SHUNK
YOU'RE DEAD, DOMINO!
OH CRAP.

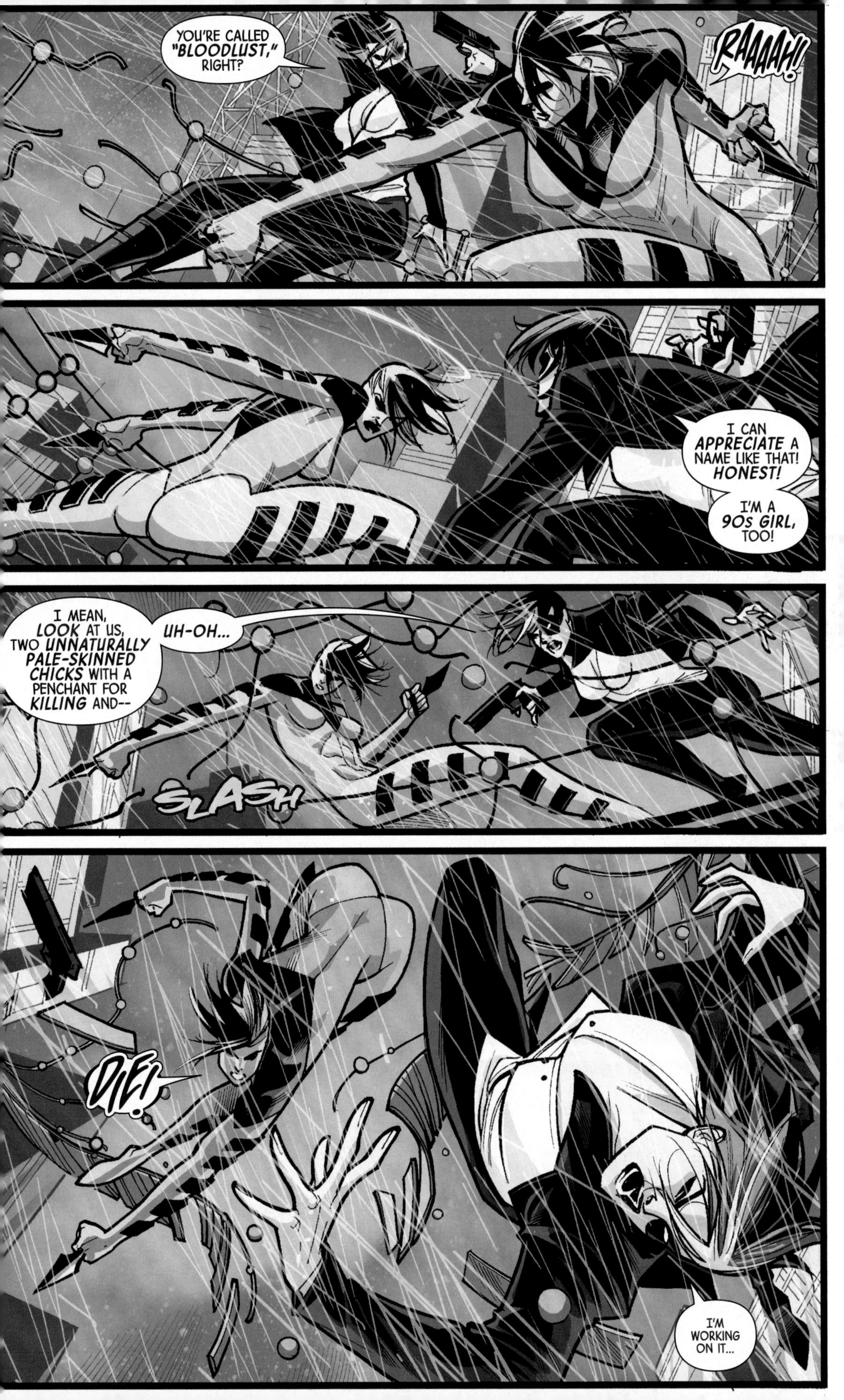
YOU'RE CALLED "BLOODLUST," RIGHT?
RAAAAH!
I CAN APPRECIATE A NAME LIKE THAT! HONEST!
I'M A 90s GIRL, TOO!
I MEAN, LOOK AT US, TWO UNNATURALLY PALE-SKINNED CHICKS WITH A PENCHANT FOR KILLING AND--
UH-OH...
SLASH
DIE!
I'M WORKING ON IT...

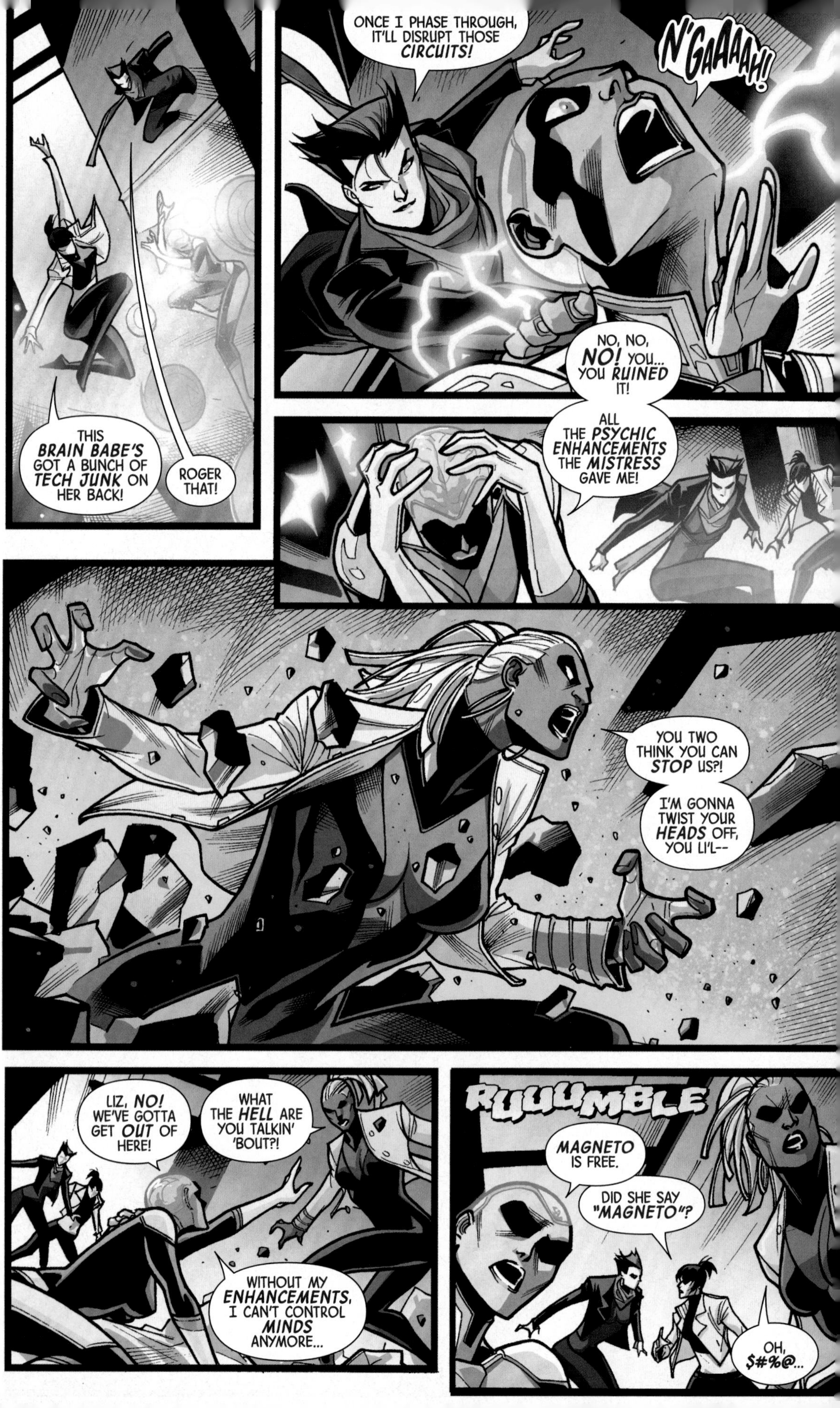
THIS BRAIN BABE'S GOT A BUNCH OF TECH JUNK ON HER BACK!
ROGER THAT!
ONCE I PHASE THROUGH, IT'LL DISRUPT THOSE CIRCUITS!
N'GAAAAH!
NO, NO, NO! YOU... YOU RUINED IT!
ALL THE PSYCHIC ENHANCEMENTS THE MISTRESS GAVE ME!
YOU TWO THINK YOU CAN STOP US?!
I'M GONNA TWIST YOUR HEADS OFF, YOU LI'L--
LIZ, NO! WE'VE GOTTA GET OUT OF HERE!
WHAT THE HELL ARE YOU TALKIN' 'BOUT?!
WITHOUT MY ENHANCEMENTS, I CAN'T CONTROL MINDS ANYMORE...
RUUUMBLE
MAGNETO IS FREE.
DID SHE SAY "MAGNETO"?
OH, $#%@...

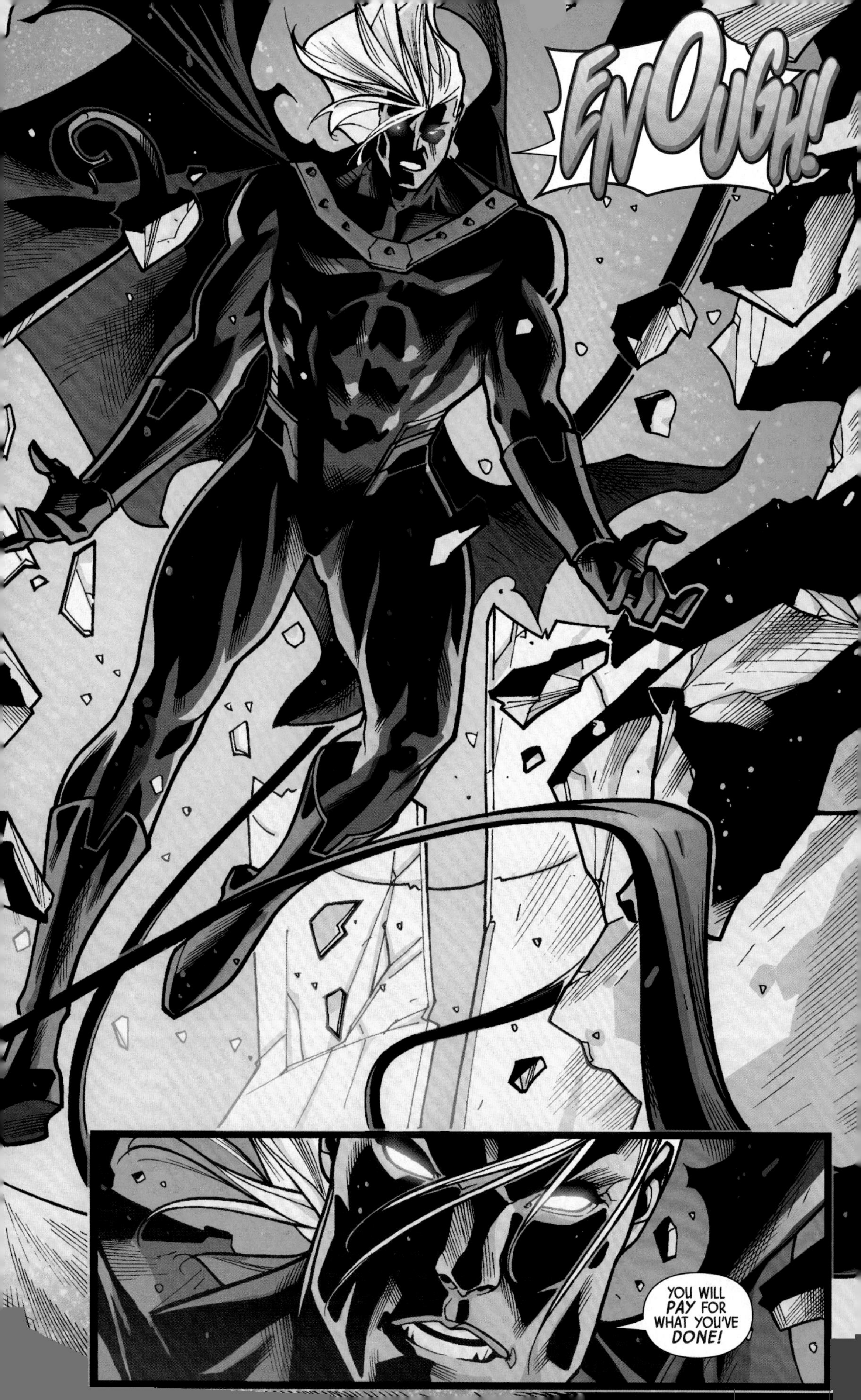
ENOUGH!
YOU WILL PAY FOR WHAT YOU'VE DONE!

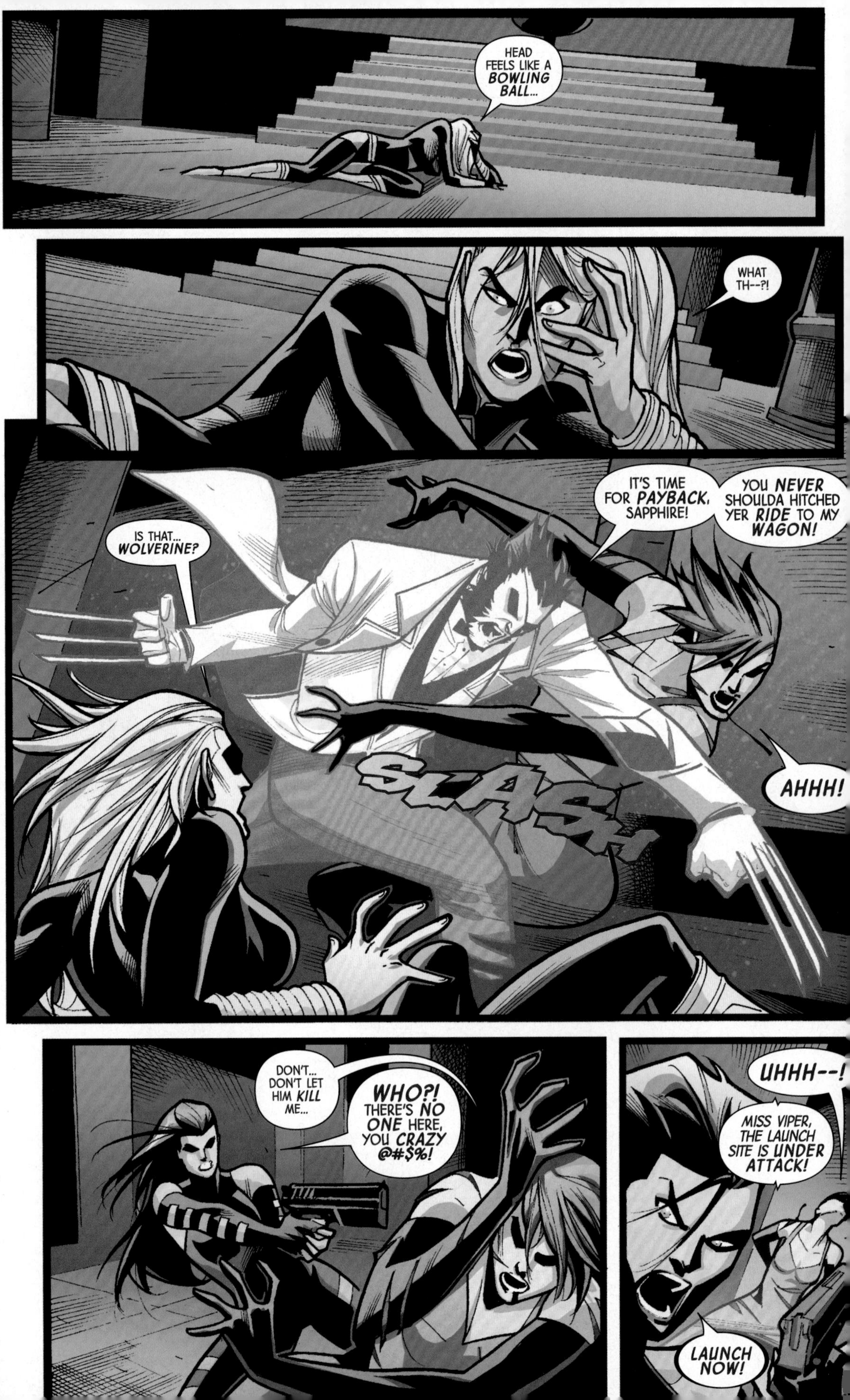
HEAD FEELS LIKE A BOWLING BALL...
WHAT TH--?!
IS THAT... WOLVERINE?
IT'S TIME FOR PAYBACK, SAPPHIRE!
YOU NEVER SHOULDA HITCHED YER RIDE TO MY WAGON!
SLASH
AHHH!
DON'T... DON'T LET HIM KILL ME...
WHO?! THERE'S NO ONE HERE, YOU CRAZY @#$%!
UHHH--!
MISS VIPER, THE LAUNCH SITE IS UNDER ATTACK!
LAUNCH NOW!

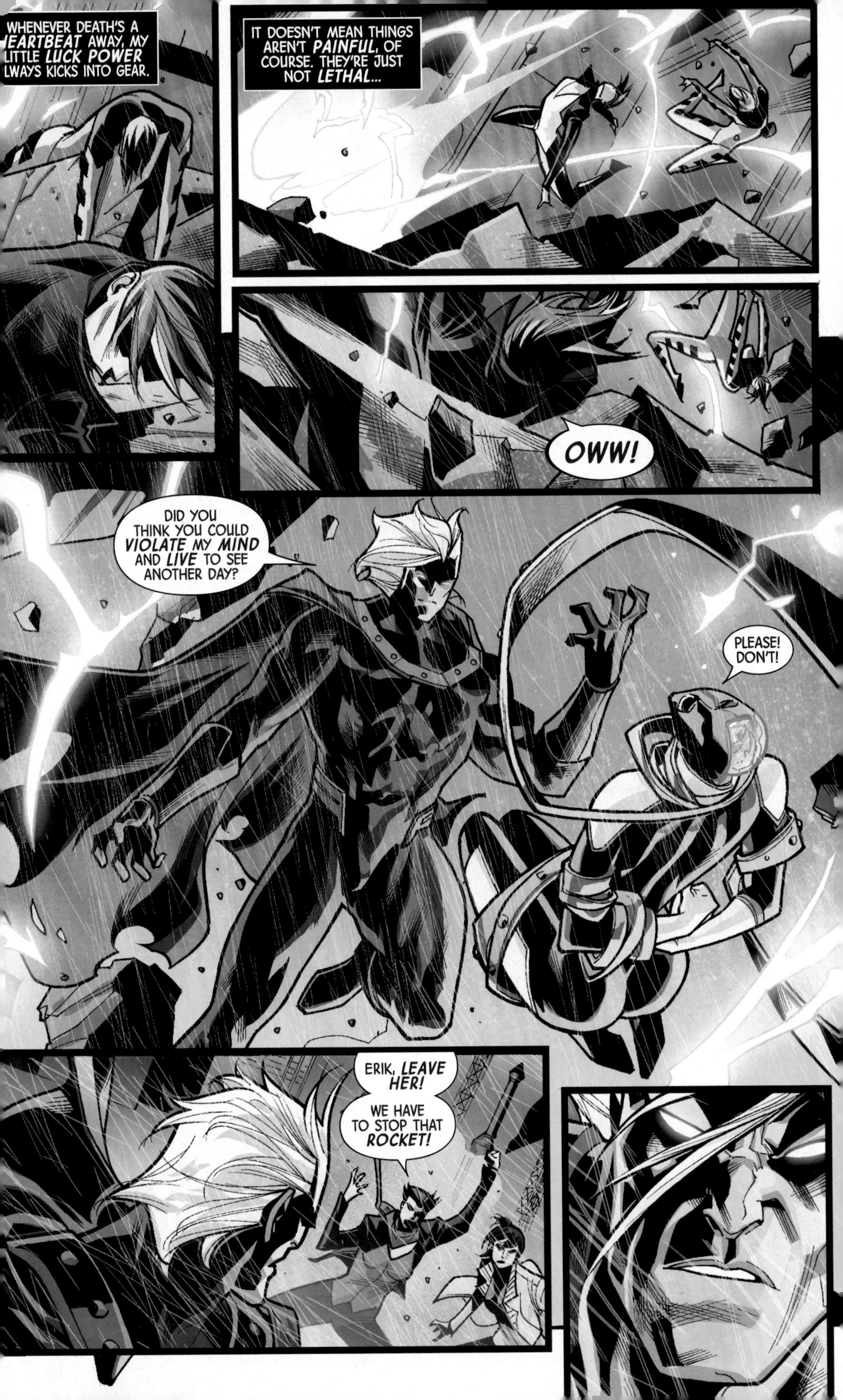

WHENEVER DEATH'S A
EARTBEAT AWAY, MY
LITTLE LUCK POWER
LWAYS KICKS INTO GEAR.
IT DOESN'T MEAN THINGS AREN'T PAINFUL, OF COURSE. THEY'RE JUST NOT LETHAL...
OWW!
DID YOU THINK YOU COULD VIOLATE MY MIND AND LIVE TO SEE ANOTHER DAY?
PLEASE! DON'T!
ERIK, LEAVE HER!
WE HAVE TO STOP THAT ROCKET!

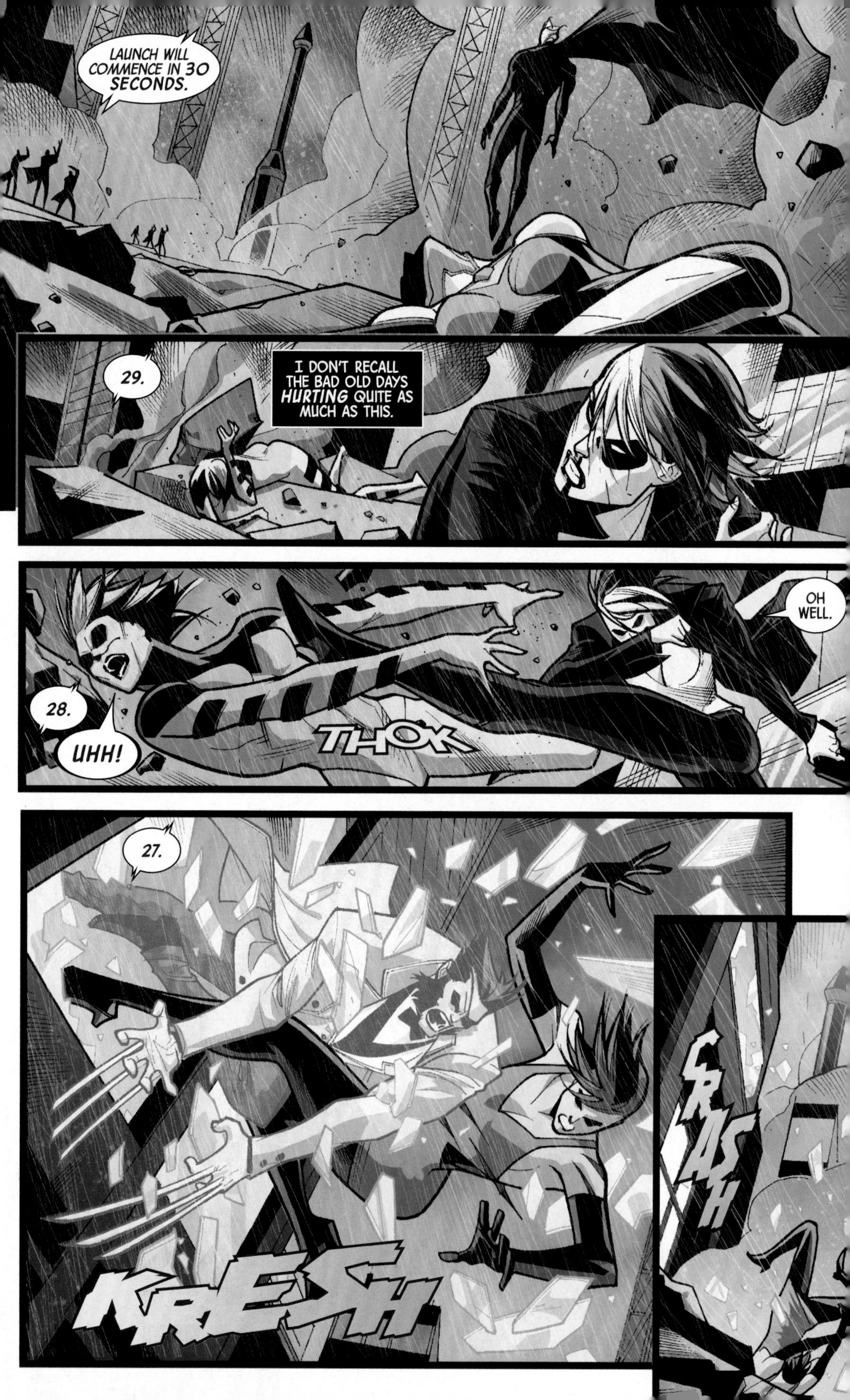
LAUNCH WILL COMMENCE IN 30 SECONDS.
29.
I DON'T RECALL THE BAD OLD DAYS HURTING QUITE AS MUCH AS THIS.
OH WELL.
28.
UHH!
THOK
27.
KRESH
CRASH

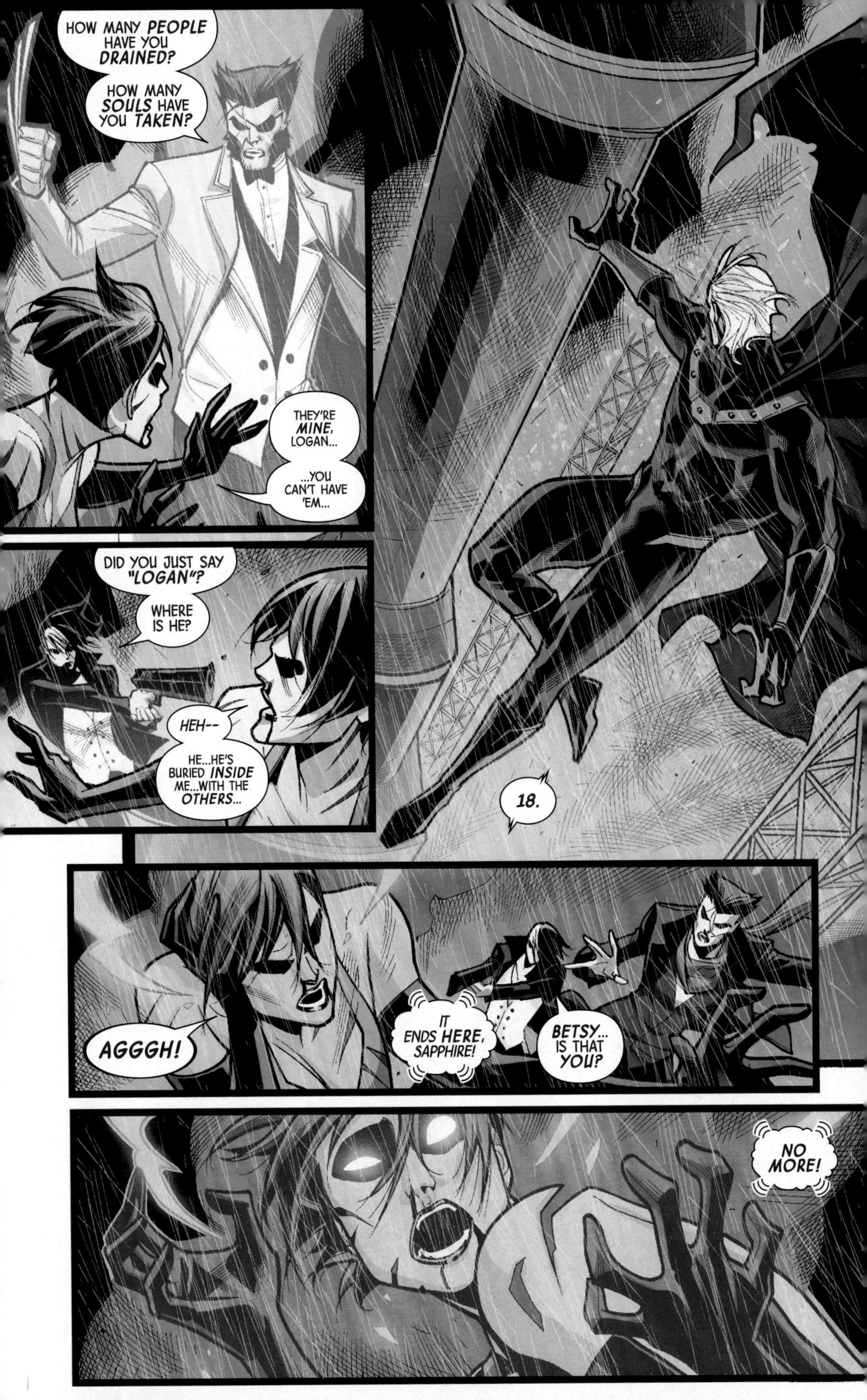
HOW MANY PEOPLE HAVE YOU DRAINED?
HOW MANY SOULS HAVE YOU TAKEN?
THEY'RE MINE, LOGAN...
...YOU CAN'T HAVE 'EM...
DID YOU JUST SAY "LOGAN"?
WHERE IS HE?
HEH--
HE...HE'S BURIED INSIDE ME...WITH THE OTHERS...
18.
AGGGH!
IT ENDS HERE, SAPPHIRE!
BETSY... IS THAT YOU?
NO MORE!

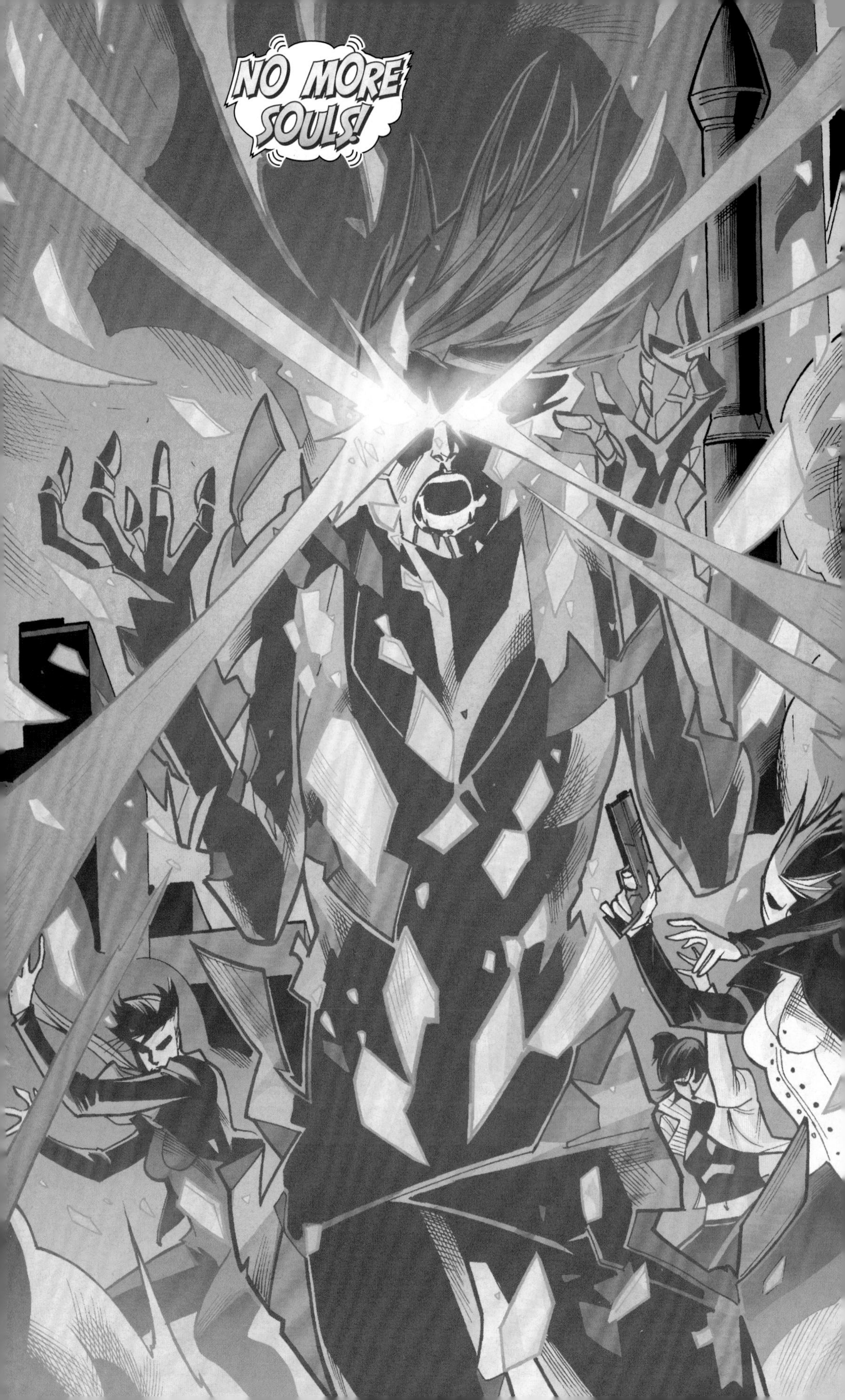
NO MORE SOULS!

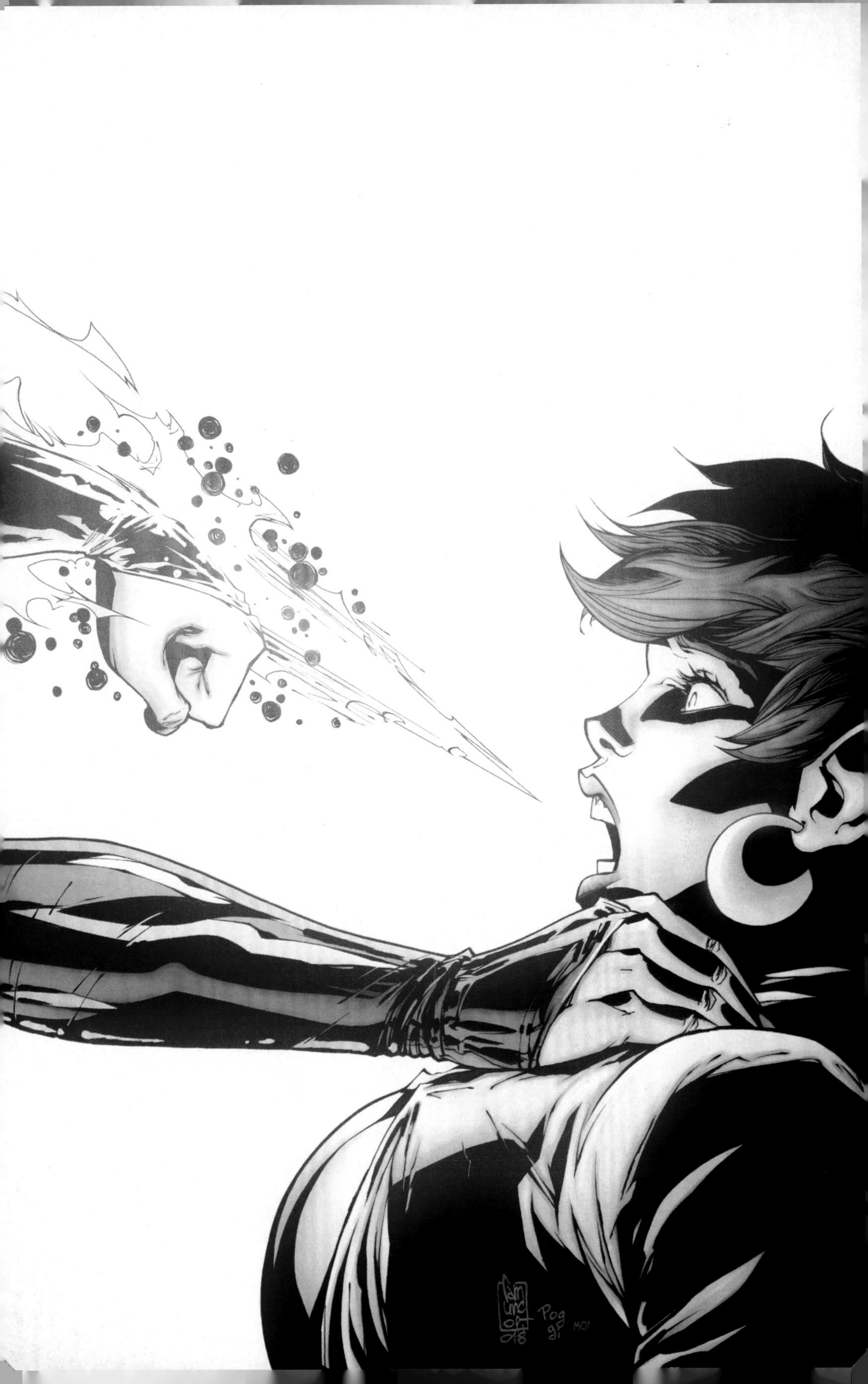

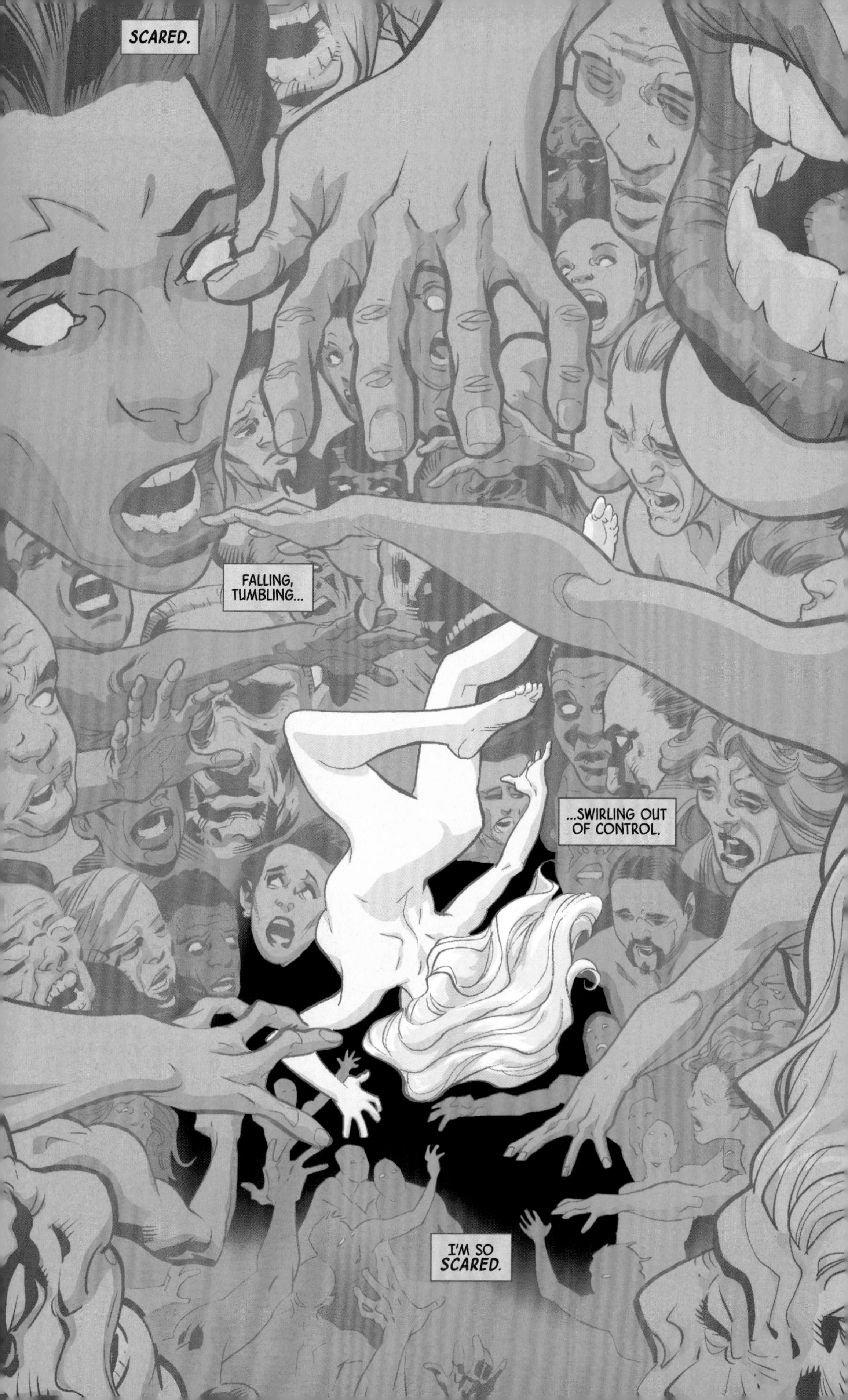
SCARED.
FALLING, TUMBLING...
...SWIRLING OUT OF CONTROL.
I'M SO SCARED.

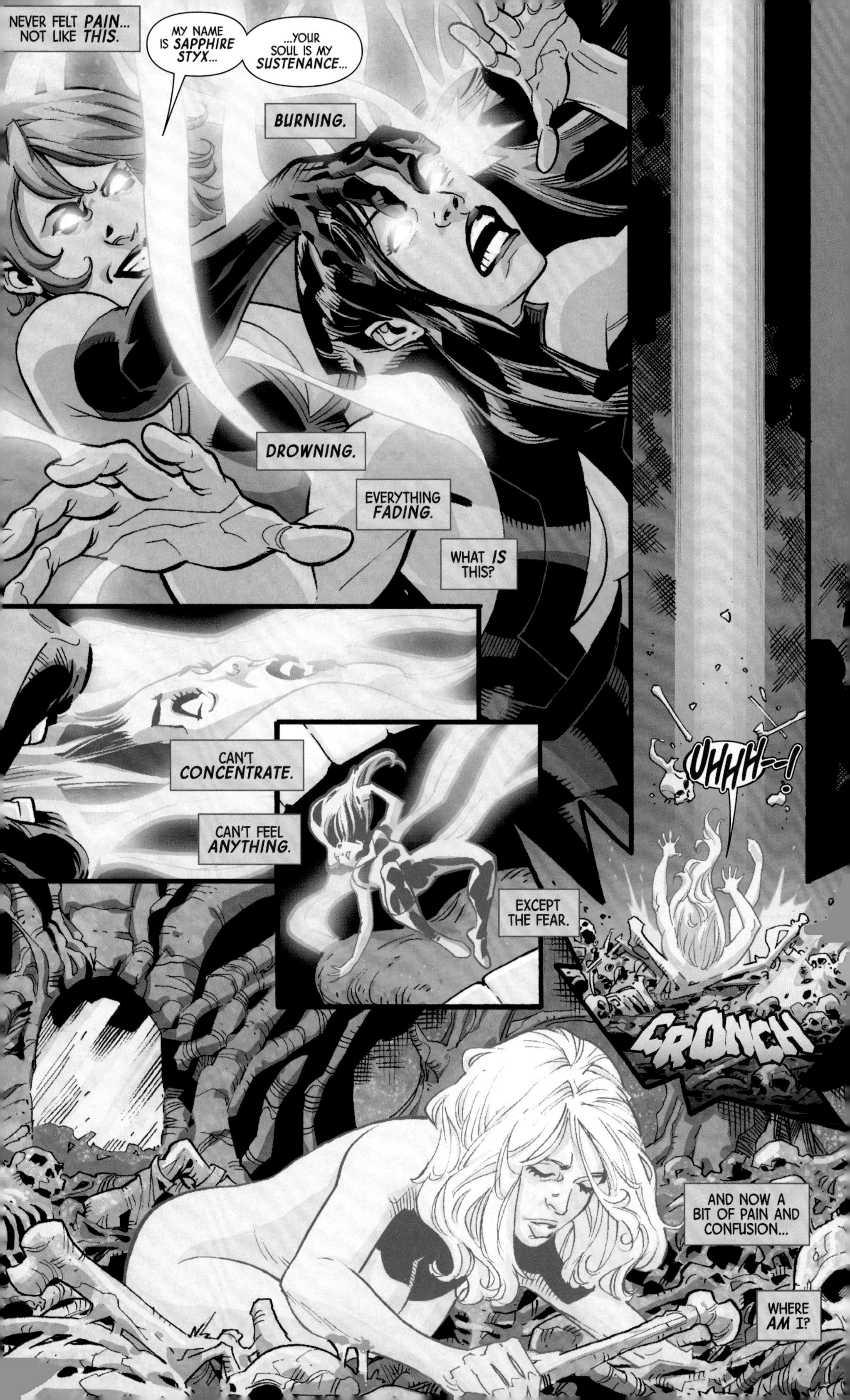
NEVER FELT PAIN... NOT LIKE THIS.
MY NAME IS SAPPHIRE STYX...
...YOUR SOUL IS MY SUSTENANCE...
BURNING.
DROWNING.
EVERYTHING FADING.
WHAT IS THIS?
CAN'T CONCENTRATE.
CAN'T FEEL ANYTHING.
EXCEPT THE FEAR.
UHHH--!
CRONCH
AND NOW A BIT OF PAIN AND CONFUSION...
WHERE AM I?

AND, FOR THAT MATTER...

...WHO AM I?

STOP THAT.

STOP.

EVEN HERE, TORN AWAY FROM YOUR PHYSICAL FORM....

...YOU ARE YOURSELF.

YOU ARE *BETSY BRADDOCK.*

IT FEELS LIKE A *LIFETIME* AGO.

IT *WAS...*

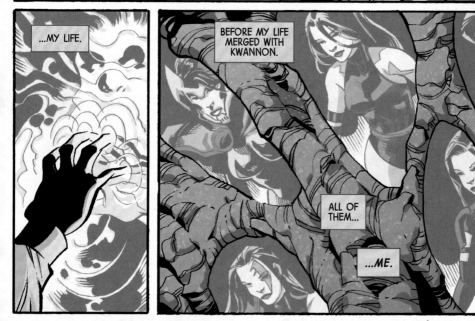

...MY LIFE.

BEFORE MY LIFE MERGED WITH KWANNON.

ALL OF THEM...

...ME.

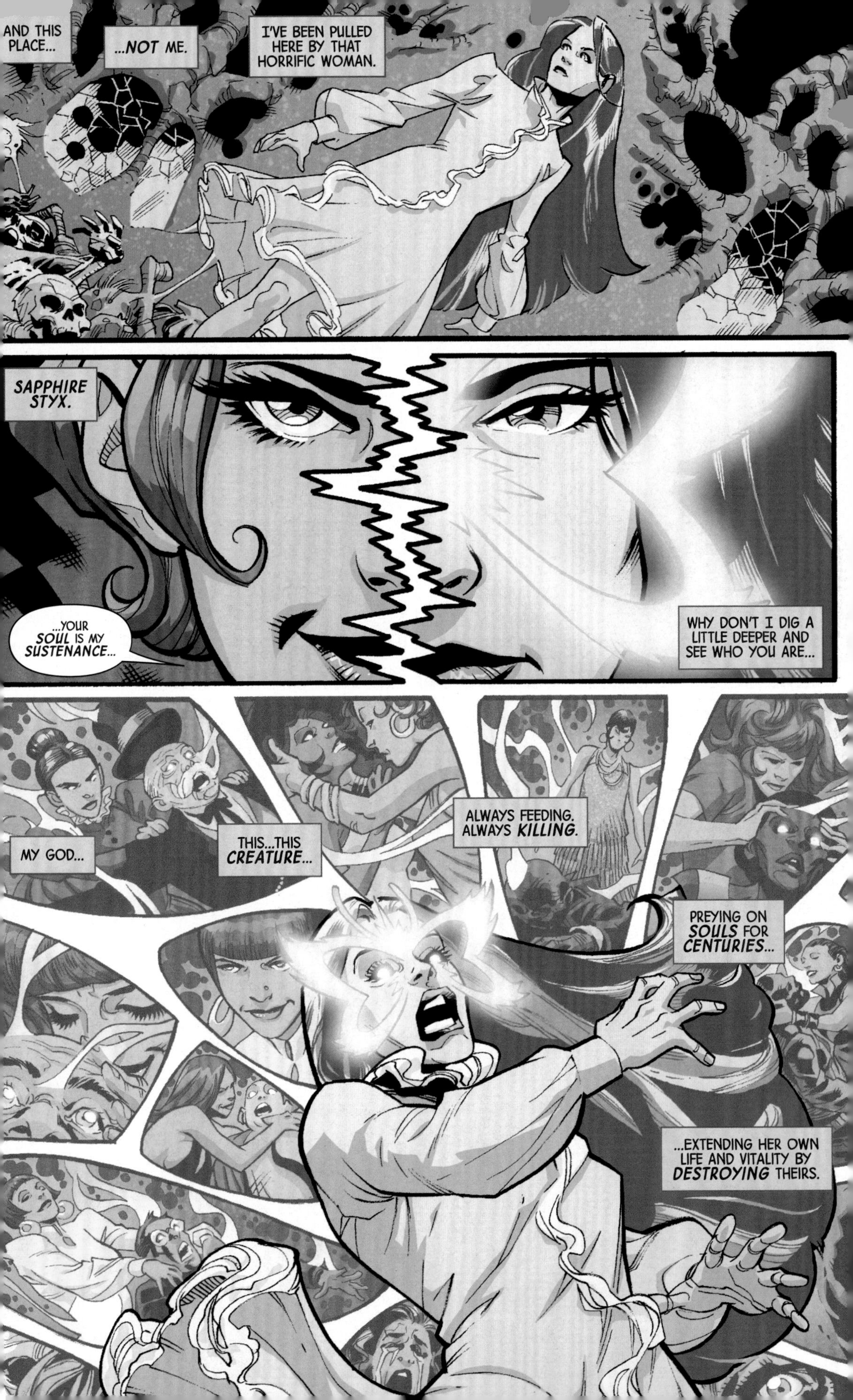
AND THIS PLACE...
...NOT ME.
I'VE BEEN PULLED HERE BY THAT HORRIFIC WOMAN.
SAPPHIRE STYX.
...YOUR SOUL IS MY SUSTENANCE...
WHY DON'T I DIG A LITTLE DEEPER AND SEE WHO YOU ARE...
MY GOD...
THIS...THIS CREATURE...
ALWAYS FEEDING. ALWAYS KILLING.
PREYING ON SOULS FOR CENTURIES...
...EXTENDING HER OWN LIFE AND VITALITY BY DESTROYING THEIRS.

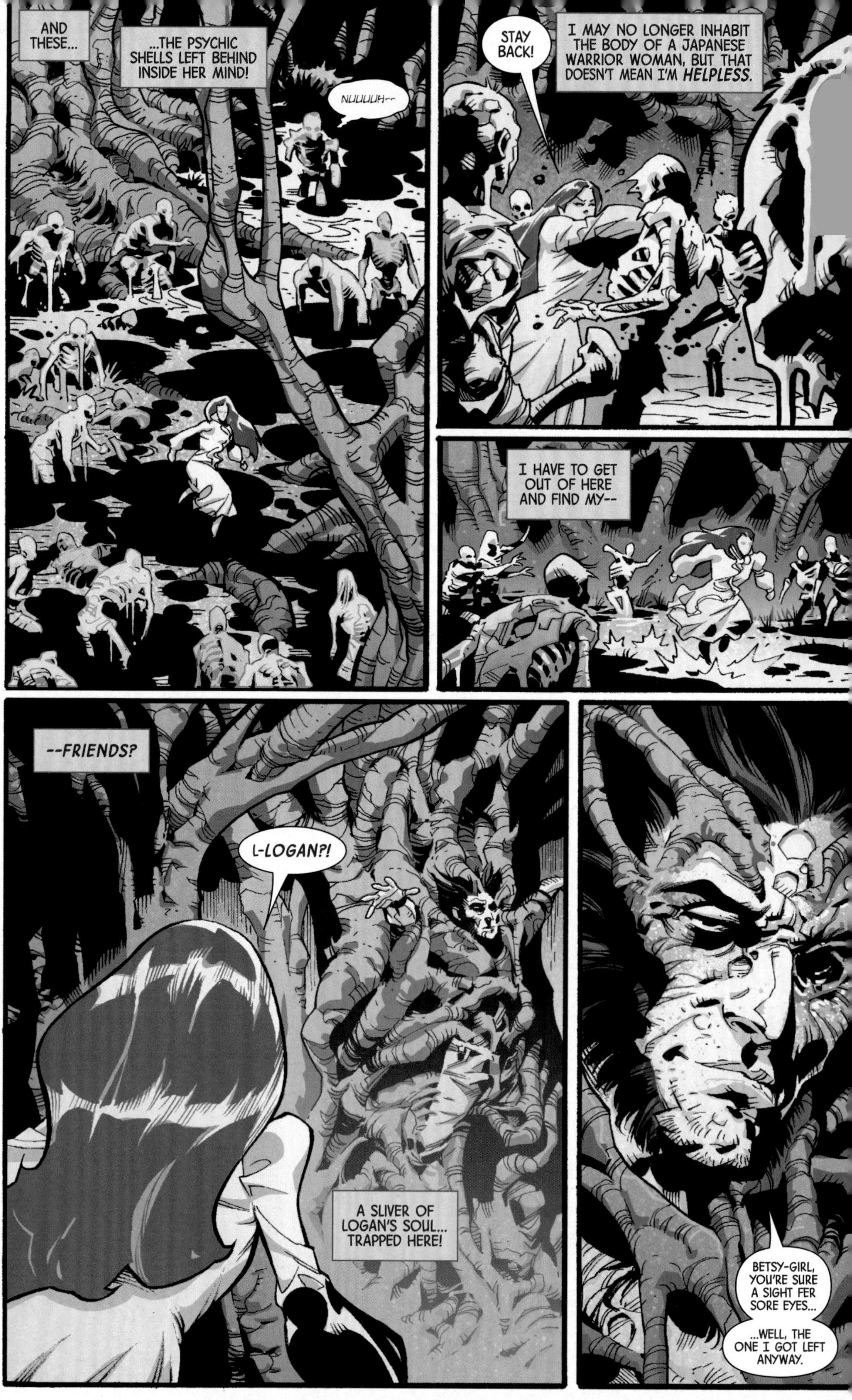

AND THESE...
...THE PSYCHIC SHELLS LEFT BEHIND INSIDE HER MIND!
NUUUUH--
STAY BACK!
I MAY NO LONGER INHABIT THE BODY OF A JAPANESE WARRIOR WOMAN, BUT THAT DOESN'T MEAN I'M HELPLESS.
I HAVE TO GET OUT OF HERE AND FIND MY--
--FRIENDS?
L-LOGAN?!
A SLIVER OF LOGAN'S SOUL... TRAPPED HERE!
BETSY-GIRL, YOU'RE SURE A SIGHT FER SORE EYES...
...WELL, THE ONE I GOT LEFT ANYWAY.

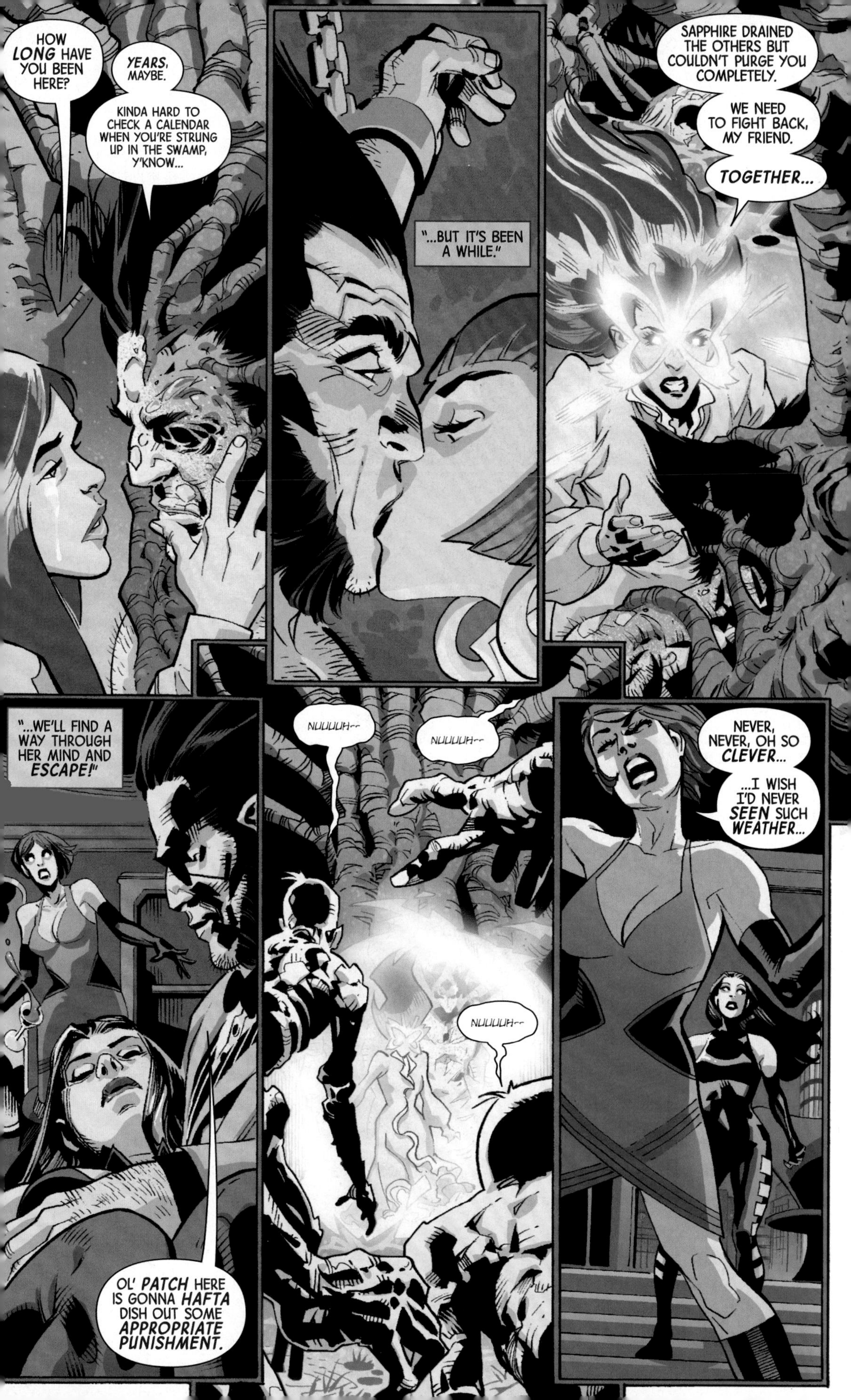
HOW LONG HAVE YOU BEEN HERE?
YEARS, MAYBE.
KINDA HARD TO CHECK A CALENDAR WHEN YOU'RE STRUNG UP IN THE SWAMP, Y'KNOW...
"...BUT IT'S BEEN A WHILE."
SAPPHIRE DRAINED THE OTHERS BUT COULDN'T PURGE YOU COMPLETELY.
WE NEED TO FIGHT BACK, MY FRIEND.
TOGETHER...
"...WE'LL FIND A WAY THROUGH HER MIND AND ESCAPE!"
OL' PATCH HERE IS GONNA HAFTA DISH OUT SOME APPROPRIATE PUNISHMENT.
NUUUUH--
NUUUUH--
NUUUUH--
NEVER, NEVER, OH SO CLEVER...
...I WISH I'D NEVER SEEN SUCH WEATHER...

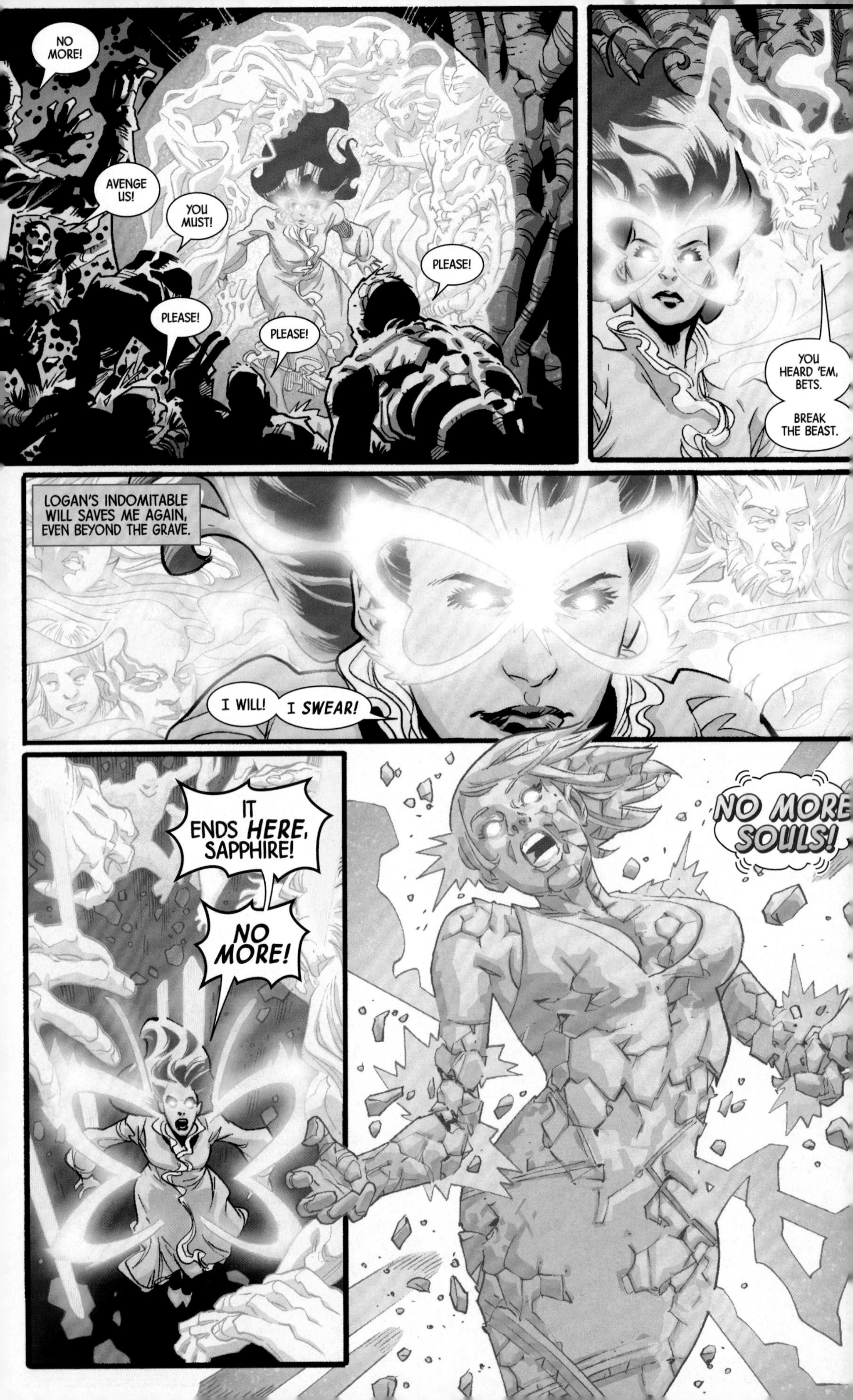
NO MORE!
AVENGE US!
YOU MUST!
PLEASE!
PLEASE!
PLEASE!
YOU HEARD 'EM, BETS.
BREAK THE BEAST.
LOGAN'S INDOMITABLE WILL SAVES ME AGAIN, EVEN BEYOND THE GRAVE.
I WILL!
I SWEAR!
IT ENDS HERE, SAPPHIRE!
NO MORE!
NO MORE SOULS!

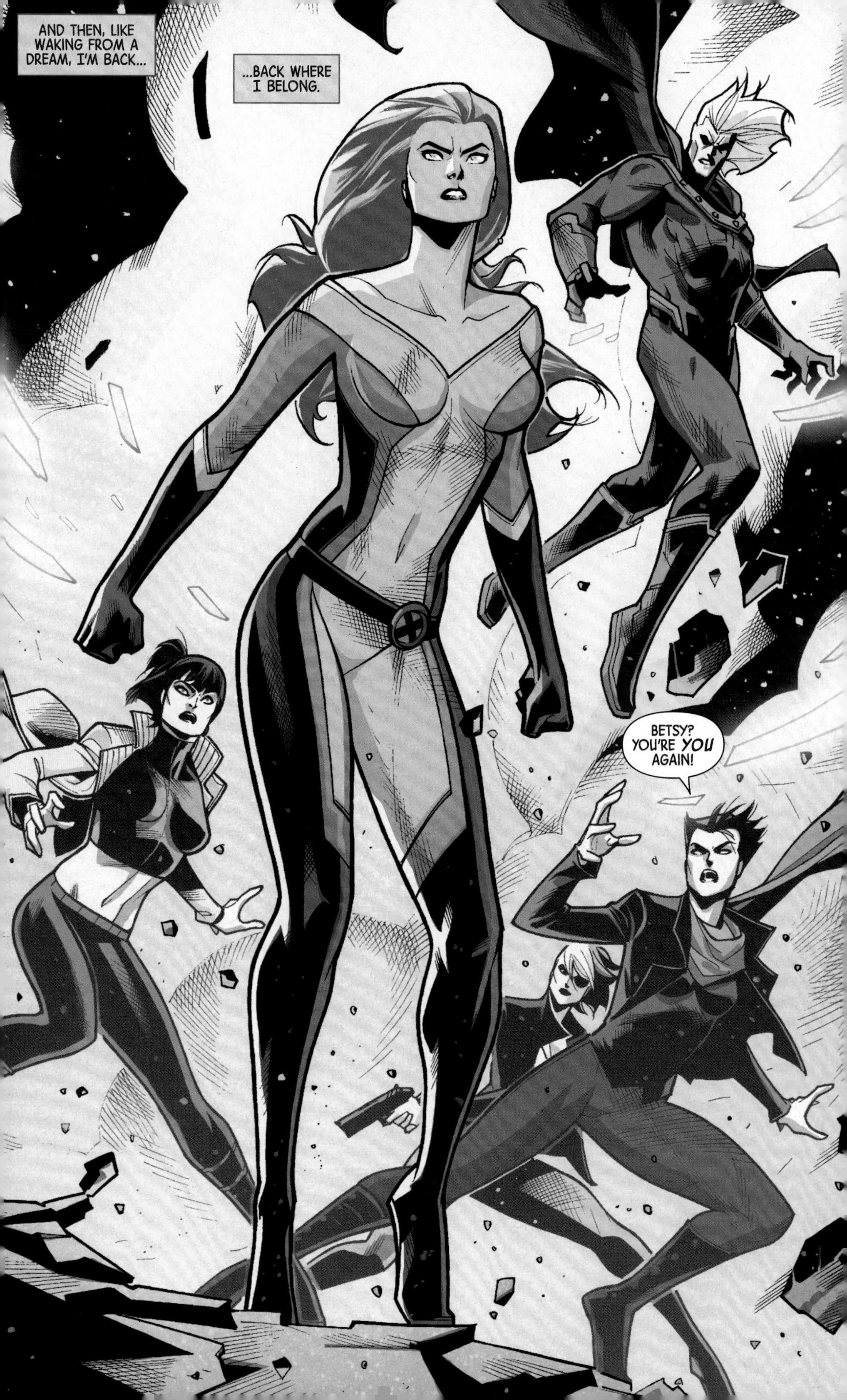
AND THEN, LIKE WAKING FROM A DREAM, I'M BACK...
...BACK WHERE I BELONG.
BETSY? YOU'RE *YOU* AGAIN!

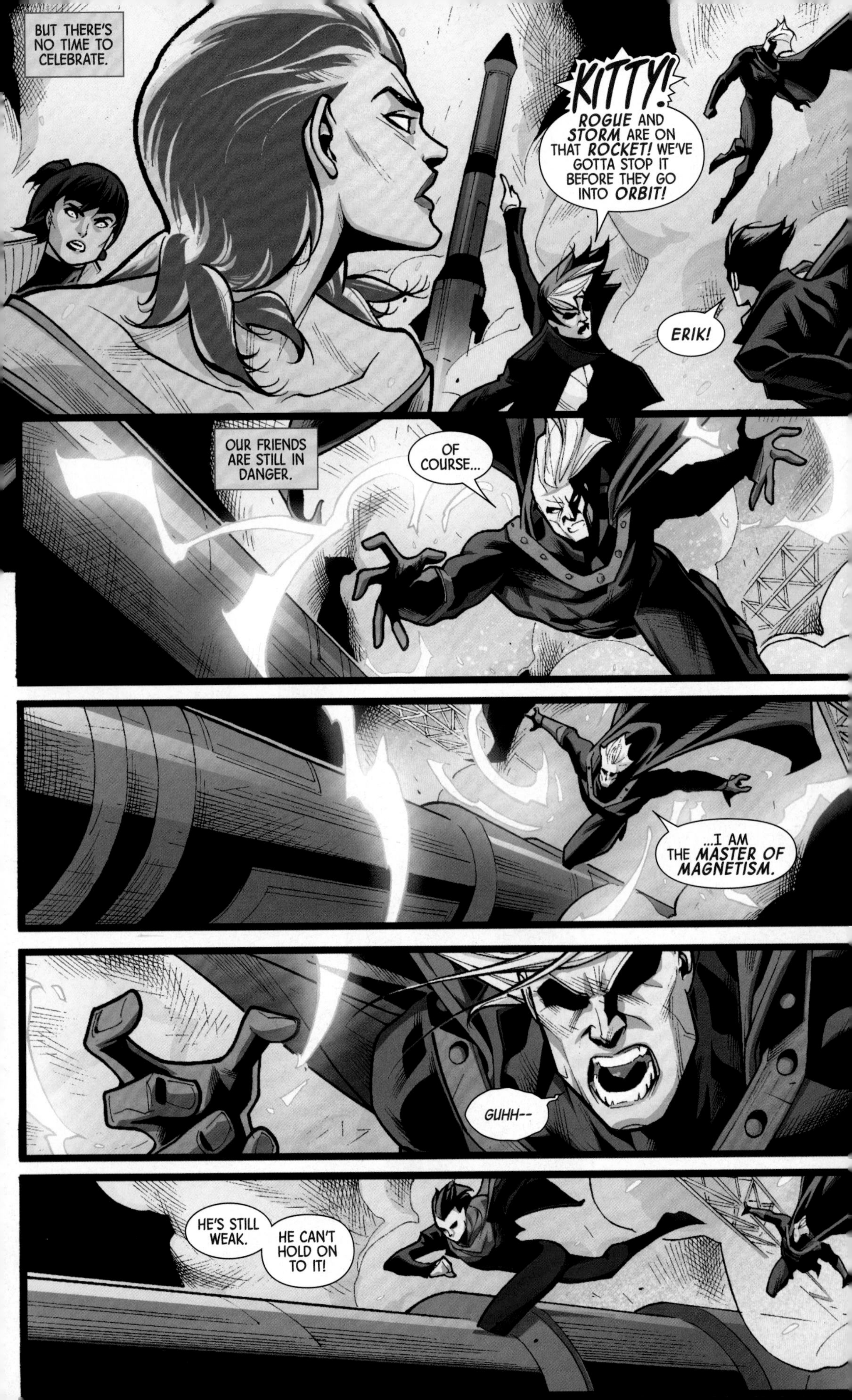
BUT THERE'S NO TIME TO CELEBRATE.
KITTY!
ROGUE AND STORM ARE ON THAT ROCKET! WE'VE GOTTA STOP IT BEFORE THEY GO INTO ORBIT!
ERIK!
OUR FRIENDS ARE STILL IN DANGER.
OF COURSE...
...I AM THE MASTER OF MAGNETISM.
GUHH--
HE'S STILL WEAK.
HE CAN'T HOLD ON TO IT!

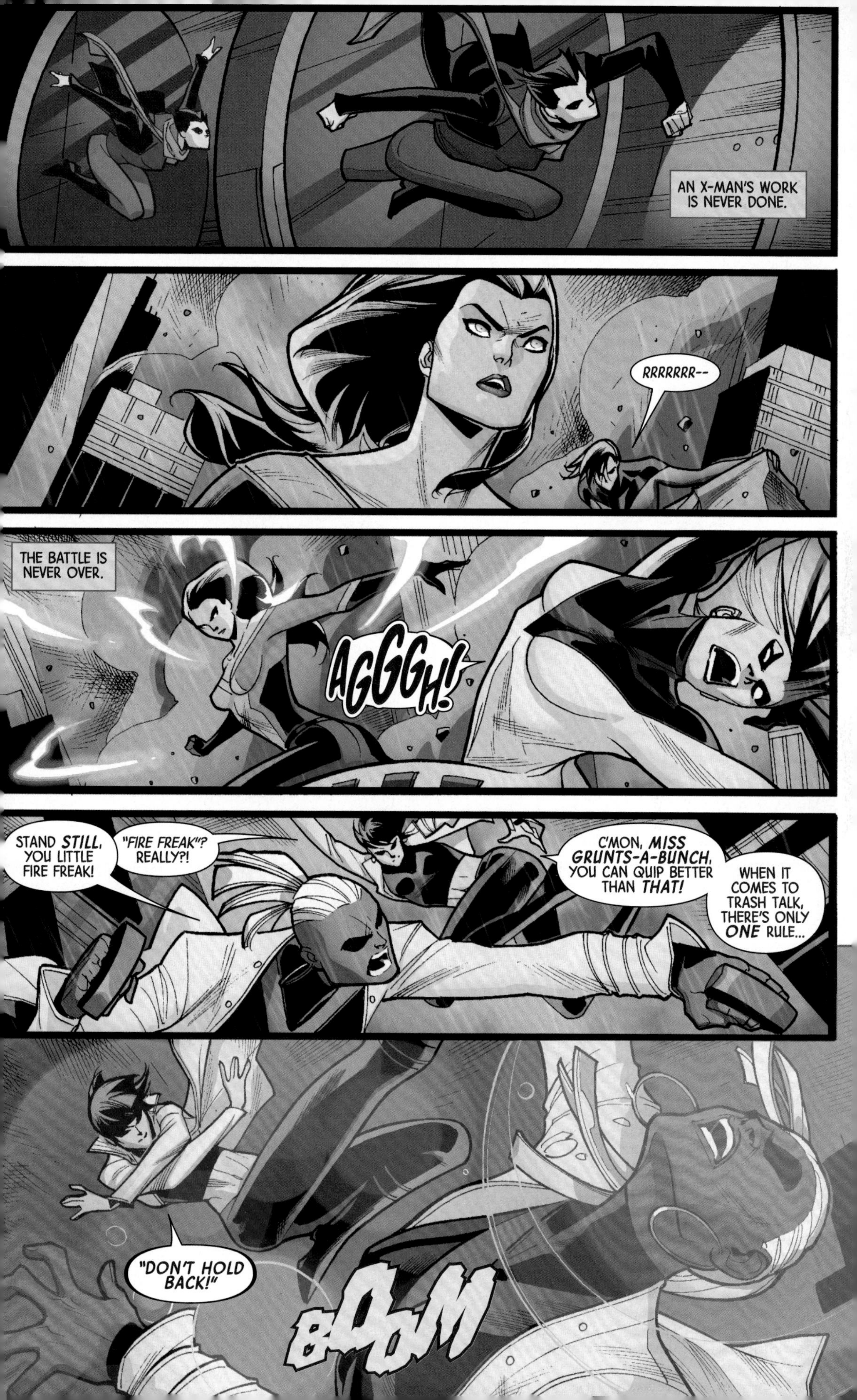
AN X-MAN'S WORK IS NEVER DONE.
RRRRRRR--
THE BATTLE IS NEVER OVER.
AGGGH!
STAND STILL, YOU LITTLE FIRE FREAK!
"FIRE FREAK"? REALLY?!
C'MON, MISS GRUNTS-A-BUNCH, YOU CAN QUIP BETTER THAN THAT!
WHEN IT COMES TO TRASH TALK, THERE'S ONLY ONE RULE...
"DON'T HOLD BACK!"
BOOM

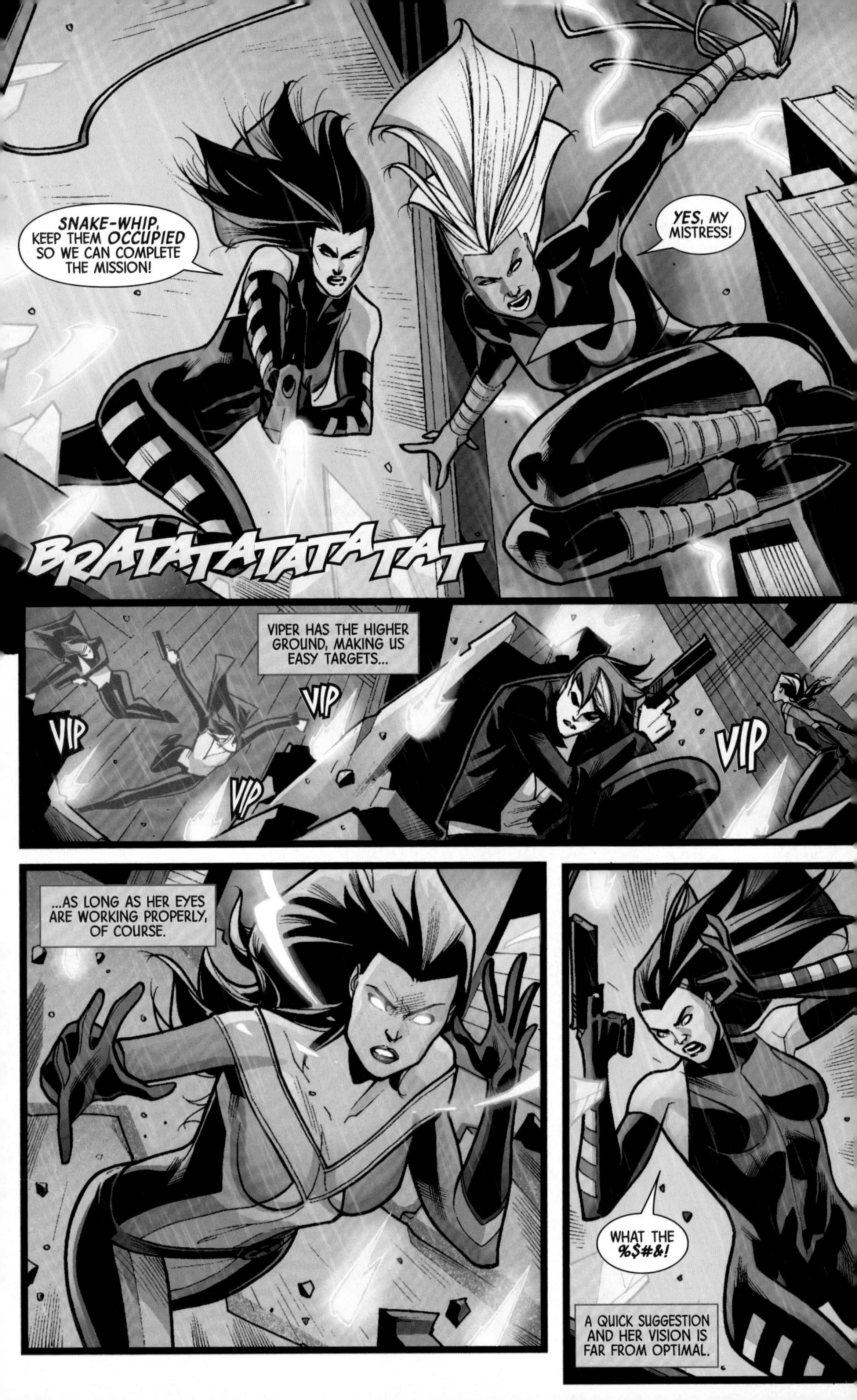
SNAKE-WHIP, KEEP THEM OCCUPIED SO WE CAN COMPLETE THE MISSION!
YES, MY MISTRESS!
BRATATATATATAT
VIPER HAS THE HIGHER GROUND, MAKING US EASY TARGETS...
VIP
VIP
VIP
VIP
...AS LONG AS HER EYES ARE WORKING PROPERLY, OF COURSE.
WHAT THE %$#&!
A QUICK SUGGESTION AND HER VISION IS FAR FROM OPTIMAL.

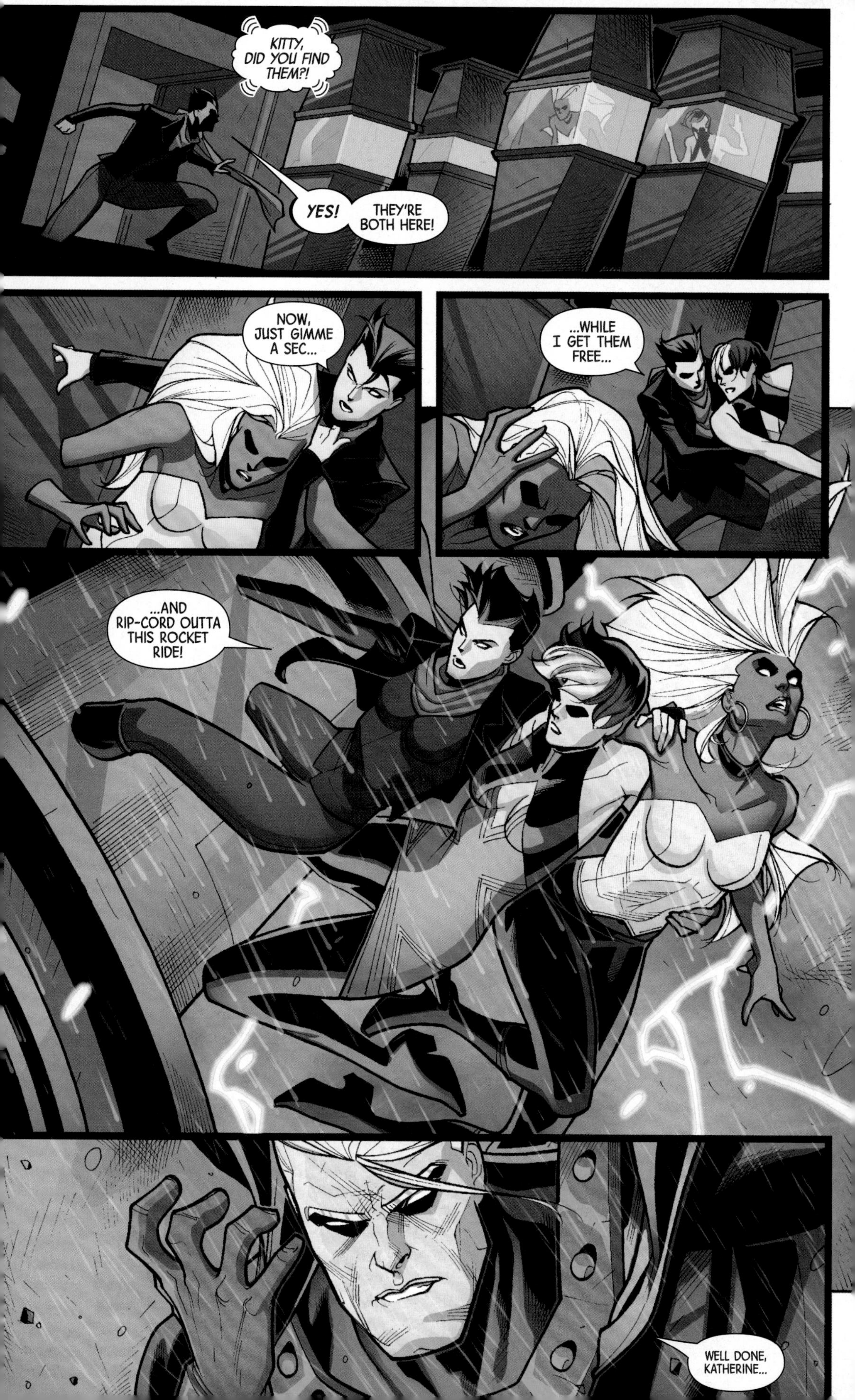
KITTY, DID YOU FIND THEM?!
YES!
THEY'RE BOTH HERE!
NOW, JUST GIMME A SEC...
...WHILE I GET THEM FREE...
...AND RIP-CORD OUTTA THIS ROCKET RIDE!
WELL DONE, KATHERINE...

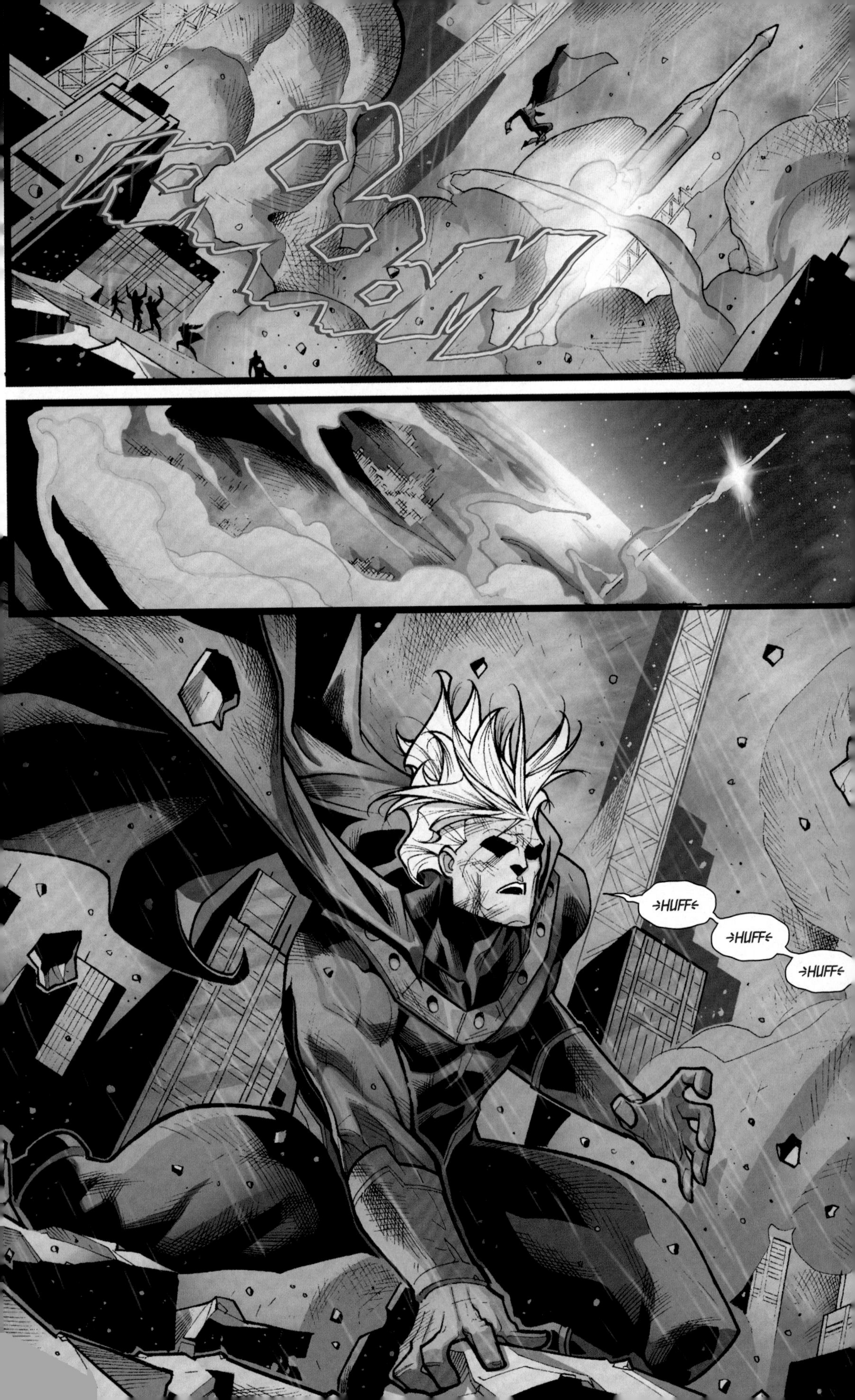

→HUFF←
→HUFF←
→HUFF←

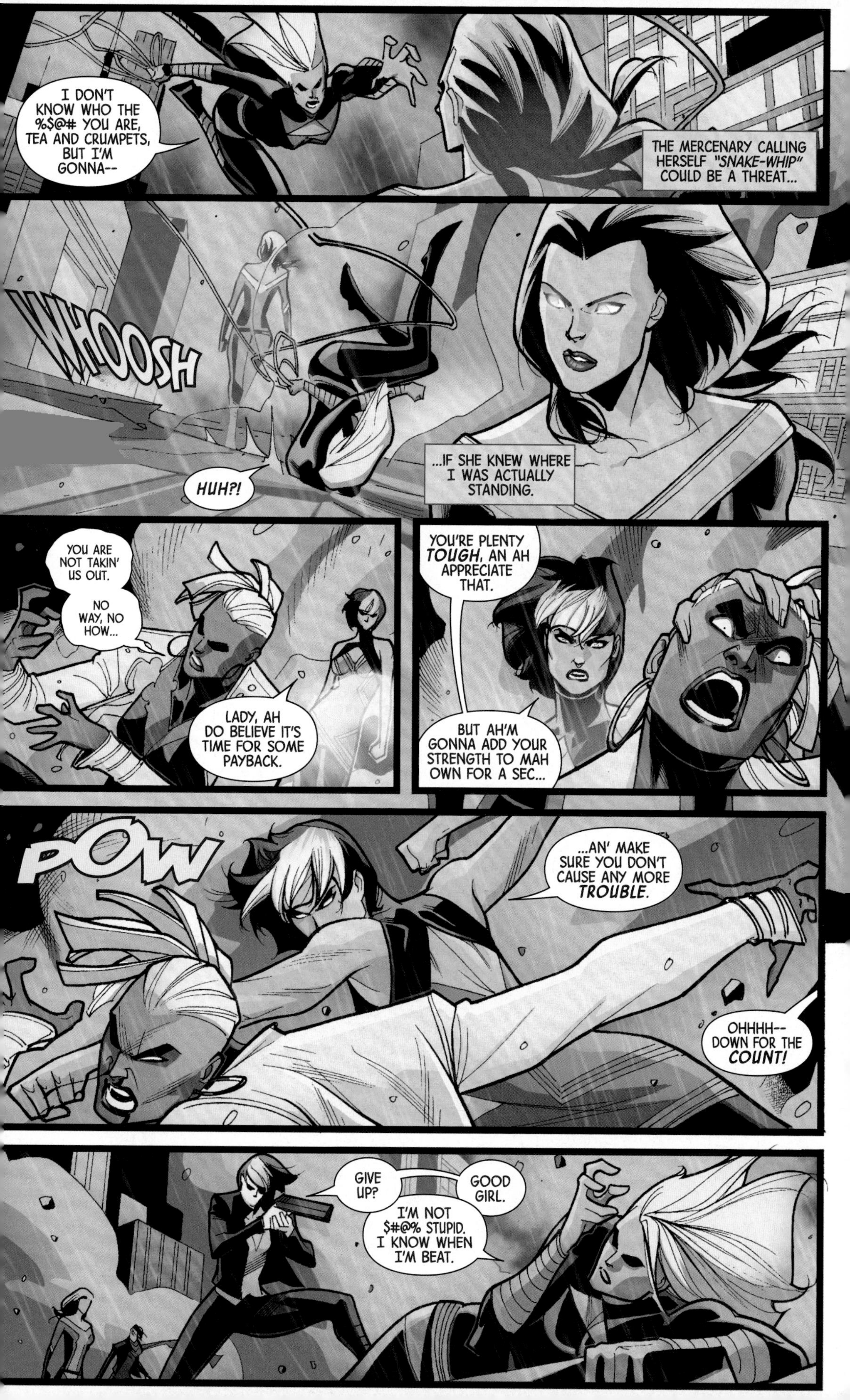
I DON'T KNOW WHO THE %$@# YOU ARE, TEA AND CRUMPETS, BUT I'M GONNA--
THE MERCENARY CALLING HERSELF "SNAKE-WHIP" COULD BE A THREAT...
WHOOSH
HUH?!
...IF SHE KNEW WHERE I WAS ACTUALLY STANDING.
YOU ARE NOT TAKIN' US OUT.
NO WAY, NO HOW...
LADY, AH DO BELIEVE IT'S TIME FOR SOME PAYBACK.
YOU'RE PLENTY TOUGH, AN AH APPRECIATE THAT.
BUT AH'M GONNA ADD YOUR STRENGTH TO MAH OWN FOR A SEC...
POW
...AN' MAKE SURE YOU DON'T CAUSE ANY MORE TROUBLE.
OHHHH-- DOWN FOR THE COUNT!
GIVE UP?
GOOD GIRL.
I'M NOT $#@% STUPID. I KNOW WHEN I'M BEAT.

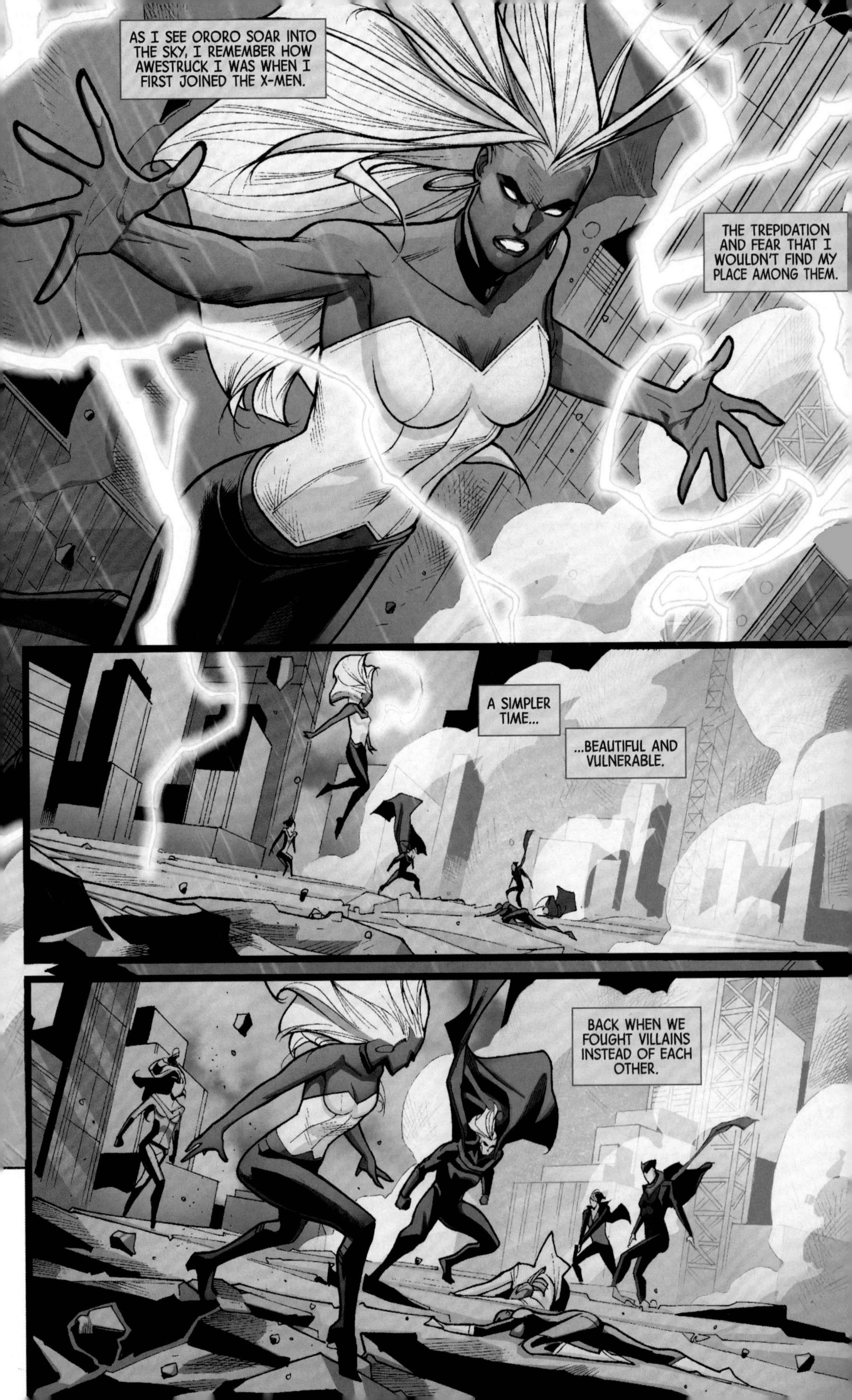
AS I SEE ORORO SOAR INTO THE SKY, I REMEMBER HOW AWESTRUCK I WAS WHEN I FIRST JOINED THE X-MEN.
THE TREPIDATION AND FEAR THAT I WOULDN'T FIND MY PLACE AMONG THEM.
A SIMPLER TIME...
...BEAUTIFUL AND VULNERABLE.
BACK WHEN WE FOUGHT VILLAINS INSTEAD OF EACH OTHER.

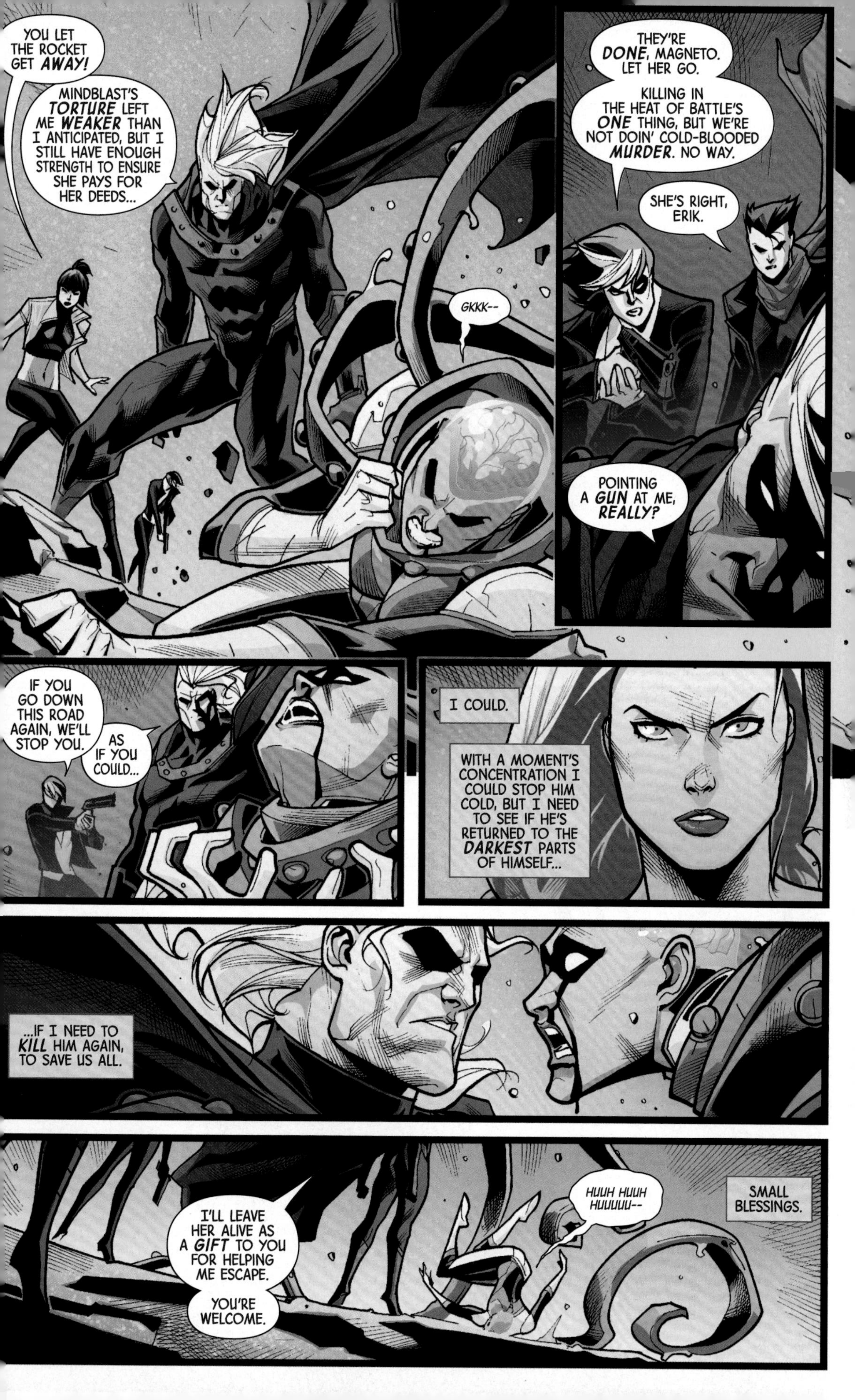
YOU LET THE ROCKET GET AWAY!
MINDBLAST'S TORTURE LEFT ME WEAKER THAN I ANTICIPATED, BUT I STILL HAVE ENOUGH STRENGTH TO ENSURE SHE PAYS FOR HER DEEDS...
GKKK--
THEY'RE DONE, MAGNETO. LET HER GO.
KILLING IN THE HEAT OF BATTLE'S ONE THING, BUT WE'RE NOT DOIN' COLD-BLOODED MURDER. NO WAY.
SHE'S RIGHT, ERIK.
POINTING A GUN AT ME, REALLY?
IF YOU GO DOWN THIS ROAD AGAIN, WE'LL STOP YOU.
AS IF YOU COULD...
I COULD.
WITH A MOMENT'S CONCENTRATION I COULD STOP HIM COLD, BUT I NEED TO SEE IF HE'S RETURNED TO THE DARKEST PARTS OF HIMSELF...
...IF I NEED TO KILL HIM AGAIN, TO SAVE US ALL.
I'LL LEAVE HER ALIVE AS A GIFT TO YOU FOR HELPING ME ESCAPE.
YOU'RE WELCOME.
HUUH HUUH HUUUUU--
SMALL BLESSINGS.

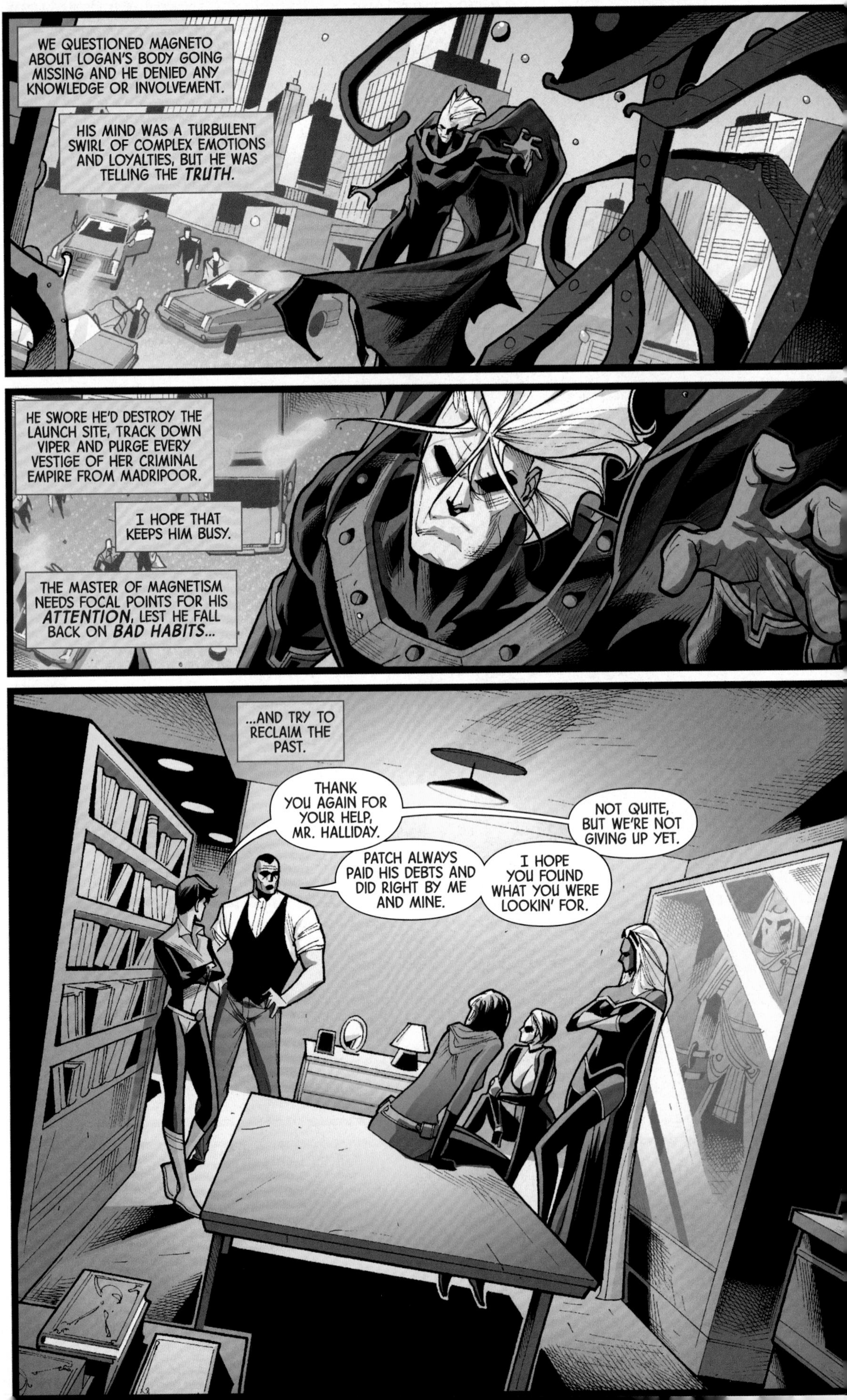
WE QUESTIONED MAGNETO ABOUT LOGAN'S BODY GOING MISSING AND HE DENIED ANY KNOWLEDGE OR INVOLVEMENT.
HIS MIND WAS A TURBULENT SWIRL OF COMPLEX EMOTIONS AND LOYALTIES, BUT HE WAS TELLING THE *TRUTH*.
HE SWORE HE'D DESTROY THE LAUNCH SITE, TRACK DOWN VIPER AND PURGE EVERY VESTIGE OF HER CRIMINAL EMPIRE FROM MADRIPOOR.
I HOPE THAT KEEPS HIM BUSY.
THE MASTER OF MAGNETISM NEEDS FOCAL POINTS FOR HIS *ATTENTION*, LEST HE FALL BACK ON *BAD HABITS*...
...AND TRY TO RECLAIM THE PAST.
THANK YOU AGAIN FOR YOUR HELP, MR. HALLIDAY.
PATCH ALWAYS PAID HIS DEBTS AND DID RIGHT BY ME AND MINE.
I HOPE YOU FOUND WHAT YOU WERE LOOKIN' FOR.
NOT QUITE, BUT WE'RE NOT GIVING UP YET.

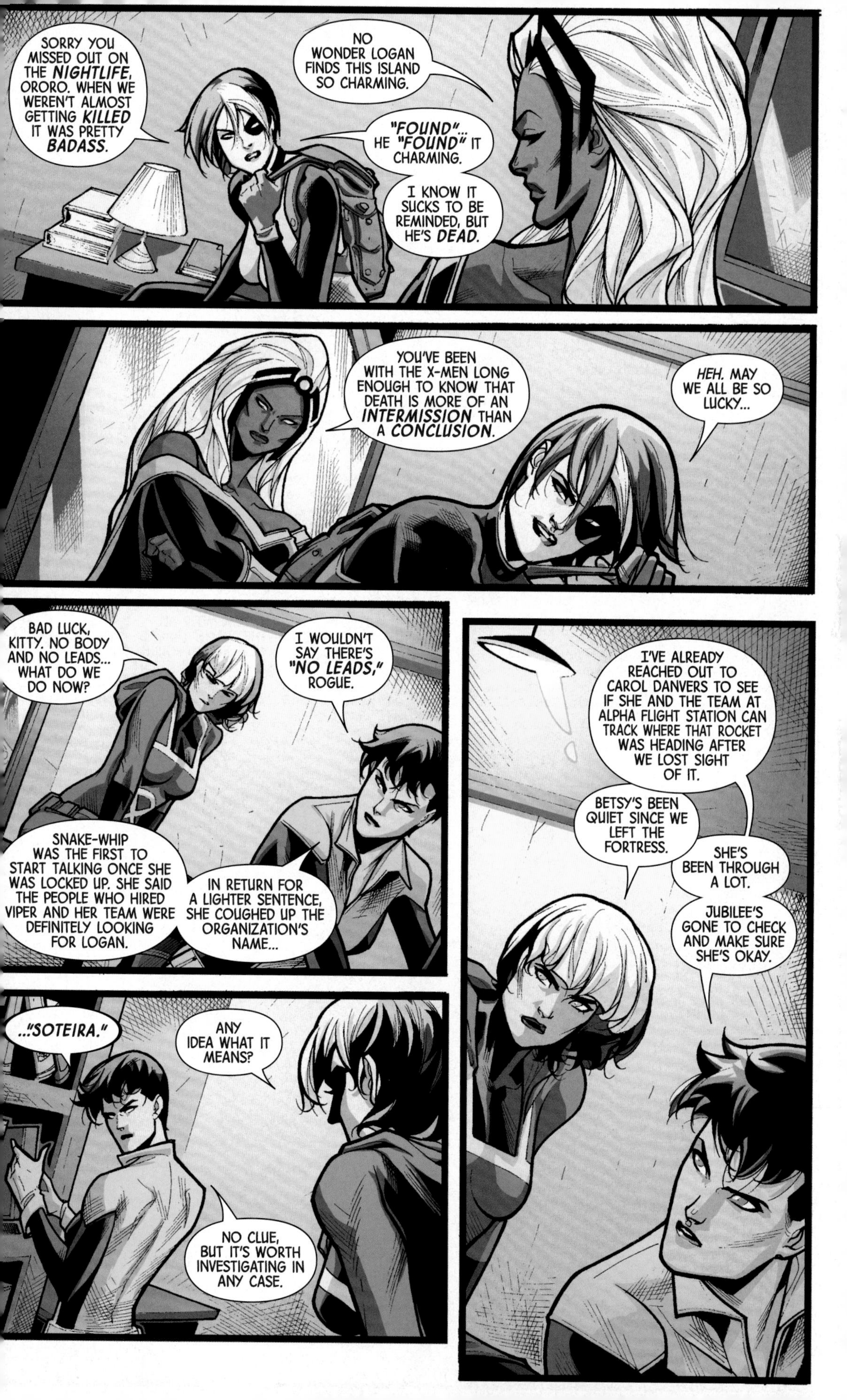
SORRY YOU MISSED OUT ON THE NIGHTLIFE, ORORO. WHEN WE WEREN'T ALMOST GETTING KILLED IT WAS PRETTY BADASS.
NO WONDER LOGAN FINDS THIS ISLAND SO CHARMING.
"FOUND"... HE "FOUND" IT CHARMING.
I KNOW IT SUCKS TO BE REMINDED, BUT HE'S DEAD.
YOU'VE BEEN WITH THE X-MEN LONG ENOUGH TO KNOW THAT DEATH IS MORE OF AN INTERMISSION THAN A CONCLUSION.
HEH. MAY WE ALL BE SO LUCKY...
BAD LUCK, KITTY. NO BODY AND NO LEADS... WHAT DO WE DO NOW?
I WOULDN'T SAY THERE'S "NO LEADS," ROGUE.
SNAKE-WHIP WAS THE FIRST TO START TALKING ONCE SHE WAS LOCKED UP. SHE SAID THE PEOPLE WHO HIRED VIPER AND HER TEAM WERE DEFINITELY LOOKING FOR LOGAN.
IN RETURN FOR A LIGHTER SENTENCE, SHE COUGHED UP THE ORGANIZATION'S NAME...
..."SOTEIRA."
ANY IDEA WHAT IT MEANS?
NO CLUE, BUT IT'S WORTH INVESTIGATING IN ANY CASE.
I'VE ALREADY REACHED OUT TO CAROL DANVERS TO SEE IF SHE AND THE TEAM AT ALPHA FLIGHT STATION CAN TRACK WHERE THAT ROCKET WAS HEADING AFTER WE LOST SIGHT OF IT.
BETSY'S BEEN QUIET SINCE WE LEFT THE FORTRESS.
SHE'S BEEN THROUGH A LOT.
JUBILEE'S GONE TO CHECK AND MAKE SURE SHE'S OKAY.

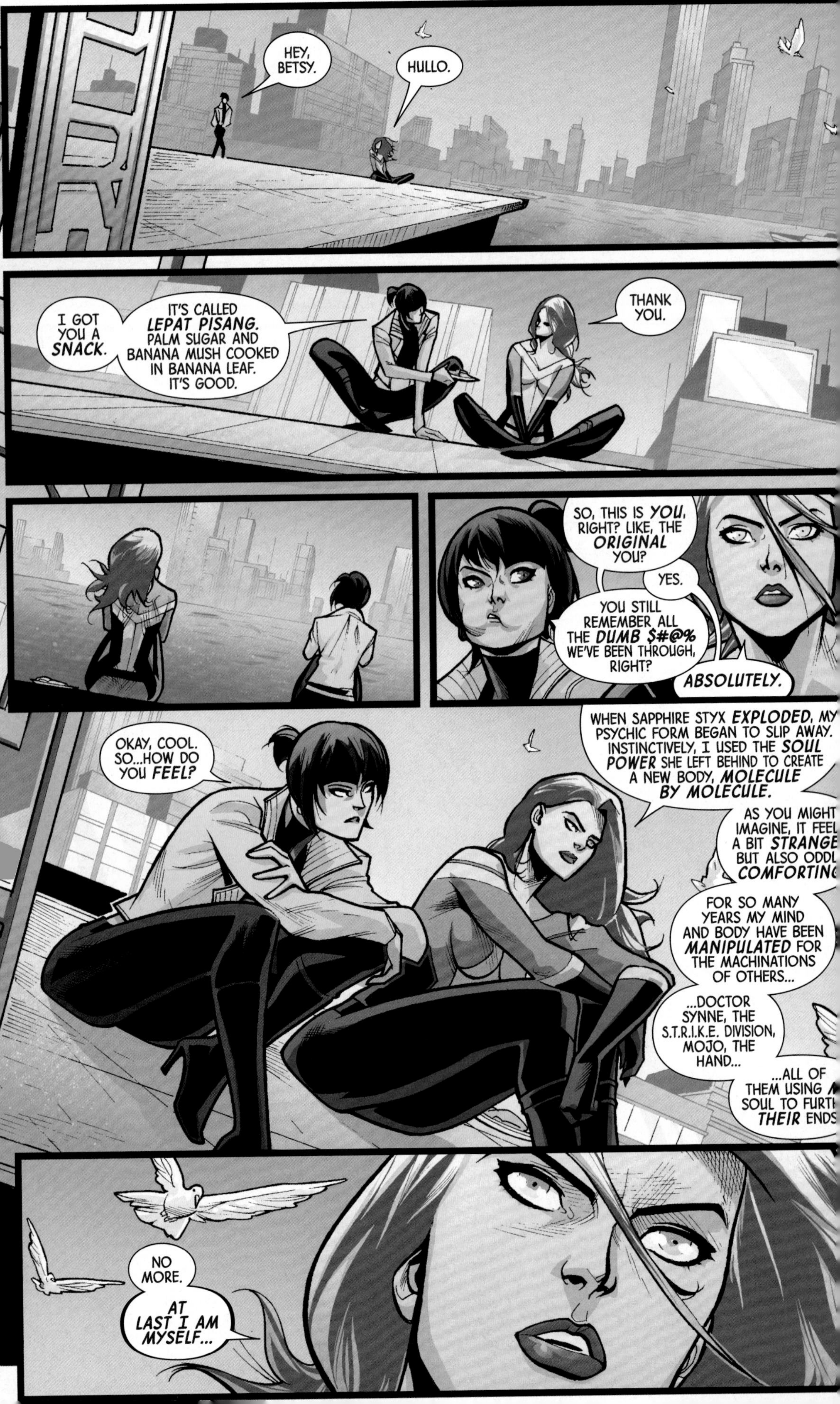
HEY, BETSY.
HULLO.
I GOT YOU A SNACK.
IT'S CALLED LEPAT PISANG. PALM SUGAR AND BANANA MUSH COOKED IN BANANA LEAF. IT'S GOOD.
THANK YOU.
SO, THIS IS YOU, RIGHT? LIKE, THE ORIGINAL YOU?
YES.
YOU STILL REMEMBER ALL THE DUMB $#@% WE'VE BEEN THROUGH, RIGHT?
ABSOLUTELY.
OKAY, COOL. SO...HOW DO YOU FEEL?
WHEN SAPPHIRE STYX EXPLODED, MY PSYCHIC FORM BEGAN TO SLIP AWAY. INSTINCTIVELY, I USED THE SOUL POWER SHE LEFT BEHIND TO CREATE A NEW BODY, MOLECULE BY MOLECULE.
AS YOU MIGHT IMAGINE, IT FEEL A BIT STRANGE BUT ALSO ODDL COMFORTIN
FOR SO MANY YEARS MY MIND AND BODY HAVE BEEN MANIPULATED FOR THE MACHINATIONS OF OTHERS...
...DOCTOR SYNNE, THE S.T.R.I.K.E. DIVISION, MOJO, THE HAND...
...ALL OF THEM USING SOUL TO FURT THEIR ENDS
NO MORE.
AT LAST I AM MYSELF...

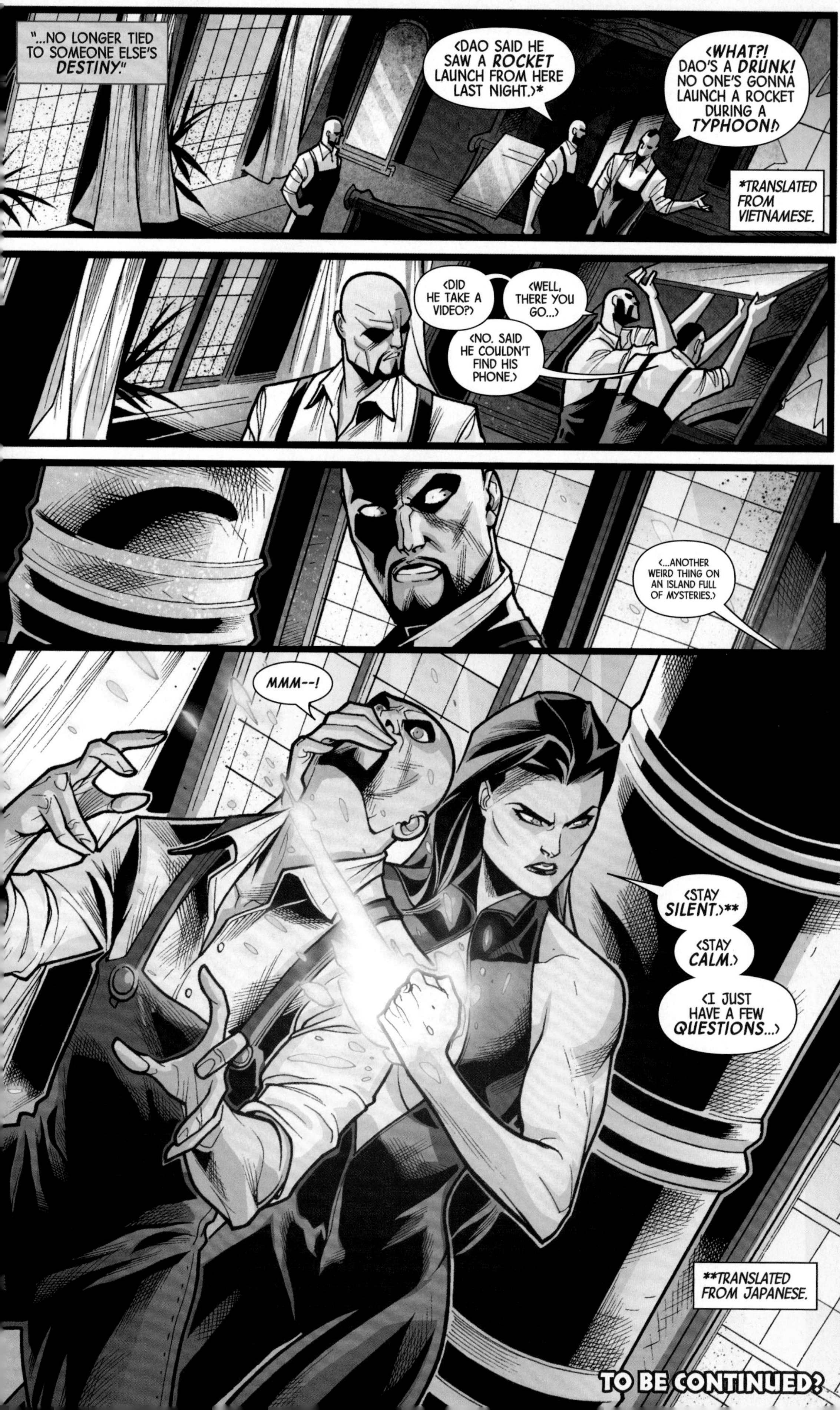
"...NO LONGER TIED TO SOMEONE ELSE'S DESTINY."
<DAO SAID HE SAW A ROCKET LAUNCH FROM HERE LAST NIGHT.>*
<WHAT?! DAO'S A DRUNK! NO ONE'S GONNA LAUNCH A ROCKET DURING A TYPHOON!>
*TRANSLATED FROM VIETNAMESE.
<DID HE TAKE A VIDEO?>
<WELL, THERE YOU GO...>
<NO. SAID HE COULDN'T FIND HIS PHONE.>
<...ANOTHER WEIRD THING ON AN ISLAND FULL OF MYSTERIES.>
MMM--!
<STAY SILENT.>**
<STAY CALM.>
<I JUST HAVE A FEW QUESTIONS...>
**TRANSLATED FROM JAPANESE.
TO BE CONTINUED?

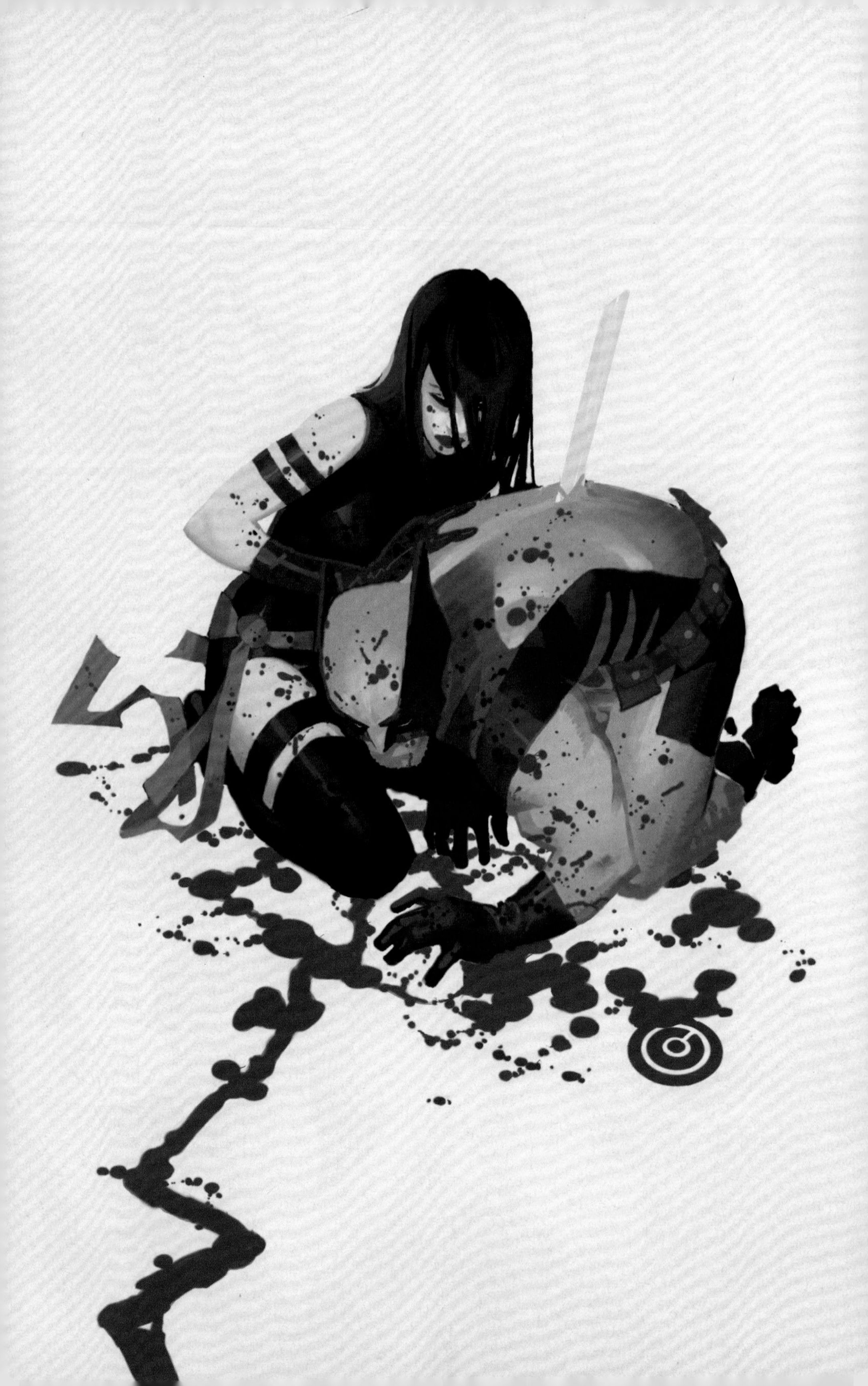

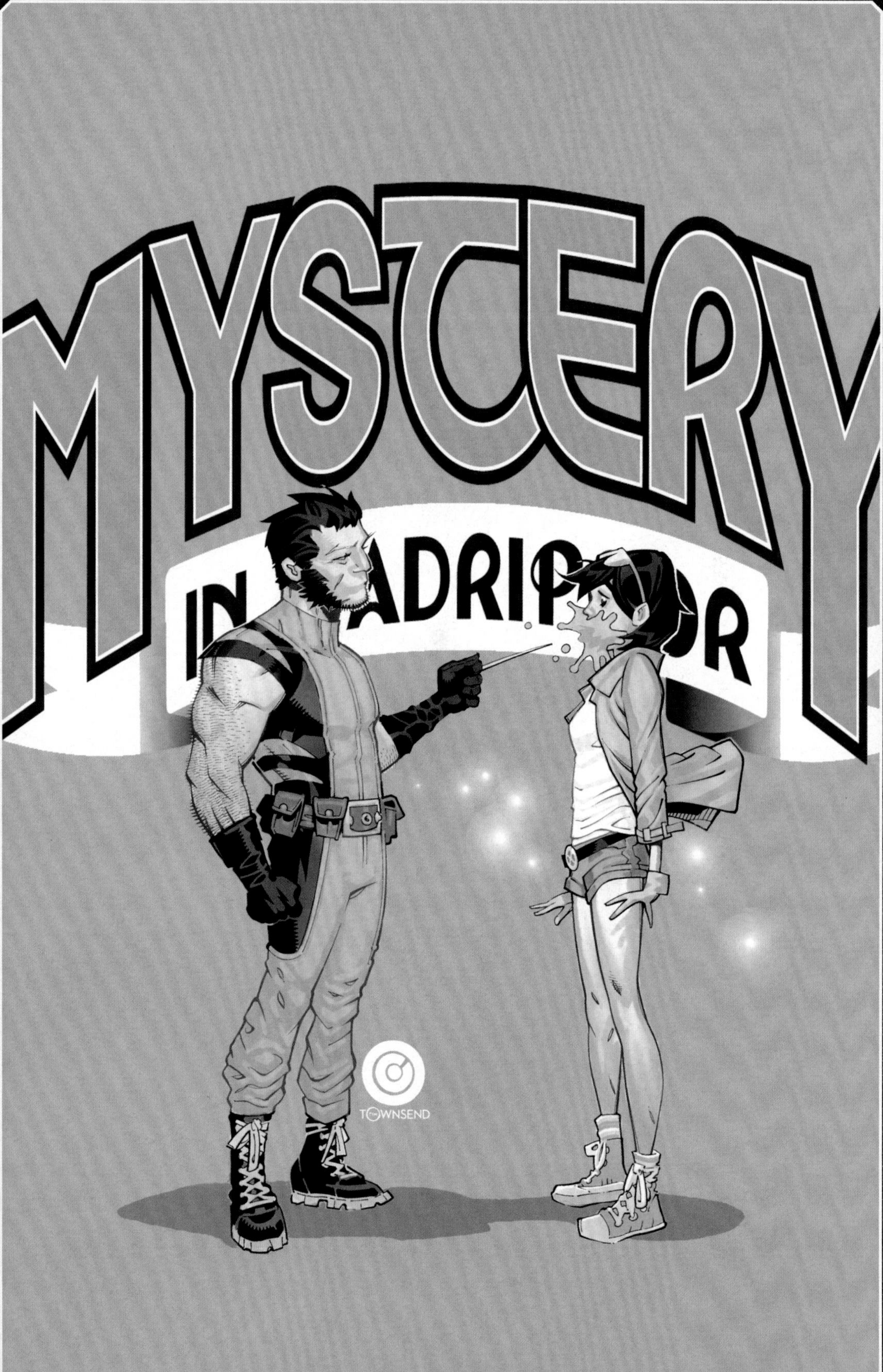
MYSTERY
TOWNSEND

Chris Bachalo & Tim Townsend

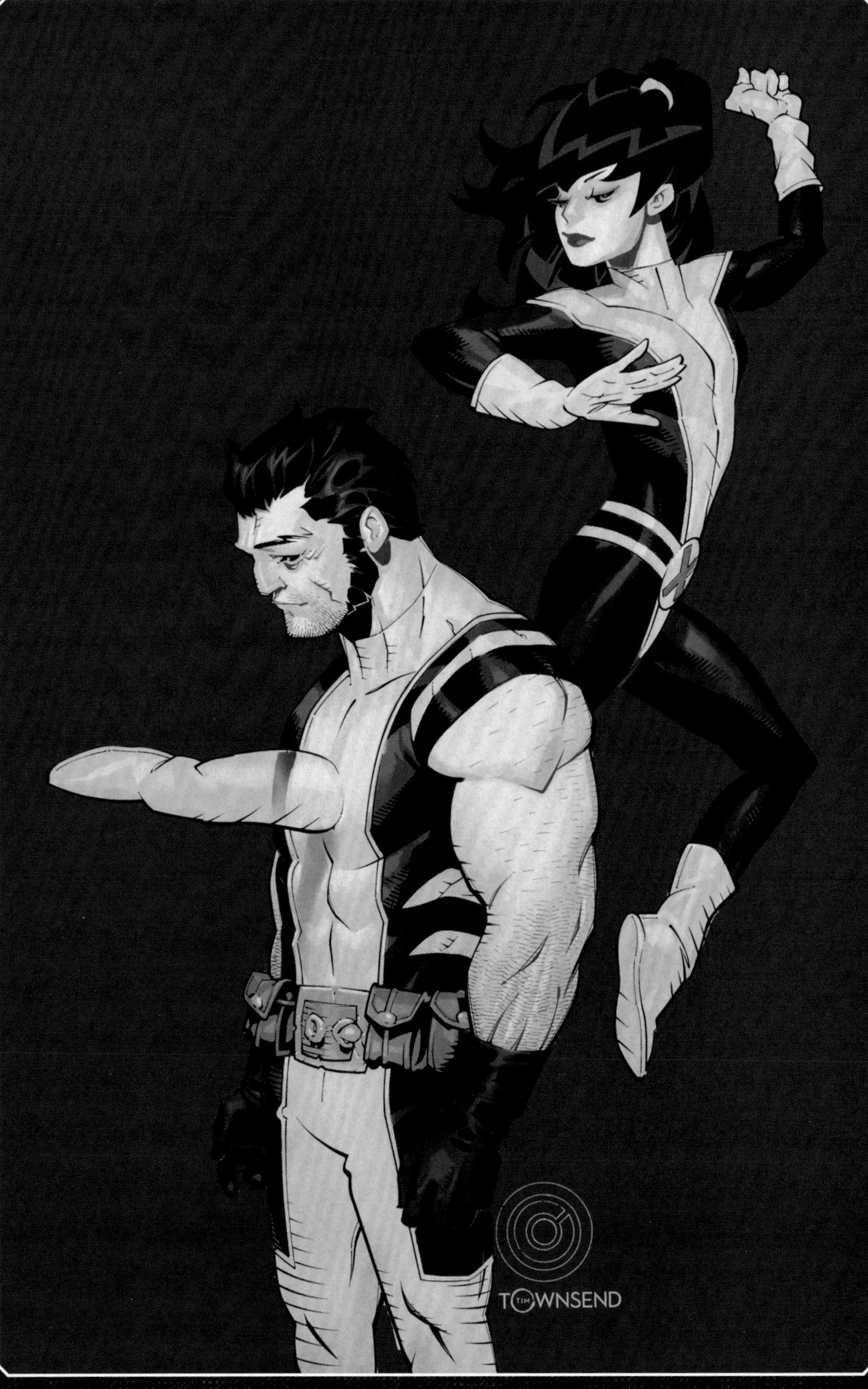
TIM TOWNSEND

Chris Bachalo & Tim Townsend

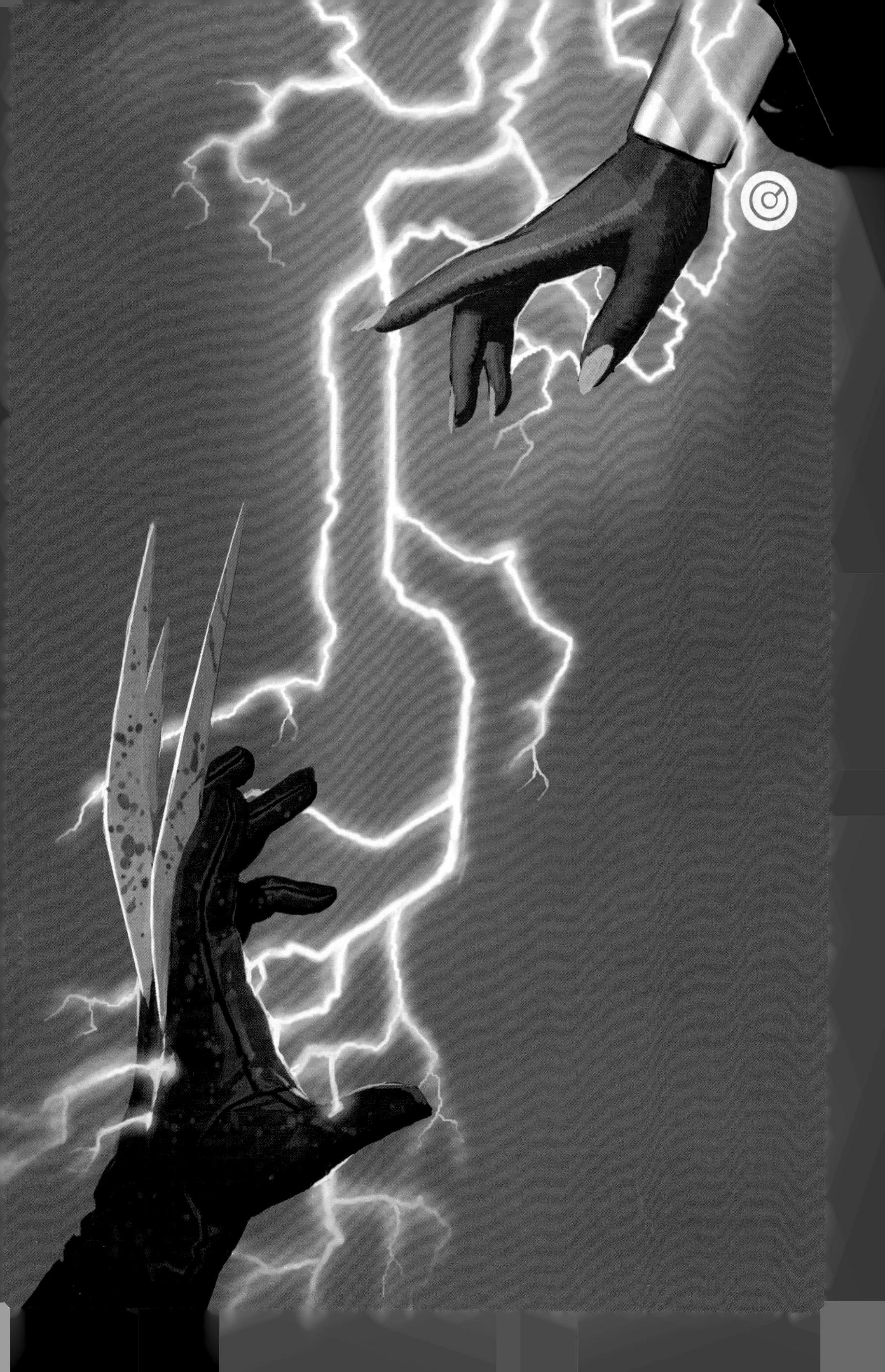

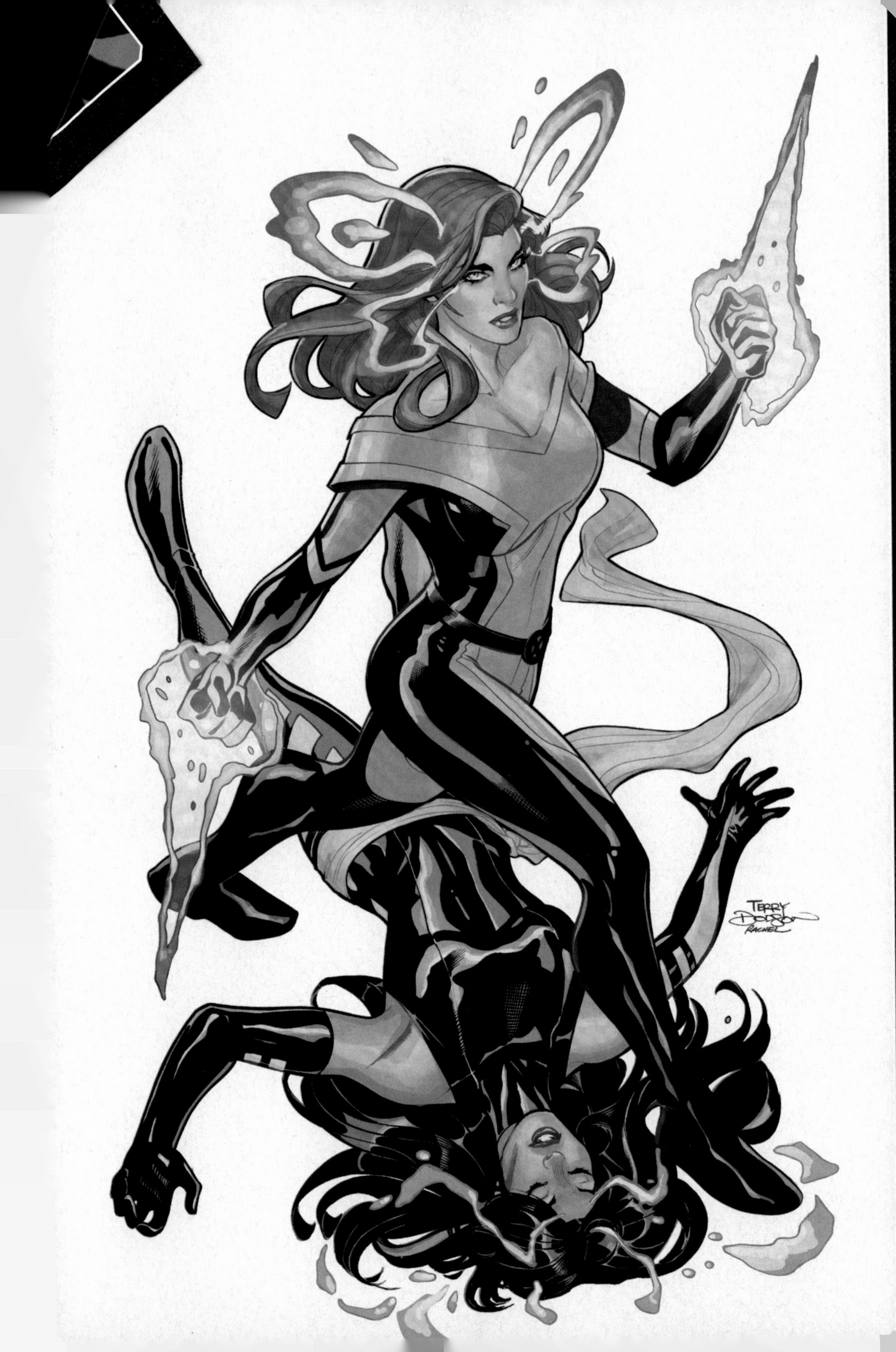
TERRY DODSON RACHEL